Peer Violence in Children's Residential Care

Also by Christine Barter

INVESTIGATING INSTITUTIONAL ABUSE OF CHILDREN: An Exploration of the NSPCC Experience

PROTECTING CHILDREN FROM RACISM AND RACIAL ABUSE: A Research Review

Also by David Berridge

CHILDREN'S HOMES

CHILDREN'S HOMES REVISITED (*Author with I. Brodie*)

WHERE TO TURN? FAMILY SUPPORT FOR SOUTH ASIAN COMMUNITIES – A CASE STUDY (*Author with T. Qureshi and H. Wenman*)

Also by Pat Cawson

CHILD MALTREATMENT IN THE FAMILY: The Experience of a National Sample of Young People

CHILD MALTREATMENT IN THE UNITED KINGDOM: A Study of the Prevalence of Child Abuse and Neglect (*Author with C. Wattam, S. Brooker and G. Kelly*)

Peer Violence in Children's Residential Care

Christine Barter,
Emma Renold,
David Berridge and
Pat Cawson

© Christine Barter, Emma Renold, David Berridge and Pat Cawson 2004

All rights reserved. No reproduction, copy or transmission of this publication may be made without written permission.

No paragraph of this publication may be reproduced, copied or transmitted save with written permission or in accordance with the provisions of the Copyright, Designs and Patents Act 1988, or under the terms of any licence permitting limited copying issued by the Copyright Licensing Agency, 90 Tottenham Court Road, London W1T 4LP.

Any person who does any unauthorised act in relation to this publication may be liable to criminal prosecution and civil claims for damages.

The authors have asserted their rights to be identified as the authors of this work in accordance with the Copyright, Designs and Patents Act 1988.

First published 2004 by
PALGRAVE MACMILLAN
Houndmills, Basingstoke, Hampshire RG21 6XS and
175 Fifth Avenue, New York, N.Y. 10010
Companies and representatives throughout the world

PALGRAVE MACMILLAN is the global academic imprint of the Palgrave Macmillan division of St. Martin's Press, LLC and of Palgrave Macmillan Ltd. Macmillan® is a registered trademark in the United States, United Kingdom and other countries. Palgrave is a registered trademark in the European Union and other countries.

ISBN 1–4039–3559–9

This book is printed on paper suitable for recycling and made from fully managed and sustained forest sources.

A catalogue record for this book is available from the British Library.

Library of Congress Cataloging-in-Publication Data
   Peer violence in children's residential care / Christine Barter ... [et al.].
     p. cm.
   Includes bibliographical references and index.
   ISBN 1–4039–3559–9 (cloth)
    1. Children – Institutional care – Great Britain. 2. Children – Violence against – Great Britain. 3. Children and violence – Great Britain. 4. Violence in children – Great Britain. 5. Bullying – Great Britain. 6. Peer pressure in children – Great Britain. I. Barter, Christine.

HV751.A6P245 2004
302.3—dc22
                                           2004044362

10 9 8 7 6 5 4 3 2 1
13 12 11 10 09 08 07 06 05 04

Printed and bound in Great Britain by
Antony Rowe Ltd, Chippenham and Eastbourne

Contents

List of Tables and Figures	ix
List of Vignettes	x
Acknowledgements	xi

1 Childhood, Peer Relationships and Peer Violence   1
    Listening to children's voices   2
    Perspectives on childhood   3
    Children, young people and violence   4
    Residential care for children   8
    Bullying and peer violence in residential settings   10
    Common themes on peer violence   21
    The meaning of violence   22
    Public/private dichotomy of violence   23
    Gender and violence   23
    The present study – research methods   24
    Summary points   27

2 Mapping Peer Violence in Children's Homes   29
    Conceptualising violence   29
    Young people's evaluation of peer violence and
      verbal attacks   30
    Types and levels of violence   31
    Physical violence   32
    Physical non-contact violence   36
    Sexual violence   37
    Verbal attacks and insults   39
    Bullying   42
    Staff evaluation of peer violence and verbal attacks   44
    Peer violence in the previous month   45
    Peer violence in the past year   46
    Physical non-contact violence   47
    Bullying   50
    Sexual violence   51
    Verbal attacks and insults   54
    Developing a continuum of violence   56
    Summary points   57

3 Young People's Perspectives on Violence — 59

'We have our own rules': children's cultures and
the normalisation of violence — 60
'Seven months living here, you just get used to it':
the importance of context — 61
'Hi, I'm Ramon and I run this place': 'pecking orders'
and peer group hierarchies — 63
'He rules the place and bullies everyone': bullying
as a 'natural' and inevitable peer group dynamic? — 65
The masculinisation of physical violence — 67
Challenging and transgressing passive femininities:
girls and physical violence — 68
The sexualisation of female violence — 68
'I never hit him before he hits me': violence as social justice — 69
'Standing ground' and 'saving face': projecting, protecting
and maintaining 'hard' masculinities — 74
'He acts like a two-year-old': age and immaturity as
catalysts for violence — 76
Summary points — 77

4 Staff Perspectives on Violence — 79

'They all know their little places': hierarchical
peer group dynamics — 80
Gender and violence — 87
'Racist stuff just isn't allowed here': racial violence — 93
'The youngsters just hit whilst the older lot are more
subtle about it all': age and violence — 95
'They've never been shown how to behave properly at home,
so they just use violence to get through life': young people's
backgrounds and understandings of violence — 99
Summary points — 102

5 Shared and Different Understandings of Violence — 104

The use of vignettes — 104
Physical attack – vignette A — 106
Psychological attack – vignette B — 113
Male on female sexual attack – vignette C — 122
Male on male sexual attack – vignette D — 130
Dominant discourses on violence — 134
Linking meaning and experience — 136
Summary points — 138

6 Institutional and Organisational Factors Associated with Violence — 139
Policies and procedures — 140
Young people's assessments of policies and procedures — 142
Children's rights — 145
Young people's meetings — 146
Referrals — 149
Size and structure of the building — 154
Function of the children's home — 155
Staffing levels — 156
Relating organisational and structural factors to the violence continnum — 157
Summary points — 160

7 Evaluating Working Practices — 161
Seeking support and issues of disclosure — 161
Evaluations of staff interventions — 167
Summary points — 182

8 Responding to Violence – Methods of Intervention — 184
Sanction-based interventions — 184
Physical restraint — 187
Informal meetings — 189
Formal meetings — 190
Child protection procedures — 191
Proactive working practices — 193
Wider perspectives on reducing violence — 199
Summary points — 202

9 Conclusion — 203
Summary of the research — 204
Young people's experience of peer violence in residential care — 205
Violence as a structured element of the group culture — 206
The gendered nature of violence — 207
Seeing what really happens or what is expected? — 207
Hierarchies and the pecking order — 210
Peers as both oppressors and supports — 211
Justification narratives — 213
The permeable institution and the community culture — 214

Combating racism among young people	215
What is different about the residential setting?	216
Understanding the roots of violence	219
Tackling different levels of violence	220
Confronting peer violence – strategies and standards	221
Using the strengths of young people's culture	224
Supporting residential care	225
Peer violence: an aspect of social relations	227
Appendix A – Researching Violence	229
Appendix B – Analysing the Data	231
Definitions and conceptualisations of violence	
(what, how and why)	231
Contextualisation of violence (where and when)	231
Experience of violence (who)	231
Appendix C – Sample Breakdown	233
Young people	233
Staff	234
Bibliography	235
Index	248

List of Tables and Figures

Tables

2.1	Staff estimations of the impact of physical violence	45
5.1	Vignette sample	106
5.2	Perceptions of female culpability and the seriousness of sexual violence	127
6.1	Organisational factors and the violence continuum	158
6.2	Structural factors and the violence continuum	159
6.3	Sector and the violence continuum	159
6.4	Length of stay and the violence continuum	159
C1	Age and gender of young people	233
C2	Gender and ethnic origin of young people	233
C3	Grade and gender of staff	234
C4	Type of home by grade of staff	234
C5	Grade and ethnic origin of staff	234

Figures

2.1	Diagrammatic representation of the violence continuum	57
6.1	Diagrammatic representation of the violence continuum	157

List of Vignettes

Physical attack – vignette A 106
Psychological attack – vignette B 113
Male on female sexual attack – vignette C 122
Male on male sexual attack – vignette D 130

Acknowledgements

First, and most importantly, our deepest thanks go to all the young people who talked so openly about such a sensitive topic and who allowed us to intrude into their daily lives. Due to confidentiality their names must remain anonymous and pseudonyms have been used throughout the book.

This research was funded by the Economic and Social Research Council (ESRC) under the *Violence Research Programme*. We are very grateful for this assistance, for the support of the programme director Professor Elizabeth Stanko and for the stimulating discussions with our fellow programme researchers.

We are indebted to the local authorities, voluntary organisations and private homes, which bravely allowed us to scrutinise their working practices in such a controversial area. We extend our gratitude to the managers and staff in the homes, who shared their views and experiences and put up with our prying whilst always making us feel welcome.

Our thanks go to members of our Advisory Group, who gave us useful advice during the course of the project, namely Isabelle Brodie, Debbie Epstein, Elaine Farmer, John Rowlands, Ian Sinclair, Jo Moad and Adrian Ward. Any limitations in what follows of course remain our responsibilities. We would also like to thank Caroline Boyle, Andrea Cornelius, Emma Barrett and Lenna Lou for their administrative support over the duration of the research and beyond. Finally, we appreciate the encouragement and support of librarians and the many other helpful colleagues at NSPCC and the University of Luton. We hope you all feel that our efforts have been worthwhile.

1
Childhood, Peer Relationships and Peer Violence

Interviewer: What do you think are the best things about living here?
Shyama: Having friends.
Interviewer: And who's your best friend here?
Shyama: Michelle.
Interviewer: Yeah, and anyone else?
Shyama: Bianca and Nina.
Interviewer: Any boys?
Shyama: NO (shouts).
Interviewer: And what's good about having friends here?
Shyama: You can do stuff with them...talk to them about things, how you're feeling...Oh and I like the trips out.
(Shyama, aged 9)

Interviewer: What are some of the things you don't like about living here?
Paul: Well sometimes the other young people get on my nerves and there's a lot of competition here...peer pressure, some staff annoy me a lot, but apart from that I think it's all right.
Interviewer: When you say peer pressure, what sort of things are you thinking of?
Paul: Well, I used to get involved in things because of what other young people were doing because I felt pressured but I've grown out of that now.
Interviewer: How would that work, how would they pressure you?
Paul: Well they'd just be like, if you don't do this you're out of order...stuff like that really.
Interviewer: Did it involve threats?
Paul: No, I've never really been threatened...there's never really been any bullying in this house, like you do hear a lot like there's bullying in children's homes and stuff, but

	everyone's sort of equal here...there's no head dog in this house, do you know what I mean, everyone treats each other like they'd like to be treated.
Interviewer:	So the pressure was quite subtle then?
Paul:	Yeah 'cause mostly the people have moved out now and now we've got quite an equal group in here now they just treat each other all right, but beforehand it was bad, like when I first got here I hated it, 'cause of the young people and what they were like.

(Paul, aged 14)

Listening to children's voices

The need to listen to children and young people's voices has been recognised in a number of recent major policy developments and consultations by central and local government, affecting education, care services, youth justice, leisure and environmental services (Children and Young People's Unit 2001). Specific departments and programmes have been set up addressing the needs of children and young people and the problems of social exclusion affecting the young (e.g. Children's Fund 2001). Much of this activity has been linked to concerns about youth violence and involvement in social disorder, but there are also concerns about the safety and protection of children, in the community and when they enter public care, following a number of recent tragedies and scandals which revealed inadequacies in the services intended to protect and care for children (Laming 2003).

This book reports the results of research that aimed to develop understanding of young people's violence towards peers within residential settings, by exploring both young people's and staff's understanding of the meaning and effects of violence, children's protective strategies and the extent to which children and staff had shared reference systems for dealing with violence. This was intended to contribute to the sociology of childhood and to treat the children's perspectives as important in their own right. It is hoped that these findings will contribute to the development of policy and practice which will safeguard children in residential settings from peer violence. The research is based on interviews with children and staff in 14 children's residential units, in which they discussed experience of violence between children and young people in residential care, as victims, witnesses and perpetrators. The term 'children' can encompass the whole age range up to 18 years, but as the majority of those taking part in the study were teenagers, the term 'young people' will be used to describe them, except when specifically including or referring to younger children or citing sources which use other terminology.

The requirement to listen and take account of young people's viewpoint on their own safety and situation is now incorporated in legislation (Children

Act 1989). The importance of listening to and acting on their accounts of violence and abuse has been recognised in official reports on child protection services and residential care services (Department of Health 1995a, Kent 1997, Waterhouse 2000). Thus there exists a growing recognition within both research and practice in the public care of children that the voices of children have not been heard as they should be. Children are known to assess and manage potential safety and danger in school and community environments and to develop strategies to deal with risks (Smith and Sharp 1994, Hood et al. 1996, Harden et al. 2000). Dealing with violence in residential settings, where children live together, at times of day and night when they could be particularly vulnerable, might require different strategies to those used at school or in the neighbourhood.

The perceptions and experiences of staff working with young people on a day-to-day basis have also been largely missing from the literature. Different professionals may make different judgements, but additionally, definitions by children of their needs and problems may be very different from those of professionals (Baldwin 1990). The Support Force for Children's Residential Care (1995), set up to address some of the problems identified by the Warner Committee (1992) on staffing in children's homes, concluded in its final report that there is a need for managers, staff and children to work together to create a structure and daily living environment that provide positive opportunities whilst creating boundaries around what is acceptable behaviour. However, for residential workers to enforce these boundaries successfully they need to be perceived by children as representing a legitimate authority (Barter 1997). This will most effectively be achieved if practice is informed by a consistent and agreed framework, incorporating the users' own definitions, thresholds and especially children's own protective responses to violence.

Perspectives on childhood

Both socialisation theories and sociological studies of childhood prior to the 1970s viewed children as essentially determined by their environments (Brannen and O'Brien 1996). But within contemporary sociology a new paradigm for the study of childhood is emerging, centring upon the dissonance which exists between children's own experiences of being a child and the institutional form which childhood takes (James and Prout 1990, James 1993, Mayall 2002). The sociology of childhood views children's social relationships and cultures as worthy of study in their own right and not just in relation to their social construction by adults (James, Jenks and Prout 1998). Children are seen as being actively involved in the construction of their own social lives, the lives of those around them and of the societies in which they live. Within this the plurality of childhood must be acknowledged, for example according to class, age, gender, disability and ethnicity (Jenks 1996).

This enables children to be viewed as significant actors in, and interpreters of, a complex social world (Brannen and O'Brien 1996). Children are viewed as both constrained by structure and agents acting within and upon it. By exploring the relationship between these two levels we can then begin to elucidate the link between given and largely adult-defined social institutions and the activities which children construct for and between themselves. How we think of children as social actors and the theoretical accounts to underpin this have, however, still to be developed. These ideas are elaborated in Chapter 2.

Children, young people and violence

Almost all evidence on levels of peer violence in the United Kingdom comes from sources which predominantly reflect an adult-focused view, whether from research, practice literature or administrative sources such as inquiry and committee reports. The Gulbenkian Report (1995) on children and violence notes that children (defined as those under the age of 18) are far more likely to be the victims of violence than the perpetrators, but that children's involvement in violent offending appears to be increasing. Much recent media coverage has been given to the increase in violent crime, said to be caused primarily by children assaulting and 'mugging' other children, and there have been high profile cases of suicide by children, allegedly because they were being bullied by fellow pupils at school (Marr and Field 2001). Between 30 and 40 per cent of school pupils experience bullying in some form, and sexual assault in childhood and adolescence is more likely to be experienced from other young people than from adults (Cawson *et al.* 2000). Older teenagers form the single largest group of offenders in statistics of violent crime (Home Office 2001). The British Crime Survey found that young people were the most frequent perpetrators of assault and robbery against 12–15-year olds from the general population (Aye Maung 1995, Simmons 2002). The annual Youth Justice Board (2002, 2003) surveys of school-age children confirm that they experience high levels of physical assault and bullying, racist abuse and attack, and theft and damage to belongings, by other young people. Most of these attacks occur at school. These surveys, and others carried out recently, present a consistent picture of violence between young people, in which fighting in public places and carrying weapons are practised by substantial minorities of young males, and smaller proportions of young females (Graham and Bowling 1995, Flood-Page *et al.* 2000, Beinart *et al.* 2002). The Gulbenkian Report (1995) notes the dearth of hard evidence on the levels and types of violence involving children, beyond that of limited statistics on offending and bullying at school. Although there is now considerable quantitative data available, there is very little recent analysis of the dynamics and circumstances of this behaviour.

In spite of adult concern about levels of youth violence, little research attention has been paid to children's perspectives on violence. There is evidence that children's experience of violence, both in community and institutional contexts, may be largely hidden from adults for a variety of reasons, including social values about 'grassing' or 'telling tales' and because the young try to protect themselves from interference by adults which might curtail their freedom (Smith and Sharp 1994, Aye Maung 1995). There are difficulties in defining when children's behaviour to each other should be considered abusive, for example, the boundaries between sexual experimentation and sexual abuse (Home *et al.* 1991, Vizard, Monck and Misch 1995).

Bullying and peer abuse

One of the most notable features of discussions of aggressive behaviour between children is the lack of clarity and consistency with which the terms 'bullying' and 'peer abuse' are used. Most sources of evidence, whether from research, practice literature or inquiry reports, acknowledge that children can be vulnerable to physical, sexual and psychological threat or attack by other children, or can be perpetrators of such attack against other children. Attacks can happen in any context in which children meet each other; at home, in the community, at school, or in public care or custody. Beyond this, most sources, especially in official reports and guidance, take it for granted that there is a distinction between bullying and abuse which is obvious, generally understood, and does not need explanation. The most common distinction made is that 'bullying' is used to refer to physical or psychological threat or attack, including attacks on or theft of children's personal property, and comparatively rarely refers to sexual threat or attack. Occasionally the term 'sexual harassment' is used as a synonym for sexual bullying. 'Peer abuse', on the other hand, is nearly always used to describe sexual threat or attack, and sometimes the more serious physical attacks, but is rarely used for minor physical assaults, for psychological threat or attack, or for attacks on children's belongings. 'Bullying' carries the connotation that it is less serious than 'abuse', and is treated as such in most official reports and guidance.

The distinction in the way the two terms are used is particularly clear in the two major government reviews of safeguards for children living away from home, carried out in England and Wales (Utting 1997) and in Scotland (Kent 1997). The comprehensive literature review attached to the Scottish report (Kendrick 1997) draws on material on both bullying and abuse, but the text of the report itself maintains the distinction between the two forms of aggression. Recent government and other reports on youth offending similarly make a distinction between bullying and violent offending, building in an assumption that these are separate phenomena the meaning and difference of which are clear (Flood-Page *et al.* 2000, Beinart *et al.* 2002, Youth Justice Board 2002, 2003). In spite of the fact that 'peer abuse' is regarded more seriously, however, 'bullying' has received more attention, both in terms of its conceptualisation, and in research on its nature and prevalence.

The conceptual distinction between the terms is hard to justify, and it was necessary to set it aside for the present study in order to explore the young people's own language and thoughts, including their understanding of familiar words such as bullying. Nevertheless the discussion of the available evidence given below necessarily reflects the distinction given in the literature and is grouped accordingly. The present research uses the term 'peer violence' to refer to physical, psychological and sexual threat or attack, except when citing previous texts which use other terms.

Bullying at school and in the community

One of the major areas of research in which violence by peers has been considered is in relation to bullying at school and in the community. This is highly relevant to any consideration of peer violence in residential care, partly because residents in children's homes are also part of the local school and community, and partly for what the research shows about broader features of social relationships between young people in British culture. No universally agreed definition of bullying exists. Yet there is some consensus that bullying is an aggressive act aimed to intentionally hurt or harm another person, is repetitive and involves some form of power imbalance which makes it difficult for the victims to defend themselves (Farrington 1993). Children and young people include these elements in their own descriptions of bullying behaviour (Arora and Thompson 1987). Smith and Sharp (1994) succinctly define bullying as the 'systematic abuse of power'. Bullying can take many varied forms. This can, however, be problematic as very diverse behaviours are submerged under this uniform definition. In addition the term 'bullying' may be used to 'play down' the significance of aggressive behaviour, treating it as less serious than an identical act carried out by an adult (Cawson *et al.* 2000).

Probably the two most recognised types are physical bullying (where a child hits another) or verbal bullying (where harmful forms of teasing or verbal abuse are used), however there can also be indirect and relational bullying. Indirect bullying refers to some form of social manipulation where the bully uses others as a means of attack instead of attacking themselves. Relational bullying refers to inflicting harm on peers in ways that damage social relations, such as spreading malicious rumours or social exclusion.

Prevalence figures for bullying vary depending on the research methodology, questionnaire details, definition used, age and composition of the sample. Accounts by adults (e.g., teachers and parents) are generally viewed as less reliable than self-reports from children. The first large-scale English survey (Whitney and Smith 1993) of 6700 pupils reported that 27 per cent of primary school pupils had been bullied, with 10 per cent stating this occurred at least once a week. This was found to decrease slightly once the child reached secondary school with rates of 10 per cent and 4 per cent respectively. In relation to bullying 12 per cent of primary and 6 per cent of secondary pupils admitted taking part in bullying. Cawson *et al*'s (2000) study of 2869 young adults found that 40 per cent stated they had experienced some form of bullying in their childhood, a fifth of these said it had occurred 'regularly over the years'. Other recent studies provide slightly lower rates (Salmon *et al*. 1998). Although most pupils state they did not like bullying, a significant minority said they would join in (Smith and Sharp 1994). Recent developments in the field have included more complex understandings surrounding the differentiation of participation roles such as ring leader bully, follower, reinforcer, outsider and defender, as well as victim (Salmivalli *et al*. 1996).

Over the past decade, research has identified a number of general features surrounding the dynamics of (mostly school-based) bullying (see Rigby 1996, Smith *et al*. 1999, Smith 2000).

Who are the bullies and the bullied?

Self-reports of being bullied decline with age, whilst self-reports of bullying others do not. There is also a marked shift with age away from physical bullying to more indirect and relational forms. More boys report being bullies, whilst boys and girls are equally distributed in relation to victimisation. Boys practice and experience more physical bullying, whilst girls more indirect and relational bullying. Boys tend to be bullied by other boys and girls by both girls and boys. Girls are more likely to experience bullying involving sexual harassment (Duncan 1999). However there is some evidence to suggest that girls' bullying, while less frequent than boys', may be more difficult to tackle (Eslea and Smith 1998).

A number of victim risk factors have been identified including; having few or low social status friends (Hodges *et al*. 1997), having an over-protective family background (Smith and Myron-Wilson 1998), having a disability or special educational needs (Smith and Sharp 1994), the latter also being a risk factor in relation to perpetrating bullying. Cawson *et al*. (2000) found that the most commonly stated reason why children were bullied was size (height and weight), followed closely by 'class' and intelligence. Children from minority ethnic groups have been shown to experience more racist name-calling and discrimination from peers (though not necessarily other forms of bullying) than white children (Barter 1999, Cawson *et al*. 2000, Cline *et al*. 2002). Research has also shown that children may be teased and physically assaulted due to their sexual orientation (Rivers 1995). Recent work by one of the current authors (Renold 2001) found that a third of 10–11-year-old pupils had been bullied for not fitting in with the gender stereotypes of their peers.

Bullies have been shown to come from families that are lacking in warmth, where violence and abuse is common and discipline inconsistent (Olweus 1993, Smith and Myron-Wilson 1998), while Cawson (2002) found that young people who were abused and neglected in their families were also more likely to report being bullied by peers. Although some bullies may lack social skills, ringleader bullies may have good 'theory of mind' abilities (understanding of others' mental states) and be skilled social manipulators (Sutton *et al.* 1999).

Experiences of being bullied have been correlated with anxiety, depression, suicidal feelings and low self-esteem (see Salmon *et al.* 1998, Hawker and Boulton 2000 for detailed reviews of this area). Cawson *et al.* (2000) found that a quarter of those bullied (one in ten of the total sample) reported suffering long-term effects.

Coping strategies

Many victims do not tell an adult about their bullying experiences. This proportion increases with age, possibly reflecting the more serious nature that victimisation takes as children become older. Children and young people adopt a wide range of coping strategies, varying by both age and gender, and which exhibit differential success rates (Smith and Sharp 1994, Hood *et al.* 1996, Harden *et al.* 2000). Overall non-assertive strategies such as crying are less successful than ignoring the bullying or seeking help, although the success of telling teachers depends on the school ethos (Kochenderfer and Ladd 1997).

Intervention

School-based research has shown that the school ethos, attitudes of teachers in bullying situations and degree of supervision of free-time appear to have a major effect on the extent of bullying. The importance of whole-school policies has been stressed. Most positive outcomes came from schools which put more time and effort into anti-bullying measures and where school policies were developed in consultation with pupils, teachers, parents and governors creating an atmosphere of shared ownership. Curriculum-based exercises, working with individuals and groups and playground work were important features in success rates. There has also been considerable interest in peer support and mediation as an approach. A recent survey (Naylor and Cowie 1999) shows the benefits of such school-based initiatives including; having someone to talk to, increased peer helpers' confidence and improvements in the atmosphere of schools generally. Problems included some hostility to peer helpers from other pupils, difficulty in recruiting boys as peer supporters, and issues of power-sharing with staff. However, the effectiveness of school-based programmes, which do not take into account wider community dynamics, has been questioned (Pitts 1995, Randall 1996).

Residential care for children

In order to understand the context in which violence between young people living in children's homes occurs, we need to provide some background to children's residential care. Residential care for children looked after by local authorities ('in care') arouses much controversy. Whereas boarding education for the affluent is perceived positively by its purchasers, and seen to confer educational and social benefits, its equivalent for young people experiencing family breakdown and demonstrating emotional and behavioural problems is viewed more critically. As a consequence, over the past 25 years, the number of residents living in children's homes in England on any one day has tumbled from some 20000 to nearer 6000 (Berridge 1985, Department of Health 2003). This has occurred for a variety of reasons. On the one hand, though the evaluation of outcomes is a complex issue (Parker et al. 1991, Berridge 1994), the benefits arising from residential placements for young people have been questioned. Sinclair and Gibbs' (1998) national study of 48 homes, for example, discovered that whatever progress was made during residence generally disappeared following departure. What the researchers defined as 'good' homes did not produce better outcomes. Factors such as staffing levels and qualifications, which had previously been assumed to be central, were found to be unrelated to the success of homes. The Department of Health's (1998a) overview of 12 residential research studies concurred with this general view and concluded that, in order to be more effective, there was a need for residence to be better integrated into the continuum of services for children in need. More effective specialist supports for young people were required, including education and health. It is important for residence to be effective as its costs are very significant, estimated in the mid-1990s at around half a billion pounds annually (Sinclair and Gibbs 1998).

Although relatively small numbers are now in residential care at any one time, a rather different picture is obtained from the figures on movement in and out of placement. These suggest that a high proportion of young people will spend part of their period in public care in a residential placement, often while waiting for a foster home to become available, or in an emergency following placement breakdown or a family crisis (Department of Health 1998a). Nevertheless the use of long-term residential care has greatly declined compared to a generation ago, and this has meant that many of the children formerly so placed are now in family settings. Children's homes have increasingly come to be used for the comparatively small group of children deemed 'hard to place', because they had experienced frequent placement breakdowns elsewhere, or because their behaviour was thought to make them unsuitable for foster care (Berridge and Brodie 1998).

The findings from recent research on children's homes reveal the complexity of problems with which they are having to deal (Sinclair and Gibbs 1998). Residents, with an average age of about 14 years, bring with them a troubled past. Most have experienced physical, sexual and/or emotional abuse in their families. Inconsistent parenting is a common feature and family life has often broken down leading to separation. Relationship problems abound and parents often find that their teenagers are out of control. Young people, in turn, are frequently confused, angry and living in despair. Schooling suffers and many pupils underachieve, attend sporadically or are excluded. Other ways of occupying time and achieving status can be substituted, including offending and drug use. Their social exclusion and marginality provide a poor trajectory into adult life.

The children's homes they join are often poorly placed to address these problems: standards vary considerably and facilities can be lacking specific objectives and underlying philosophies (Brown *et al.* 1998). Referrals may occur to where there is a vacancy rather than a facility ideally suited to meet a young person's needs. Homes are stigmatised and often unpopular in neighbourhoods. Staff may sometimes be transitory and, in comparison with other areas of social work, less well trained and poorly paid. Young people pose considerable challenges in their behaviour and self-esteem and their daily control can override longer-term needs.

Nonetheless, many young people say that they like the children's home in which they live and most adolescents, at least, see residential care as preferable to the alternatives (Berridge 1994). Research over many years shows considerable variation between residential institutions which nominally carry the same label and admit residents with similar characteristics and histories, and demonstrates that it is possible to identify well run establishments which are the most successful at meeting young people's needs during residence (Bullock *et al.* 1993). Demonstrating that these benefits carry over into successful outcomes after leaving care is a different matter, especially now that the average length of stay is less than two years (Sinclair and Gibbs 1998). The main difficulty is that, in itself, a brief residential stay is unlikely to overcome the major personal and structural problems that have accumulated over the years. There is also evidence, from research over the past 40 years, that peer dynamics intervene in residential settings, and are major influences on young people's happiness and progress (Millham, Bullock and Cherrett 1975, Millham *et al.* 1978).

Bullying and peer violence in residential settings

In spite of the many recent scandals concerning the abuse of children in residential homes and schools (Wolmar 2000, Colton 2002), there has, surprisingly, been no major empirical research specifically focused on the prevalence of abuse of children in residential settings in the United Kingdom. Evidence comes from a few local studies and from the reports of enquiries set up following some of the major incidents. Kendrick's (1997) literature review for the Scottish Office is particularly helpful. Most of the accounts described below address the issue of peer violence in residential settings in the context of research on or inquiries into broader aspects of residential care or education.

The conceptualisation of peer violence in previous research falls within four separate traditions: the social work, sociological, psychological and social administrative approaches. The social work perspective, reflected in the few studies focused specifically on peer abuse in residential care and in more recent inquiry reports, sees it as a child protection problem, concerned with identifying risk to children and safeguarding them from harm. The sociological analysis, primarily represented by the Dartington Social Research Unit studies, sees violence as an organisational and structural feature of social and power relationships in residential communities, linking the separate but parallel worlds of staff and children and reflecting status within the children's world (Lambert *et al.* 1970, Millham, Bullock and Cherrett 1975). The psychological analysis, based largely on children's case histories, sees violence as the result of individual pathology, caused by children's previous experience of destructive and abusive relationships and faulty learning, affecting their ability to develop positive contact with peers, or to find non-violent, constructive solutions to conflict. The social administrative perspective views peer violence as a problem of maintaining order, with the emphasis on staff competence and training, appropriate disciplinary structures and on management providing leadership and support. Most research, however, takes an eclectic and pragmatic approach, and draws on a mixture of these explanations.

Peer violence as a child protection concern

Surprisingly, there has been little previous research addressing peer violence in a specific child protection context. In view of the growing concern in the 1980s and 1990s about the problem of institutional abuse, it was perhaps surprising that the programme of 20 research studies on child protection funded by the Department of Health (1998a) did not include any specific study with a residential focus. This is indicative of the way in which both policy and research are often constrained by artificial administrative boundaries. The inquiries into institutional abuse scandals have noted that young people's complaints about abuse were frequently ignored or discounted because of assumptions that were made about the character, behaviour and truthfulness of the young people placed in residential care (e.g. Levy and Kahan 1991). These assumptions may also have contributed to the lack of interest in research on the protection of young people in residential care.

The primary focus of the enquiry reports has been on the actual or potential abuse by *staff*, the reason which led to the setting up of the inquiries in the first place. Yet although the abuse by staff has hit the headlines, due to its appalling nature and persistence over many years, much of the available evidence has indicated that residents are most often at risk from *other young people* in the home or school.

One of the authors of this report examined the independent investigations over a two-year period of all National Society for the Prevention of

Cruelty to Children (NSPCC) teams into abuse in residential or day care settings (Barter 1998). This revealed 36 investigations concerning allegations made by 67 children against 50 abusers. A fifth of these involved abuse by other residents. Six of the ten concerned sexual abuse, mostly female residents complaining about male peers. Over a quarter of all allegations of sexual abuse in residential settings involved peers. This work built on an earlier statistical survey by the NSPCC into this problem, in which all regions had been asked for details of cases of institutional abuse they had dealt with in the previous year (Westcott and Clement 1992). Information was provided on 84 children abused in 43 residential settings. Almost two-thirds were male and half of them were 15 years of age or above. Four-fifths of the cases involved some kind of sexual abuse and one-fifth involved physical abuse (not mutually exclusive). Half occurred in children's homes and two-fifths in residential schools. Half of the perpetrators were peers and 43 per cent staff. An overwhelming majority were male (81 per cent). The report highlighted the particular vulnerability of disabled children to institutional abuse: over a third of those abused were reported to have a learning difficulty and 1 per cent were physically disabled.

Elsewhere, Lunn (1990a,b) reported that Nottinghamshire County Council had discovered that a worrying number of its 380 children in residential homes were being abused by other residents. Twenty-six young people who had been placed in care because of sexual abuse were found to have been further abused by their peers; and another six suffered sexual abuse for the first time at the hands of other residents. Twenty-three boys had been placed with known histories as sexual abusers, and sixteen young people had come into care as victims of abuse and had gone on to sexually abuse others. The authority was said to be developing two separate facilities for sexually abused girls and sexually abused boys.

Young people's own accounts provide further evidence of the incidence and nature of institutional abuse. Morris and Wheatley (1994) investigated the calls to the dedicated phone line set up by ChildLine for children in care. In the first 6 months of its operation, 539 calls were received from young people in England and Wales. Three-quarters of callers were girls and over half between 14 and 16 years, confirming concerns about how to provide better protection for younger children who may not be able to access telephone help lines. Just over half the calls were from residents in children's homes and a third were living in foster care. For the resident group, the most significant problem for callers was bullying or other forms of violence from peers in the home (10 per cent). Again, most perpetrators were male. The behaviour ranged from teasing or being picked on, to physical attacks. Calls concerned small as well as large homes.

Young people felt that communal living created inevitable conflict and that arguments or fights would sometimes erupt, which then released tension. Responses involved trying to ignore the problem, distancing themselves from the perpetrator so they would be untouched by the intimidation or retaliation. In extreme cases, young people would withdraw completely from interaction with the other residents or request a change in placement. Most callers stated that they had informed staff but felt that their concerns had been ignored. Children had been advised to ignore the teasing or name-calling. Physical fights were usually unobserved by staff, who were reluctant to act on the basis of children's accounts alone.

Another 25 callers to the special phone line concerned allegations of current sexual abuse, 9 of which were against male residents and 8 against male residential staff. Young people said that staff usually reacted to their complaints with scepticism. Two callers added that staff thought the abuser was their boyfriend. The report concluded that bullying is a persistent feature of residential homes.

A parallel phone line was set up specifically for pupils living in boarding schools (La Fontaine and Morris 1992). In 6 months this received 1012 calls, 20 per cent classified as bullying and 15 per cent were sexual abuse. Attacks were very often serious and a number of pupils were clearly terrified. Girls were more likely to have been subjected to 'psychological bullying', usually with individuals or groups of girls in the same class. The researchers acknowledged the difficulty in differentiating between sexual abuse and sexual harassment. In contrast to the care population, almost all the sexual abuse reported involved staff of the schools, but 13 per cent was attributed to other pupils. A quarter of the sexually abused callers reported that other children were being abused by the same person. A further study of calls from boarding school pupils in 1995–96 produced similar figures for bullying but a much reduced figure for sexual assaults at school, especially by fellow pupils (ChildLine 1997).

The statistics are complemented by personal accounts from young people in care. A report of the work of a therapeutic community stated that a quarter of children on entry were regarded as 'bullies' (Little and Kelly 1995). However, a young woman's account of her experiences at the community does not convey that this was a problem. Children were under close surveillance from staff and seemed more preoccupied with resolving their own problems than venting their frustrations on others. In contrast, Fever's (1994) pessimistic and moving account of his upbringing by a voluntary agency tells of his sexual abuse between the ages of 7 and 10 by a teenager with whom he was made to share a bedroom. He was threatened with castration if he told anyone.

The evidence presented to the major reviews of residential services which were set up in response to a series of scandals also indicated high levels of violence from young people. Members of the Children's Safeguards review team covering England and Wales held meetings with young people from 20 local authorities and reported that the danger most often referred to was that from other children, especially bullying, physical abuse and theft

(Utting 1997). Less was said by the young people about the danger to personal safety from staff. Indeed, the report estimated that 'possibly half the total of abuse reported in institutions is peer abuse' (p. 99). Yet only 1 brief final paragraph out of 12 in the section on 'abusers' refers to children. A separate part of the report discusses 'bullying', implying a clear distinction both conceptually and in practice between the two behaviours. This report echoes some of the concerns previously raised in connection with bullying in schools, that adults may regard it as a 'normal' feature of children's behaviour and social relationships. The report states that:

> ...so little was said to the Review about bullying in children's homes – except by children and young people experiencing past or present anxieties about their personal safety... Just as worrying is the acceptance of these consequences by staff and managers – as if casual violence, sexual molestation, threats and racial abuse characterise 'normal' adolescent behaviour and were therefore neither more nor less than could be expected in a children's home. (p. 105)

The Scottish review team made a similar distinction between bullying and peer abuse, using the latter term to refer only to sexual abuse, although noting in a different section of the report that physical abuse could include injuries inflicted by other young people (Kent 1997).

Violent 'cultures' in residential homes and schools

Evidence from these few sources focusing on abuse is consistent with the findings of research looking more broadly at the regimes and cultures of residential care and boarding schools. Many studies of children's residential settings have touched on the subjects of bullying and peer violence, although few focus primarily on it. Most give indications that peer violence could be a feature of the regime.

Research in boarding schools in the 1960s revealed that bullying was common and some schools could be particularly hostile (Lambert 1968). The sociological analysis considered it primarily as a feature of organisational life, which serves a variety of functions, rather than as a child protection issue. Pupils felt that the benefits of boarding outweighed any disadvantages. Homosexual behaviour was depicted as common in all-male boarding schools but not especially exploitative ('I get sick of the boys who are constantly making passes at me. It is highly embarrassing' [p. 271]). Concerns about inappropriate behaviour by masters were seldom raised by pupils in the book. This presents a very different picture from that given by callers to the Boarding School Helplines in the 1990s, cited earlier (La Fontaine and Morris 1992, ChildLine 1997).

Detailed research was undertaken on 18 boys' approved schools for young offenders in the 1970s, focusing on their regimes (Millham, Bullock and

Cherrett 1975). In contrast to the revelations since about residential malpractice in some former approved schools, most of those in the study were portrayed as essentially harmonious and boys were mainly positive about their experiences. In a chapter on the boys' informal world, the researchers concluded that there was little evidence of the '...violence, exploitation and hostility which are supposed to characterise such groups' (p. 170) but point out that '...in those few approved schools where the boys' informal worlds had coercive and brutish qualities' (*ibid*), they did little to conceal the fact. Boys were reported to have developed a 'pecking order' in most schools, resembling staff hierarchies, but this was mainly linked to the fact that those who had been at the school longest felt they should benefit most in everyday life – such as access to the television. Boys with the highest informal status, especially in the most effective schools, were '...not thugs or manipulators but frequently the more mature, thoughtful and responsible members of the group' (p. 172). The Dartington Social Research Unit returned to the subject of residential care with their observer–participation study of structure and culture in nine children's homes (Brown *et al.* 1998). The report contains little discussion of resident violence, with residents in six of the nine homes telling researchers that the behaviour of their peers was 'reasonable'.

A study of secure provision for boys (Millham *et al.* 1978) reported that outbursts and conflicts were said to be rare when children were locked up, possibly linked to the high level of adult surveillance. This report contains a more detailed discussion of violence in residential institutions, as the two factors that led to the demand for an increase in secure units was a perception that violent behaviour and absconding were becoming more significant problems in open units. Violence was defined as 'the use of force in a social situation in a way that those in power define as illegitimate' (p. 59). This, and the accompanying discussion, implies that violence is equated with *physical* acts; that behaviour that was officially condoned could not be 'violent', such as a headteacher encouraging one boy to fight another; and that (senior) staff cannot themselves be responsible for 'violence'.

The regimes adopted by institutions were said to influence the level of violence: the more relaxed the regime, the greater the incidence of aggressive behaviour of all sorts. However, the number of 'serious' incidents was said to be very small. We do not know how boys themselves defined 'serious'. Violent incidents were said to cluster and in the senior approved schools this was felt to be linked with changes in the leading group among residents. Elsewhere (Millham *et al.* 1976) the same researchers added that three-quarters of violent incidents recorded in the four schools studied in detail were between children themselves.

In all the Dartington studies of public residential care, as distinct from boarding schools, sociological analysis of the staff and resident 'cultures' concluded that the children's culture was weak and fragmented, partly due to high levels of staff control and surveillance, and partly because the residents were for the most part too immature and disturbed to co-operate in establishing a coherent and dominant pattern of control and conformity.

An observer–participation study of 20 children's homes in the early 1980s reported that 1 in 6 residents were said by staff to pose 'major control problems' within the homes, about a third presented 'minor' problems yet half caused few noticeable difficulties (Berridge 1985). However this covered a range of behaviours, including verbal aggression and defiance towards staff, and not just peer relations. The study concluded that there was an element of 'moral panic' about unruly behaviour in children's homes and '…lethargy and boredom rather than uncontrollable behaviour tend to be the more pressing problems' (p. 83). Berridge and Brodie's (1998) study of 12 children's homes reported that bullying was referred to explicitly in three establishments. But, it appeared that, for adolescents, subcultures operated more in relation to social networks *outside* the home, involving care leavers and other groups of youths.

The relationship between aggressor and victim

The study of the secure units (Millham *et al.* 1978) pointed to the complex relationship between perpetrators and victims of violence:

> Particularly interesting also is the whole relationship between the hitter and the hit. It is not necessarily one of constant and mutual hostility. Often the fight is part of an ongoing friendship, sometimes an intense relationship, and only in rare cases the result of carefully nurtured hostility or indifference…Not only did highly aggressive boys have a wider friendship network but they were more likely to be involved in conflicts with their reciprocating friends. (p. 64)

Similar conclusions were reached in a sociological analysis of racism in the lives of primary school pupils, where white children could resort on occasions to extremely offensive racist name-calling against minority ethnic children who, in other respects, appeared close friends (Troyna and Hatcher 1992).

Browne and Falshaw (1996) noted the degree of overlap between bullying and bullied in a secure unit, where 30 per cent of young people were both bullies and victims. They found a relationship between being bullied in the secure unit and having previously been bullied in schools, and depict a pattern of personal histories associated with bullying very similar to that outlined earlier in studies of bullying in schools.

Changing behaviour or a changed context for peer violence?

During the 1990s research appeared to show different patterns of relationships between young people in residential care, compared to those of the earlier studies. Research on young people going missing from residential and foster homes contained evidence on the extent to which running away was related to unhappiness and exploitation in placements (Wade *et al.* 1998). Indeed, young people involved stated that an important reason for going missing was the powerful peer culture in some homes. The researchers commented that power relations within peer cultures could have a more significant effect on young people's behaviour than staff interventions. Entering a residential home could be particularly unsettling. An important aspect of developing strategies to prevent young people going missing was to tackle bullying in homes.

Recent research on children in residential care indicates that young people may be significantly more at risk of physical and sexual violence from other residents than from staff. Sinclair and Gibbs' (1998) study is the main source of recent information about young people's violent experiences in children's homes. It gives a disconcerting account of the dynamics of everyday life in many establishments and of the unhappiness of residents. Forty-four per cent of the 223 residents interviewed stated that they had been bullied during their stay at the home. This raises questions about exactly what is meant by 'bullied' and whether all young people and adults share a common definition. It is also unclear how much of this violence took place within the home itself rather than at school or in the wider community. Nonetheless, it is a high figure and the incidence was greatest for the youngest residents. Seventy per cent of those aged 12 years or under said they had been bullied since arrival at the home, compared with nearly half of 13- and 14-year-olds and just over a third of the remainder. For many, these experiences were a continuation of experiences prior to entry to residential care and not experienced solely in the care system: 41 per cent said they had been bullied beforehand, and these young people were more likely also to have been bullied while in the children's home. Furthermore, Sinclair and Gibbs asked residents about their main worries. Problems were identified concerning health, education and leaving the residential home but the main anxiety expressed related to 'getting on with peers' – 81 per cent said this worried them 'a lot', 15 per cent 'some' and only 4 per cent not at all.

Peer sexual assault and exploitation in residential homes

Two studies explored the sensitive issue of sexual exploitation of young people by peers in children's homes. Sinclair and Gibbs (1998) found that 23 per cent of females and 7 per cent of males reported that someone had tried 'to take sexual advantage' of them, with peers rather than staff being apparently responsible for this. As with bullying, those who had experienced sexual harassment prior to admission were more likely to have experienced it while in the home, leading the researchers to suggest that some young people were particularly vulnerable to bullying or harassment. Farmer and Pollock's (1998) research into sexually abused and abusing children in substitute care discovered that children who had been abused at home were more likely to be placed in residential care, whereas those who had abused others mostly went to foster homes, where it was assumed they would be less of a risk. There were extensive gaps in information passed on to caregivers, insufficient attention was paid to whether or not the child would be a 'good match' with others in placement and it was not uncommon for abusers to share bedrooms with other children. Consequently, half the sexually abused children in the sample went on to abuse others, mostly involving peers in foster and residential placements.

While levels of reported bullying and other peer violence in recent children's homes research seem comparable to those found in studies of schools and community settings, Millham *et al.* (1976) cautioned against uncritically transferring what is known about violence in one context to another. The impact of attack in the place where young people live, and from fellow residents, may be experienced quite differently from that of violence elsewhere. In Sinclair and Gibbs' study, most residents felt that they had been helped in some way to deal with their problems by their stay at the home. But the depth of residents' unhappiness was illustrated by their responses to other questions: between a third and two-thirds gave answers that indicated they were worried, depressed, had a low opinion of themselves or thought they were going nowhere in life. An alarming four in ten claimed that they had considered killing themselves in the previous month. Previous experiences of bullying and sexual abuse were significantly associated with unhappiness but incidents since admission were even more strongly linked. Being bullied was felt to be a probable cause of poor adjustment in the longer term. Though staff were generally perceived as kind and helpful, Sinclair and Gibbs concluded that a more important determinant of young people's welfare was the resident group and how young people got on with them.

It is not clear whether the greater prevalence of peer violence suggested in more recent reports and studies represents a worsening of actual levels of violence – perhaps linked to a change in population in children's homes as the most troubled young people are concentrated in a much smaller number of establishments – or is it the result of a change in the approach towards examining and assessing violent behaviour by young people? It could also result from a more open approach taken by researchers towards young people's accounts of their experience. In many respects the past two decades have seen changing attitudes towards violence of all kinds, with lessened tolerance leading to new legislative and policing responses to domestic violence, sexual violence and child abuse. The change has been most notable with respect to violence in the private rather than the public arena. There is greater protection in law than formerly, more resources allocated to helping victims of violence, and an apparently greater willingness to report some forms of violence.

Publicity given to the harm caused by bullying in schools has led to school-based initiatives to acknowledge and tackle behaviour, which seems formerly to have been considered by adults as a trivial problem (Smith and Sharp 1994). The debates about physical punishment of children, in school and in the family, and about violence in the media, have focused attention on the ways in which children respond to models of violence, and the messages they receive when they see or experience violence from adults. While there is little evidence that levels of interpersonal violence have substantially decreased (Simmons 2002, Stanko 2002) it is possible that the more open discourse within which violence is now considered has made it easier for researchers and others to address and identify peer violence which was previously hidden. Yet, though young people may be more willing to tell researchers about experience of violence, all the evidence suggests that they are still often reluctant to confide in parents, professionals or other adults in their network.

Policy and guidance on peer violence in children's homes

Child care policy has had little to say about violence between young people in children's homes. The guidance available has largely reflected the social administrative perspective that it is primarily a matter of maintaining order, and the primary concern was always with violence towards, or abuse by, staff rather than on behaviour between young people. The then Department of Health and Social Security sponsored a series of seminars and a publication on violence in the mid-1970s in response to concerns about maintaining order in approved schools (Tutt 1976). In the early 1980s, the Dartington Social Research Unit looked at issues of control in residential care where the focus once more returned to violence between children (Millham *et al.* 1981). Guidance on residential care was produced to accompany the introduction of the Children Act 1989 (Department of Health 1991). This contained helpful good practice material but the section on maintaining good order and discipline makes no mention of peer relationships. In addition, Sir William Utting conducted two detailed reviews of residential childcare in the 1990s. The first, in response to the Pindown report discussed above (Levy and Kahan 1991), alludes to peer violence but gives much greater prominence to violence by staff (Department of Health 1991). The second review 6 years later, followed continuing publicity about physical and sexual abuse in institutions over the previous 20 years, and focused on the issues of safeguarding children and young people. The report is remembered for its pithy statements, references to 'sexually and physically abusive terrorists' (p. 5) and the review being at times '...a crash course in human (predominantly male) wickedness and in the fallibility of social institutions' (p. 7, Utting 1997). Although, as cited earlier, the report identified abuse by peers as a major issue in residential settings, and the recommendations mention peer violence, little detail is given. Action to address peer violence is excluded from the list of principal recommendations.

Reports along similar lines were also commissioned in Scotland (Kent 1997) and Wales (Waterhouse 2000). Once again the former, though acknowledging the problem of peer abuse, makes no particular mention of it in the list of recommendations.

Another important policy initiative in the 1990s was the work of the Warner Committee on staffing in children's homes (Department of Health 1992), also set up in response to a major scandal (Kirkwood 1993). The Committee's remit was concerned with the protection of children and young people from abuse by staff. It reported that, though there is some US research, there was no full-scale study of the abuse of children in institutions in the United Kingdom. The only evidence the committee cited was a small-scale exercise by the National Association of Young People in Care (NAYPIC), based on 50 young people, mostly living in institutions, who had complained to them about abuse. About half the perpetrators of abuse were staff (mostly male) and half were other young people (Department of Health 1992, p. 20). The attention of the Committee focused on the selection, development and management of staff and none of its 83 recommendations concern abuse by children.

A main government initiative to raise standards in the management and delivery of children's social services has been *Quality Protects* (Department of Health 1998b), set up following the Children's Safeguards review of children living away from home (Utting 1997). Under this initiative £875 million is being made available to local authorities over five years (1999–2004) to improve services for children, with a particular emphasis on care services for 'looked after' children (Department of Health 2002b). A series of publications have been produced outlining various objectives, sub-objectives and a 'Performance Assessment Framework' (PAF). An underlying principle of the initiative, as the title suggests, is that children's safety will be enhanced by an improvement in overall standards of social care rather than solely through particular measures. Thus, for children looked after by local authorities, *Quality Protects* covers, for example, areas such as the stability of placements, educational achievements, health, offending, re-registrations on the child protection register, proportions in family placements, unit cost of services and rates of adoption. Once again the focus is on the competence and effectiveness of professionals and there are no specific indicators concerning institutional abuse or violence between young people as measures of quality in residential services.

Young people in custody

Although there has been media attention to violence in custodial institutions for young people, often following deaths of young people due to suicide and occasionally homicide, there has been even less research than on the care system. However the available evidence from the few research studies and from official reports, including the published reports of inspections of young offenders' institutions (Chief Inspector of Prisons 1997), present a similar picture to that of other group settings, in which violence and bullying are common features of young people's experience, with a substantial group being both bullies and bullied (Edgar and O'Donnell 1997) and an oppressive hierarchy or 'pecking order' (Howard League 1995). Kendrick (1997) summarises the evidence and shows that the prison system appears to be unusual among residential institution services in having a stated policy and clear, positive strategy to combat bullying and violence. Methods include anti-bullying agreements signed by young prisoners, anti-bullying committees of prisoners, and a positive strategy for peer support with 'Listener' schemes which use 'trained and trusted inmates to advise and counsel other inmates' (Tattum 1995 cited in Kendrick 1997, p. 209). Inspection reports and local research studies suggest that these approaches can be successful in improving physical safety and reducing self-harm and suicide attempts in a well-managed institution, but there has yet to be research on how widely they are used in the prison system, or on their effectiveness in reducing, as distinct from containing, bullying.

Common themes on peer violence

There are a number of common themes which emerge from this examination of the evidence on peer violence. In all contexts there seems to be agreement that approximately 30–40 per cent of children and young people experience threat or attack of some kind from peers; that the younger they are, the more likely they are to be victimised; that violence is usually hidden from adults both by perpetrators and victims; that power hierarchies are an important feature of the situation; that gender and ethnicity are both important factors associated with power dynamics and types of attack; that a substantial minority will be both aggressor and victim on different occasions; that family and personal factors may be important issues associated with being aggressors and victims; that being a victim in one context may increase vulnerability for the future; and that there are both immediate and long-term harmful effects of peer violence, up to and including self-harm and suicide.

There are also indications that the response of adults may have important effects on the likelihood and seriousness of violence. In both day and residential contexts the level of staff surveillance has been identified as a significant influence. It is noted that staff often do not take peer violence seriously, but that where positive intervention strategies do exist there is some evidence that they are effective in reducing levels of bullying. Some studies suggest that in well-managed services, the more mature and constructive young people are likely to have most influence on the group, with the implication (not tested in research) that poor management may have the opposite effect.

In planning the present research, the insights from earlier studies have been used in conjunction with recent developments in theorising violence. It was clear that the focus of the study could not be restricted to physical violence, since previous evidence demonstrated that threats, intimidation and indirect methods of attack were inextricably linked with, and supported, both individual acts and general climates of physical violence.

The meaning of violence

Theoretical understandings of the term violence are under-developed and remain problematic (Richardson and May 1999). Kelly (1988) argues that traditional 'common sense' definitions of violence reflect a focus on male behaviour that is considered to be a direct threat to public safety. Gabe and others (2001) continue that these 'common sense' understandings emphasise the visible and quantifiable aspects of violence to the exclusion of less visible manifestations. The implication of this is that apparent physical injury takes precedence over psychological harm (Featherstone and Trinder 1997). However, feminist scholars have pointed out that such definitions may omit acts which many people understand and experience as violence, such as verbal and/or 'psychological' abuse (Hanmer and Saunders 1984, McNeil 1987, Wise and Stanley 1987, Kelly 1988, Stanko 1990, 1995, Maynard 1993). Consequently these commentators, among others, have attempted to develop a broader social definition of violence that encompasses a wider spectrum of behaviours not restricted to legal codes or 'expert' accounts. Debates about violence often become conflated with assumptions that the overt seriousness of violence dictates its impact on people's lives. Thus long-term verbal abuse is often depicted as annoying but not fear-provoking, nor a blight on individual lives. However evidence suggests otherwise, for example in relation to racist insults (see Sibbitt 1997, Barter 1999). Scientists have shown that social rejection triggers a similar response in the brain as physical pain (Eisenberger *et al.* 2003). In addition verbal sexual pestering, comments and daily verbal abuse have been shown to contribute greatly to creating a climate within which other forms of violence can fester (Gardner and Brooks 1995, Madriz 1998). Reflecting this complexity Stanko defines violence as:

> ... any behaviour by an individual that intentionally threatens, attempts to inflict, or does cause, physical, sexual or psychological harm to others or to her/himself. (Stanko 2000: 246)

The Association of Directors of Social Services (ADSS) describe violence very simply: 'behaviour which has a damaging effect either physically or emotionally on other people' (Kemshall and Pritchard 1996: 162).

It is important to recognise that debates surrounding how violence is defined are not simply intriguing academic exercises, but have practical implications. The scope of such definitions is important as they determine how an act is labelled by both individuals and institutions, which in turn affects whether the behaviour comes to the attention of someone authorised to intervene and to assist the victim or assailant (Kelly 1988, Glass 1995, Hoyle 1998). Ultimately, it is the capacity of individuals and institutions to determine which acts are defined as 'violence' that determines the social character of violence (Stanko 2000).

Public/private dichotomy of violence

Historically, researchers and academics have concentrated on male acts of physical violence in the public domain, but this domination has now been successfully challenged, predominantly by feminist writers. Through work on socially unrecognised and hidden forms of 'private' violence (such as the sexual abuse of children and domestic violence), the central position that violence holds within the private sphere has been widely recognised (Bell 1993, Plummer 1995, Maynard and Winn 1997). Although the distinction between the two spheres has been challenged in social theory for being false (Walby 1990) and the inter-relationship between public and private violence has been acknowledged, this does not diminish the importance of recognising the 'ideological and normative power' of the public/private divide (Cooper 1993). This is of central importance in relation to residential care, which occupies a position in what has been termed the 'intermediate zone' where the public world of work and the private domain of the family overlap and merge (Stacy and Davis 1983).

Gender and violence

It is well established that males account for most homicides and violent assaults (Newburn and Stanko 1994). Hence violence is acknowledged as a problem and a consequence of certain forms of masculinities (Braithwaite and Daly 1994, Connell 1995). In contrast physical violence perpetrated by females is uncommon, as girls rely more on psychological and verbal forms of attack (Batchelor *et al.* 2001). This is despite the recent spate of (unfounded) media depictions of girls as the 'new lads', whose use of indiscriminate, physical, gang-based violence is depicted as a new and growing social problem (see Brinkworth and Burrell 1994, Cohen 1994). Female perpetrators of physical violence are castigated as being 'unfeminine' (transgressing gender expectations) and pathological, whereas some forms of male physical violence are viewed as an 'acceptable' expression of masculinity (Heidensohn 1995). Certain forms of violence are viewed as transgressions of social norms and boundaries and are, therefore, more likely to attract social opposition (Richardson and May 1999). This can include violence by children, as evidenced by the public outcry over cases where children commit homicide, compared to the attention given to murder by adult males (see e.g. Jackson 1995, Sereny 1998). Violence by adolescent males, however, arouses a different response according to context, whether it is seen as just 'silly kids' – as in aggressive horseplay in the playground or sports field – or as a threat to the social order, as in violent street crime or violence to teachers.

The present study – research methods

As stated earlier, theorisation of the term 'violence' remains underdeveloped and problematic (Richardson and May 1999). In response, we drew upon a broader and more inclusive social definition of violence that encompasses a wide spectrum of behaviours that is rooted in and can cope with the complexity of experience from the standpoint of the individual concerned. Defining violence in such a way was fundamental to our project of which a central aim is the representation of children's experiences of violence, whose voices (and thus experiences) have historically remained silent and marginalised.

We drew upon Kelly's (1987) inclusive framework for violence as a continuum of harm in which physical, sexual, emotional and psychological abuses of power at individual and group levels allows for a much more fluid theorisation of violence. In this, a whole range of behaviours can be understood according to participants' own evaluations and interpretations. Indeed, we were increasingly aware during the fieldwork how violence needs to be understood within a continuum that recognises its multi-faceted and often contested status if young people's accounts are to be incorporated and acknowledged. For example, a continuum can include a diverse range of violent behaviours from isolated flashes of physical violence to systematic, prolonged verbal attacks. It was also important to investigate both incidence and impact if we were to tease out the meanings and roles that different forms of violence play in young people's lives. Consequently, in addition to our theoretical framework, we needed to develop a methodology in which young people (and staff) could define and contextualise their own personal experiences of violence. Given the loaded nature of the term 'violence' a decision was taken early on not to describe our research interest using this term, but as an investigation into 'the positive and negative aspects of residential life' more widely. Indeed, we were very keen to use the research process in enabling children to articulate their experiences as they are significant and meaningful to them and, furthermore, allow them to wield some control over the focus and direction of the research (see Alldred 1998).

Developing appropriate methodology: prioritising children's experiences

In addition, we needed to develop a methodology that could: engage children to participate in 'sensitive research'; enable a discussion both of personal experiences of violence and types of violence that participants may not have directly encountered; explore the interpretations and meanings different actors ascribed to different situations and courses of actions; and, additionally, provide children with a greater level of control over the research interaction. Two complementary techniques were employed to fulfil these diverse aims. First, *semi-structured interviews* were used in which children could identify, define and contextualise their own personal experiences of violence. Staff were similarly asked about their experiences and management of violence between children in their care. Participants were asked to recall both their most recent experiences (within the last month) and their longer term evaluations of peer violence to determine if levels of violence fluctuated over time within each of the homes, and if so why. Second, *vignettes* were employed to depict different forms of violence to which children and adults could respond. Alongside these formal data collection techniques, researchers spent a considerable amount of time in each setting informally observing and interacting with participants. This aspect of the study was extended after feedback from the pilot stage of the project, which indicated that children needed more opportunity to get to know the researchers before they felt comfortable discussing their experiences of violence with them.

Much methodological literature exists concerning the use of qualitative semi-structured interview techniques, which we shall not rehearse here. Portraying 'active listening' and a 'non-directive stance' (Whyte 1984), and making efforts to convey a non-judgmental attitude (Hill 1997), avoiding asking 'leading questions' (Lofland and Lofland 1995) and instead asking 'contrasting', 'descriptive' and sometimes 'structural' questions (Spradley 1979) were all central components in our interview techniques (see Appendix A). In contrast, although vignettes have been used by researchers to explore diverse social issues, little methodological writing exists which examines the use of this technique within social research (but see Barter and Renold 1999, Schoenberg and Ravdal 2000) and, particularly, its application within qualitative research with children. In qualitative studies, vignettes have been increasingly used to elicit cultural norms derived from participants' attitudes to and beliefs about a specific situation and to highlight ethical frameworks and moral codes. Hughes (1998:384) states that 'vignettes highlight selected parts of the real world that can help unpack individuals' perceptions, beliefs, and attitudes to a wide range of social issues'.

Within our study, four written vignettes were used. Each depicted a different aspect of behaviour including sexual, emotional, physical and verbal forms of violence and was based on children's 'real' experiences derived from earlier pilot interviews and data from previous research (Barter 1996). Each vignette was adapted to use with younger children (aged 6–12 years) and adolescents. Questions following each vignette included how they thought characters in the story would feel and behave, and how they themselves might feel and respond if presented with a similar scenario and why. The reasons surrounding each response were then freely explored with each participant, thus allowing them the space to redefine contexts and behaviours by drawing on their own and others' experiences. Due to the flexibility of this technique within the interview we were able to adapt the data collection to fit individual participants' needs. Using the vignettes in this way compensated for some young people's lack of direct experience, and gave others the opportunity to decide when and if they wished to interject their vignette responses with personal experiences. This gave them greater control over the research interaction. For a comprehensive overview of our use of vignettes in our study of peer violence see Barter and Renold (1999, 2000).

All interviews were tape-recorded and fully transcribed for detailed analysis using the qualitative data analysis software package NUD*IST4 (see Richards 1995). Full details regarding the approach to analysis are included in Appendix B.

Sample

Thirteen homes took part in the study, 1 of which had 2 separate house units on 1 campus, making 14 residential units (9 local authority, 3 private and two voluntary homes). Nine were mixed, four all-male and 1 all-female. Twelve units were for adolescents and 2 for younger children. Homes reflected the national balance between the sectors, including establishments from across England, and in urban and rural areas.

Seventy-four children and young people were interviewed but three interviews were excluded due to doubts about their validity. Of 71 valid interviews, there were 41 young people from local authority homes, 19 from private homes and 11 from voluntary homes. As with the national distribution of young people in residential care, more were male (44) than female (27). Nearly a quarter of the sample (16) were from minority ethnic groups, 12 males and 4 females. Ages ranged from 6 to 17 years but the majority were teenagers, with 14 children aged 12 or less. Most (55) young people lived in homes with 7 or more places; 16 in smaller homes for 6 or less. About half had been in their current placement for six months or more, with 11 there for less than one month.

Seventy-one staff were interviewed: 39 women and 32 men. There were 47 from local authority homes, 14 from private homes and 10 from voluntary homes. Most were from homes for more than 6 children and 26 from smaller homes. Those interviewed included 20 with management responsibilities, 10 senior/team leaders and 41 residential social workers. Most (53) were white British, with 18 staff of other ethnicity, including African Caribbean, Irish, South Asian and African (see Appendix C for a full sample breakdown).

All staff and most young people were interviewed individually, but eight children who wished it were interviewed jointly with a friend or sibling.

Ethical safeguards for young research participants

Following the British Sociological Association's *Statement of Ethical Practice* 'special care' was taken with young research participants who are vulnerable by factors of 'age, social status and powerlessness' (Morrow and Richards 1996). Introductory meetings were held in each home with both staff and young people. All participants were sent leaflets before we visited explaining the aims of the research, the voluntary nature of participation, confidentiality and researchers' phone contact numbers alongside their photographs. The younger children, who might have had limited reading ability, were given audiotapes explaining the research. A form detailing participants' rights within the research (for example their right to end the discussion whenever they wished, or to revoke their consent for their discussion to be used upon completion of the interview) were provided which young people signed to indicate their understanding. Leaflets were also produced for parents and external social workers detailing the research project. Participants were assured that information would be confidential to the research team, unless researchers were told of circumstances in which children were in 'immediate serious danger'. These situations would be reported to an appropriate senior person (preferably with the young person's consent), and a suitable management contact was negotiated in each managing agency. Throughout the fieldwork we reminded young people of these rights and especially the limitations of confidentiality, to ensure young people did not disclose information which they may later regret. This process is described by Thorne (1980) as 'renewed consent'. All of the managers of the children's homes were assured anonymity in any reports arising from the research, consequently individual homes are not named.

The text of the book is organised as follows: Chapter 2 is concerned with mapping peer violence in children's homes. Chapter 3 then discusses young people's perspectives on violence, followed in Chapter 4 by staff views. In Chapter 5 we contrast young people's and staff views by using vignettes. Chapter 6 considers institutional and organisational factors associated with violence. Next, Chapter 7 evaluates working practices, followed by methods of intervention in Chapter 8. The final chapter summarises the main findings and draws out some conclusions.

Summary points

- There has been relatively little research on peer violence except for that on bullying at school, which has led to statistical studies and some intervention programmes. Definitions vary, but studies are united in indicating that it is a very common experience both to bully and to be bullied, with

figures of around 30–40 per cent of school pupils being bullied as the norm.
- A summary of research identified the characteristics of those most at risk, including younger children, those with problems in their family, those who have few friends. Bullying often targets children's social background, physical appearance and ethnicity. It causes considerable distress and there have been some indications of longer term harm and of bullying-related suicide.
- There has been no research specifically focused on the prevalence of abuse in residential care, in spite of the major scandals and public inquiries in recent years.
- In conceptualising violence for the present study we are operating within the sociology of childhood, and using a model which treats children and young people's relationships and cultures as being worthy of study in their own right.
- Violence is used to mean physical, sexual and psychological attack or threat, including indirect and relational attacks.
- Fourteen residential units took part in the research and 71 young people and 71 staff at different levels were interviewed. Semi-structured interviews explored children's and staff's experience, and vignettes of common violent scenarios were used to open up the discussion and explore personal experience and perspectives. No formal definition of violence was used and the focus of research was on wide-ranging aspects of behaviour between young people in children's homes, in order to look at violence in its context and to include psychological and indirect attack as well as direct physical violence.

2
Mapping Peer Violence in Children's Homes

> No-one would ever say anything about my mum because I would get up and hit them so hard, I would flip out at of them, I wouldn't care.
> (Alex, aged 14)

> I think getting, having names called to you is worse...because it hurts you more and it's, like if you had a fight and you cut yourself, the pain goes and it heals, but having, being called whatever is always at the back of your head.
> (Fiona, aged 14)

Conceptualising violence

This chapter describes in more detail the framework used to map and categorise young people's and staff's accounts of peer violence. As explained earlier, no pre-definition of violence was given, but broadly worded questions and vignettes were used to explore definitions and explanations for different forms of threat or attack. Kelly's (1987) conceptualisation of a continuum of violence involving the abuse of power, and insights from the literature outlined in Chapter 1 were used to inform the shaping of questions and choice of incidents used in the vignettes.

The literature suggested that there were some dimensions particularly important in understanding how violence is manifested between young people. In particular, gender appeared relevant to all types of threat or attack, not only sexual but physical and psychological violence also. Evidence of fluctuating relationships between antagonist and victim, and the way that individuals could be either, on different occasions, indicated that neither violent behaviour nor vulnerability were fixed properties of individual personalities, but that the context of specific incidents could affect the roles adopted on different occasions. Although it seemed that there was no evidence, in general, that peer violence was more frequent or serious in residential institutions than in other settings where young people interact, there seemed potentially greater vulnerability to long-term harm for young people in public care, due to their likelihood of having previous experiences of violence and abuse, and their separation from familiar support systems available to other young people. This indicated that the availability of all forms of support was likely to be a crucial issue to discuss with young people and staff in the research. Evidence on the roles played by adults suggested that for a variety of reasons much peer violence was hidden from adults, even from those seen as caring or supportive; and that the level of positive awareness and engagement in addressing it by staff would be potentially important in understanding the presence or absence of violence in a children's home.

Young people's evaluation of peer violence and verbal attacks

At the start of the interview, the researchers reiterated the objectives of the research: to explore and understand the way that young people in residential care behaved towards each other and their experience of living in groups of young people. After obtaining basic personal identifying data, interviews with young people began with a general investigation of their experience of residential settings in their present and previous placements. Young people were asked about everyday life in their present home, and about the advantages and disadvantages of living in a group of young people. Young participants gave examples of both. Advantages commonly mentioned were the friendship available from fellow residents and the contact with other young people who had faced similar difficulties to the ones they had themselves experienced. But among the disadvantages, all those interviewed mentioned the problems of bullying, 'hassle', hostility or aggression from other young people. The word 'violence' was rarely used in this generic context.

It was not the objective of the present research to monitor the frequency of each type of behaviour in the children's homes. Our concern was to understand the meaning of the incidents to young people, as recipients, bystanders and perpetrators. Young people were therefore not asked for a complete account of their experience of peer violence, but instead initially asked to focus on a specific incident in their experience, with the discussion then being widened into other personal experiences if they chose to do so. The illustrations given by young people were followed up in detailed discussion, with vignettes used to open up the issues further and to explore their understanding of different forms of peer violence. Incidents described in the vignettes in turn often triggered further discussion of similar incidents from personal experience. The incidents described could have involved the young person as victim, bystander or perpetrator, and could be from the present, or a previous, placement. The interviews explored the context of each incident discussed, with its triggers, sequence of events and consequences, discussion of the young people's understanding of the reasons for what happened, their feelings about it, their strategies for dealing with it and whether they had received any support from adults or peers following the incident.

Types and levels of violence

Analysis following pilot interviews showed that Kelly's (1987) framework needed refinement. Children's experiences and evaluations produced a continuum of violent behaviours that required recognition of their multi-faceted and contested status. Sexual violence, for example, could consist of physical acts, including assaults and gestures, or verbal threats and insults, but these were experienced as qualitatively different from non-sexual assaults or 'verbals'. Additionally, not all violence which occurred was an abuse of power. The final categories used were:

Physical contact violence: all forms of violence between young people involving direct physical assault. Examples from young people's accounts included: 'hitting', 'fighting', 'beating', 'kicking', 'pushing', 'slapping', 'stabbing', 'tying-up' and 'punching'.

Physical non-contact violence: physical acts that harmed young people emotionally rather than physically. They included intimidation via looks or gestures, written threats, forceful invasions of personal space and attacks on personal property. Examples given by young people were: a boy whose room was regularly 'trashed' by other residents, and one boy who was systematically physically, verbally and emotionally abusing other residents, reported to have used dots of white correction fluid on bedroom doors to signify his target that night.

Sexual violence: unwelcome behaviours, experienced as both abusive and sexual by young people, were categorised separately as sexual violence. Examples of sexual violence included 'flashing', sexual assault (e.g. grabbing a girl's breast), rape, inappropriate touching, unwanted sexual gestures and remarks.

Verbal violence: spoken words hurting or intended to hurt. Verbal attack predominantly took the form of name-calling concerning gender, sexuality, ethnicity, family and physical or sartorial appearance.

During the fieldwork the researchers became aware that there seemed to be very different levels of peer violence in the homes in the study, and this will be discussed in detail later. Examination of the log-books in homes gave a good flavour of daily life, but could not be used as a reliable guide to the frequency of violence, since staff did not necessarily know of or record all incidents. It was also possible that levels of violence in individual homes fluctuated considerably over time due to changes in population or other reasons. The normal pattern in children's homes is for the more mature and settled young people to return home or move on to foster care or independent living, being replaced by new admissions who may arrive in a distressed and turbulent state following a breakdown of their family life or previous placement. The log-books gave a good illustration of the different thresholds used for recording at the time of the fieldwork. In some homes the log recorded minor squabbles over which TV programme to watch, of a kind that might be normal domestic interaction between children in a family, while in other homes such matters would be regarded as insignificant, and physical fights or damage to property were recorded on almost a daily basis.

Because we were not monitoring the frequency of different types of behaviour, the figures given below cannot be used as a measure of the levels of violence in the children's homes in the sample, nor in residential care generally. By no means all of the incidents described came from the young people's present placement. The figures are given to demonstrate the extent to which young people had direct personal experience of receiving, carrying out or observing peer violence in residential settings; in short that they knew what they were talking about, and were extremely capable at describing and analysing their experience. The examples below illustrate the approach which was taken by the researchers to categorising and mapping the different forms and levels of threat and attack. Themes introduced will be returned to in more detail in subsequent chapters.

Physical violence

From our sample of 71 young people, 62 reported experiencing some form of physical violence during their time in residential children's homes: 38 young people as recipients of physical violence, 24 as perpetrators. Of the 62, 21 young people described incidents in which they were both recipients *and* perpetrators and 13 as bystanders. All young people described incidents that had taken place in their current placement, although many also described incidents occurring in other children's homes.

One of the most interesting findings was the lack of gender differences in involvement, with both boys and girls reporting incidents as perpetrators and victims of physical violence. However, there were gender differences in relation to how different types of physical violence were perpetrated and experienced by young people, particularly in terms of the impact and social context and dynamic in which the violence took place. We have identified differences between 'low' and 'high' level physical violence by relating the type of violence to its reported and perceived impact upon young people.

Low-level physical violence

Low-level violence was perceived by young people as having no significant long-term impact on their lives and was not a major feature of their residential experience.

> Well, there are little fights like that but they are minor in my eyes, do you understand what I mean, it was a squabble kind of thing, you know, it's like a…, like a little scrap or something, or you know, it's never anything proper serious… (Lisa, aged 16)

This form of violence was infrequent and often an isolated event that was quickly resolved. Many of the examples given included being pushed, tripped up, play-fighting and being lightly punched or kicked, but rarely involved a severe use of physical force. It was seen quite differently from similarly infrequent, yet more dangerous, examples of stabbing and injuries which resulted in severe bruising or the breaking of bones (which were classified as high-level violence). Low-level physical violence was not usually targetted or planned and was often used or received as a response to an isolated argument, or from another young person 'winding them up'.

> She was winding us up on purpose to make us hit her so she could go and tell staff and get us in trouble for it… She would really get on our nerves… We're told to ignore what she does but how can you ignore someone who's right in your face winding you up and saying stuff… she's always really in my face so I end up blowing up and losing me temper with her then I get in trouble… so… I was walking away at first but then she goes on at me and I can only take so much and I just end up hitting her. (Bianca, aged 13)

A key indicator of low-level physical violence was that those instigating the violence were often not perceived as a serious threat to a young person's safety. This was particularly the case in young people who reported being physically attacked by much younger children, or when young women physically attacked their male peers. More significantly, such low-level incidents were not situated in wider power dynamics or part of a cycle of other forms of abuse. In fact most of the incidents reported and categorised as low level were conducted within friendship groups, between siblings, or in homes that appeared to have a positive, supportive and stable peer group culture.

> Well sometimes, the other young people get on my nerves and there's a lot of competition here… peer pressure… I mean like you do hear a lot like there's bullying in children's homes and stuff, but everyone's sort of equal here… there's no head dog in this house, do you know what

I mean, everyone treats each other like they'd like to be treated...
(Christine, aged 14)

In relation to gender dynamics, about half of the girls', yet only a quarter of the boys' experiences of physical contact violence was categorised as low impact. Indeed, many of the boys' reports were qualitatively different from the girls' accounts. Girls, for example, reported being subject to, or perpetrating, isolated and infrequent attacks in response to particular provocations, such as arguments that turn into 'play-fights' and then 'get out of hand'. Most of the girls would provide coherent justifications for their actions, particularly in terms of retaliation, protection and defence framed within a discourse of rights. Boys' deployment of physical violence, however, was more about an expression and projection of a particular 'macho' masculinity. Most of the boys' accounts discussed low-level physical violence as 'just messing about', which had the effect of normalising such behaviours, often coupled with the phrase, 'it's what boys do'. As one boy stated: 'people will always fight no matter what'. Many of the incidents, particularly in homes where the majority of residents were male, were in fact conducted in the full view and knowledge of staff. Knowing that staff would immediately intervene, thus preventing any serious physical harm, provided a context in which there could be a safe instigation of violence. In these situations, boys could position themselves as the 'aggressor' and confirm their masculinity to others.

While some girls did engage in similar practices in which they projected, as one girl put it, 'a hard exterior' to others, thus camouflaging any sign of physical or emotional pain, girls did not usually perceive fighting as normal and the physical sparring engaged in by the majority of boys was not part of their everyday worlds or social interaction. How boys use different physical violence as a means of constructing particular masculinities is discussed in more depth in the following chapter.

High-level violence

High impact physical violence was categorised as such when physical force was severe, or when attacks were frequent, and when the impact on young people was viewed by the recipient as significant, often couched in terms of fear and vulnerability:

> I thought they were going to bully me, like do what happened in my past like... and like I did not like it and like I thought the kids here were going to do it (suffocate him with a pillow) because like they were looking really mean at me, staring. (George, aged 13)

Almost three-quarters (52) of the young people either engaged in, or were subject to, 'high level' physical violence. Most of these experiences occurred within their current placement and within single-sex groups. There were only 15 incidents involving mixed-sex physical violence. Attacks experienced by females from males usually involved more serious use of force and were categorised as 'high level', while most female attacks directed at male recipients were 'low level' attacks. Of the remainder, two-thirds of boys' and half of girls' experiences were categorised as high-level physical violence. Incidents ranged from knife attacks (by both girls and boys) and routine use of physical torture and terrorisation, to kicks and punches. Some high level attacks led to young people involving the police and bringing charges against the perpetrator. The more severe attacks would often happen in young people's bedrooms and during the twilight hours when staff surveillance was, in most cases, minimal. Other sites included corridors, kitchens, toilets, bathrooms and showers. All incidents were instrumental in wider power dynamics of the peer group and accounts from the perpetrators of high-level violence suggested that such attacks were often pre-planned, with the intention to cause harm. Indeed, while half of the incidents reported took place on a one-to-one basis, the other half took place within the group often involving the wider peer group as either active participants or passive supporters. This happened particularly in single-sex settings where peer group hierarchies were stronger. Moreover, young people's accounts almost always described as justified attacks which they had carried out. The recipients were described as deserving revenge because of a real or perceived provocation:

Interviewer: So give me an example of what happens when he (another male resident) says something to you.
Ramon: I'll beat him up. I'll bang him in his face. Kick him in his head, and I'll beat him up with a snooker cue and I'll walk off.

(Ramon, aged 12)

I don't go around looking for fights just fight when you have to fight... (Jesse, aged 16)

Like fucking being up in court over assault 'cause some girl walked past me and called me a 'scouse slapper'...so I just twatted her...don't like being called names when I'm not them. (Jane, aged 15)

As in the narratives of low-level violence, there were significant gender differences, particularly in terms of the perpetrators of high-level violence. Boys' accounts, for example, included talk about possessing what could be described as an *uncontrollable masculinity*, in which they described physical retaliation almost as a natural instinct, thus perpetuating the normalisation of physical fighting as 'what boys do'. This was especially in response to verbal attacks on their mothers and families (see later). Such accounts often led to a discussion of the way in which targetted and planned physical retaliations were all part of protecting what they perceived as 'hard' masculine exteriors, that would ultimately send messages to other young people that they were 'not to be messed with'. Indeed, only two young men were able to avoid retaliation in the form of physical violence. Their accounts will be discussed more fully in the Chapter 3.

Girls' accounts of engaging in high-level violence were more diverse. Examples included the protection of siblings or cousins, again using a language of revenge, and the use of physical violence as a 'last resort' to combat and ultimately halt the systematic physical, material and verbal bullying of other girls (and, in one case, a boy). One incident involved the use of physical violence (punching, kicking and scratching) towards another boy, justified as a form of female empowerment in an attempt to prove that 'girls can fight back'! However, very few of the girls' accounts involved the normalisation of high-level physical retaliation, which goes some way to explaining the gender difference, particularly in the numbers of males and females engaging in high-level physical violence.

Physical non-contact violence

Non-contact violence was defined to include physical behaviour that deeply harmed young people but affected them emotionally rather than causing physical pain or injury. Examples of non-contact violence include *control mechanisms* such as intimidation via looks, gestures or tone of voice, where young people exercise some form of control over another young person. Non-contact violence also included *property attacks*, which could involve the coercive invasion of personal space and the damaging or stealing of personal property. This often took place in young people's bedrooms and could range from stealing posters, CDs or clothes from a young person to spilling milk, and in one case pouring bleach and shampoo on to another young person's bed.

> Well they were... like I'm walking along the hallway and barge into me and call me names, and like, since I've been here my bedroom's been trashed three times. I've had all shampoo poured all over and under my door and where my carpet is, I've had some of my clothes stolen, money stolen, things out of my room stolen, things like that. And it really winds me up to come back off from seeing my family and I come back and it just winds me up seeing my bedroom being trashed, I come in and my bedroom's upside down, my cupboards on my floor, all my clothes are scattered all over the room, it just winds me up, posters ripped up... (Carl, aged 17)

While all could identify with this form of violence, just under half (33) of the young people interviewed reported experiencing or engaging in (but predominantly experiencing) different forms of non-contact violence. All these young people had experienced incidents within their current placement, and seven reported experiencing similar incidents in previous children's homes. However, there were three homes in which there were no reports of non-contact attacks. The most common form of non-contact violence was property attacks, making up just under half of all incidents (15). The rest included threats of physical injury, supported by physical gestures or signs, and control mechanisms which affected a young person's movement, or imposed the aggressor's will upon them, such as control of TV watching. Yet disturbingly, while one-third of incidents reported were perceived by young people as having little impact (these were often isolated cases which were quickly resolved by either young people or staff), two-thirds were categorised as having a significant impact upon young people in a similar way to the forms of high-level physical violence described above. First, they were deeply embedded within wider peer group dynamics and often involved systematic use of non-contact violence upon the same victims, by a small group, or by one or two young people. Second, different forms of 'high level' non-contact violence were part of a wider cycle of violence, in particular physical and verbal attacks. There was a strong relationship between physical violence and non-contact violence, with over two-thirds of young people experiencing high impact non-contact violence with physical violence. This finding (elaborated later) sheds some interpretative light on the impact of threats of physical violence, which may have been experienced as part of a cycle of violence of different types.

While overall there were equal numbers of males and females reporting experience of non-contact physical violence, closer analysis revealed that twice as many girls as boys experienced and engaged in property attacks. Furthermore, regardless of the perceived severity of the incident by the researchers, girls were much more likely to categorise this form of violence as having a high or significant impact than did boys. Indeed the same type of violence, such as the case described earlier of the stealing of CDs and destroying of posters, could be perceived as low impact for some boys, but high impact for nearly all girls. One possible interpretation, given that many of the incidents were carried out in young people's bedrooms, could be a result of the special attachment that many girls feel in relation to their personal property and their private space (McRobbie 1990) and, consequently, the awareness and knowledge by female (and male) perpetrators that this form of violence can deeply harm other girls.

Sexual violence

> Ryan's a little bastard man, he'd touch everyone up.
> (Megan, aged 15)

Unwanted behaviours which were experienced by young people as abusive and sexual were categorised separately as sexual violence. Examples of sexual violence included 'flashing', sexual assault often in the form of inappropriate touching, unwanted sexual gestures and remarks, pornographic letters, a boy hiding under a girl's bed without her knowledge, and one girl's experience of rape by a fellow resident in a previous placement. These behaviours categorised separately into sexual contact violence and sexual non-contact violence, although there was much overlap between experience of the two types. There were 12 reported cases of sexual contact violence, which included young people reporting 6 personal experiences and 6 experiences of other young people, and 9 reported cases of sexual non-contact violence. Each included young people as victims and as perpetrators. Most (14) of the incidents took place within the current home, and four were from previous children's homes. Sexual violence was not experienced in all children's homes, but in a total of 8 of the 14. Cases were equally divided between very recent experiences and those that took place within the last 12 months.

There were significant gender differences in terms of the type of sexual violence and its impact upon young people. Girls were three times more likely to experience both forms of sexual violence and experience the most severe form of sexual contact violence. Indeed cases that affected girls the most were usually perpetrated by boys. They were often described or experienced as isolated attacks, although some continued for longer periods, particularly those in which staff were not informed, or when accounts to staff had not been believed, and involved cases of sexual assault, sexual intimidation and one case of rape. All were coercive and most of these incidents took place in the young women's bedrooms. Most disturbingly, half of these incidents were not reported to staff, although they were disclosed to other young people.

There were some incidents of unwelcome female to male sexual behaviour. One was of a girl entering another boy's bedroom in the night and sleeping on the end of his bed. Other incidents included a group of girls sexually teasing a boy and trying to stretch a condom over his head, and kicking a boy in his genital area. While all were experienced by boys as uncomfortable or 'annoying' they were not reported to us as harmful, disturbing or threatening. However, boys may be under considerable peer pressure to minimise the impact of sexual violence, especially if perpetrated by girls. Newburn and Stanko (1994) argued that there is a widely held, but largely untested, assumption that a central element of masculinity involves an unwillingness to talk about or admit 'weakness'. They added that, within dominant discourses, males are traditionally perceived as perpetrators, not victims, of sexual violence. To admit to such victimisation not only challenges the above dichotomy, but also calls into question a boy's assertion of masculinity.

The only two cases of same sex sexual violence was one of a younger boy exposing his genitals in group situations and a more serious case (as defined by the young people involved) of group sexual intimidation towards a new resident on entry to the children's home. Here a group of girls positioned themselves as *'predatory lesbians'* and she was told that she had to share baths and sleep with them. A similar encounter was experienced by the two researchers involved! These cases, however, were disclosed to staff, as were similar, less threatening incidents of sexual intimidation and sexualised verbal abuse and teasing.

Verbal attacks and insults

> We don't, when we shout and swear at each other, we don't always mean it nasty, it's just the way we communicate sometimes, but instead of us fighting really, we shout and swear and mainly if you look at most of us when we swear, it's when we can't get our words out and we get frustrated and the first word that comes out that would be swearing. We do what everyone in this house does, swear a lot. (Reece, aged 16)

Verbal attacks and insults included any spoken words or comments intended to harm or that had the effect of harming another young person in some way. Nearly all young people experienced some form of verbal attack. Also, like many of the forms of violence discussed so far, much of it took place within rather than between groups of boys and girls. Name-calling was the most common form, and included insults relating to a young person's gender, sexuality, ethnicity, family, maturity or physical appearance.

Gender

> If you're not tough, 'cause they expect boys to be like hard in here, you get called 'women' 'cause you're not one of them. (Lance, aged 15)

Sexuality

> Interviewer: Are there certain, if someone wanted to hurt someone's feelings, are there certain names that are more hurtful than others?
> Alicia: Yeah... like whore, slag, lesbian, things like that.
> (Alicia, aged 14)

Ethnicity

> One lad called Luke who's a black lad who's really nice, dead friendly with me... em... he was picking on another lad 'cause this other lad was calling him black, whatever, and he didn't like that and he called him back. (Melissa, aged 16)

Family
> I get wound up easy or if someone cusses me mum or something and I get really angry and I will kick off. (Fergus, aged 15)
> It's very bad saying things about my family, he shouldn't say things about others, it's not very nice and it makes you upset. (Richard, aged 14)

Maturity
> He deserved it. He acts like a little two-year old, he's 16, he's older than me, and he acts like a two-year old. (Reece, aged 15)

Physical appearance and dress
> Interviewer: What sort of things do people take the mickey out of?
> Colin: Weight, looks, hairstyles, the way you dress, what size feet you have, anything.
>
> (Colin, aged 15)

From our sample of 71 young people, a total of 61 received or engaged in some type of verbal attack. However, there were marked differences in terms of the type of attack experienced and its impact upon young people. There was a general undercurrent of name-calling and swearing embedded in the social cultures of young people in all the children's homes visited by the researchers. This was acknowledged by the young people themselves as having little impact and was accepted as part of residential life. Again, as before, verbal attacks were divided into high- and low-level categories to differentiate the impact.

Low-level verbal insults

Low level name-calling was often undertaken in the wider context of good peer group relations which acknowledged boundaries, did not include insults which were known to greatly harm others, such as to young people's backgrounds and families, and was not part of wider cycles of violence. Indeed many cases were undertaken within the context of friendship and often employed as a form of entertainment, labelled by many young people as 'messing about'.

> Interviewer: Is there a lot of name-calling?
> Simon: Sometimes, yeah. We're only messing about, we don't, we're not like serious.
> Interviewer: Right, 'cause that's what we're interested in, how it affects young people, you know, does it hurt them or upset them?
> Simon: No. Don't hurt me when people say something to me. If I know they're messing around, don't hurt me.
>
> (Simon, aged 15)

Interestingly, within these contexts, both sexual and racial name-calling were interpreted by young people as unproblematic. Another factor which minimised the impact of being called names was when the name-calling was not part of the wider power dynamics, and the person issuing the names was not perceived as a threat or feared by the recipient. The most common example was when the name-caller was younger in age or smaller in size. One young man distinguished clearly between the impact of different types of verbal violence, by calling low impact verbal violence 'name-calling' and high impact verbal violence 'name-bullying' which was systematic, frequent and conducted with the intention to cause harm:

> Bullying, name-calling that's different. Name-calling is like, name-bullying, if you call people those names you would say name-calling, then it just turns into bullying by getting called it every day. (Dan, aged 15)

However, one of the grey areas in terms of being able to categorise whether an incident was high level or low level were those accounts in which the impact of name-calling was normalised to such an extent that some insults, which would greatly affect some young people, would wash over others. As one boy put it 'you just learn to live with it'.

High-level verbal attacks

Twenty-three young people and slightly more girls than boys experienced 'high-level' verbal attacks. Significantly, racist name-calling was notable in its absence amongst the experiences of young people, although many mentioned that using another person's ethnic background as a form of name-calling was a serious form of verbal abuse. The most damaging forms of verbal attack were related either to a young person's sexuality or a young person's family background. These two types of insults were more common from males (family background) and females (sexuality). Girls were six times more likely to use sexuality as a direct form of verbal insult. Boys, however, were more prone to using their family background and in particular ' mother cussing' than girls (although they too used this form of attack). As the extracts below illustrate, these two terms were deemed the worst insult a young boy or girl could experience and both would warrant immediate and often physical retaliation. This was particularly the case when boys insulted other boys' mothers (or sometimes girlfriends).

> If you really wanted to get someone, it's just, it's family really. (Richard, aged 14)

> No-one ever goes there with family because that is why we're here, because of family. (Dean, aged 15)

For any young person looked after, issues surrounding families, especially their mothers (many are from lone parent or step-families), are likely to raise conflicting feelings surrounding their experiences of abuse, support, love, care, abandonment and death. Boys appear especially sensitive to this form of name-calling, relating to predominantly male notions of protection of females, rather than themselves, and masculine codes of honour. Likewise, many of the girls talked about the importance of maintaining their sexual reputations and, thus, any challenge to their sexual status (particularly their heterosexual status) resulted in often swift forms of retaliation. These ideas will be more fully developed in Chapter 3. In sum, the impact of these types of verbal attacks for the majority of young men and women was deeply significant. They led to over a third of young people experiencing high-level verbal attacks to state that they were more harmful than physical attacks. This was particularly the case in relation to the long-lasting, emotional impact of verbal attacks:

> Interviewer: You said earlier about physical violence, that it doesn't really happen too often.
> Adrian: No it's mainly verbal. Verbal hurts more than hitting though.
> Interviewer: Verbal hurts more than hitting? You think it does?
> Adrian: I reckon it does, with hitting it's like oh a punch, the pain is over in a few seconds, but when you get verbal you know it stays in ya for quite a few days yeah.
> Interviewer: So you think having someone calling you thing stays with you?
> Adrian: Yeah hurts more yeah, because if you get hit...you know... I've been jumped before, I got jumped and if someone called me names and it keeps happening everywhere I go, then it's gonna hurt more than just hitting.
> (Adrian, aged 16)

Such a finding challenges and contradicts common assumptions about what can be counted as 'violence' when the impact of different forms of harmful behaviour are taken into account.

Bullying

Of significance in relation to young people's conceptualisations of violence was the widely used term 'bullying'. Importantly, 'bullying' could be used by young people to define a single incident, such as a young person not allowing another young person to watch their favourite TV programme, to systematic and enduring cases of verbal attacks and/or physical violence. Indeed, these accounts reflect the bullying literature which has, more recently, embraced a much broader understanding of what can constitute bullying (e.g. verbal, physical, emotional, psychological). To this end, bullying was coded in our analysis both by participants' own concepts and by the categories of violence described here, to explore the type of bullying and its diverse usage. With the exception of sexual violence, bullying was interpreted by young people as verbal insults and attacks, physical non-contact violence and non-contact violence such as property attacks, and could be perpetrated by a single individual or groups of individuals.

Bullying is:

- When someone beats up the other person
- Sometimes it's just calling names or one kid swearing at another
- A gang of people starting on another kid
- When someone trashes your room

But most young people defined bullying as a mixture of all three:

There's bullying where you go like 'move out of my way', things like that and there's different kinds of bullying like where someone is punching them for no reason at all, and then you've got bullying where you're shouting at them and telling them to do things and telling them like, 'give me your pocket money' or something like that. (Carl, aged 17)

They'd put food in your hair and stuff and just be generally nasty and boot your door down if you won't come out and stuff... they just intimidated me all the time. (Dawn, aged 13)

All the little ones he was bullying and shit... beating them up, taking their money, scaring them... real weird stuff, like mind stuff you know, telling them they couldn't do this or that or he'd beat the shit out of them that night. (Ross, aged 14)

In terms of numbers, just under half of the young people interviewed (23 boys, 10 girls) reported experiencing some form of what they defined as 'bullying'. These reports implicated 9 homes and from the 33 reported cases, all but 3 occurred in their current placement. Twenty-five of these cases were types of physical contact violence, 12 were non-contact violence, 20 were forms of verbal attacks, predominantly intimidation and threats (not mutually exclusive). However, not one young person conceptualised sexual violence as 'bullying'. As was discussed above, young people's definition of 'bullying' varied. For example, one young person described a hierarchy of bullying incidents and used the term 'big bullying' to denote the severity of some forms of bullying like:

Big bullying if like someone charges into someone's room with a screwdriver and robs their play-station or their jewellery, and then tells them to jump out of the window. (Ewan, aged 13)

Thus, each case was categorised as having high or low impact to account for such variation. Two-thirds were categorised as having a high impact in terms of the physical and emotional harm caused. Boys were more likely to categorise verbal bullying as having a high impact (particularly in the form of 'mother cussing'). Girls, however, were more likely to categorise physical contact bullying as having high impact (this could be due to the fact that high-level physical violence was rare). Victims of high impact bullying reported feeling depressed and being very scared:

> It made me feel crap, like, just really bad and depressed, so I tried to stay out a lot, but he was always here when you got back. (Neil, aged 15)

While there was a wide perception of what counted as bullying, the majority of young people who were victims of something they defined as 'bullying' used the term to denote a targeted (and to a lesser extent persistent) abuse of power (see Smith and Sharp 1994, Askew 1989).

> Someone who is weaker than you, who you can intimidate by your height, or size or strength or you just use violence or force in any type of way... that's bullying. (Rick, aged 16)

This was particularly the case in relation to the construction and maintenance of peer group hierarchies in which a singly dominant individual or group of individuals manipulate and control the peer group using a range of oppressive and subordinating tactics. These can include physical force, verbal and property attacks and psychological torture, described by one boy as 'mind games'.

Staff evaluation of peer violence and verbal attacks

Staff had generally been present in the residential homes significantly longer than many of the young people we talked with. They were able to provide not only a snapshot of the current situation at the time of fieldwork, but also provide a longer term account of violence, and estimate changes in both its frequency and nature over time. Additionally, staff accounts of incidents did not necessarily involve young people currently in the home, and they often described circumstances where young people had been moved out due to violence. Many similarities are evident between the staff and young people's accounts, although significant discrepancies also emerge. It must, however, be remembered that young people did not always disclose their experiences of violence to staff, consequently staff may present an incomplete picture due to the incidence of 'hidden' (unobserved) violence. Looking at the current level of physical violence identified by staff over 1-month and 12-month periods leading up to the fieldwork, we allocated

Table 2.1 Staff estimations of the impact of physical violence

Time Period	Category one (low level only)	Category two (low with sporadic high level)	Category three (consistent high level)
Past month	8 homes	5 homes	1 home
Past 12 months	3 homes	6 homes	5 homes

the 14 homes into three categories (see Table 2.1). As with young people's accounts, we separated violence into low and high impact using the same criteria as before.

Peer violence in the previous month

Staff in just over half of homes (8) stated that either no or only very sporadic low-level violence had occurred within the previous month. Staff in five homes stated that low-level physical violence was frequent and was periodically interrupted, to a greater or lesser extent, with isolated incidents of high-level violence. Only staff in a single residential home identified the persistent presence of high-level violence throughout this period.

Homes with low-level physical violence

For homes in category one (no violence or only sporadic low-level violence in the previous month), the majority of staff in each home generally agreed on the level of violence present. Interestingly, staff presented slightly different assessments in relation to the impact of this violence. Staff who had experience in previous establishments where greater levels of physical violence had been routinely present, generally viewed the significance of the low-level violence as being of less impact than did staff who had no direct experience of settings where physical violence occurred regularly.

Examples of low-level physical violence given by staff included; 'fisticuffs', 'a hit or a slap', 'squabbling', 'play fighting' 'getting out of hand', 'slap happy', 'a quick cuff', 'the odd thump' 'skirmishes', 'pinching' and 'restricting each others' movements'. Workers used three main criteria in their evaluation of physical violence as being low impact: lack of physical harm, outside of wider power dynamics, and the victim's own assessment of impact. Consequently when we compared workers' evaluations of low-level physical violence to young people's, we found that both groups were generally using very similar criteria in their assessments of harm. The other major example of low-level physical violence, again mirroring young people's own evaluations, concerned violence that was only initiated in staff's presence in the firm belief that staff would intervene before any physical contact was made. One male worker described it as 'handbags at 60 paces' which, upon reflection, seems a rather inappropriate analogy as very few girls in our study concerned themselves with this form of 'display' violence. This type of violence was referred to by staff in nearly all the homes, and was generally viewed as providing young men with a safe opportunity to parade a certain form of masculinity through their willingness to use violence, safe in the knowledge they would be unable to carry through their threat to completion.

Sporadic high-level physical violence homes

Moving on to homes in category two (persistent low level with isolated high-level incidents over the previous month) there appeared to be slightly less agreement amongst staff in their evaluations of the level and nature of the high-level incidents. Nearly all the staff in these homes (19 of 22) agreed that some form of low-level violence occurred routinely amongst the young people. Over two-thirds of these staff (14 of 19) thought this had little impact on the young people and positioned it as a 'normal' aspect of peer relations or at least acceptable in the context of the 'challenging' young people they were caring for. In respect to the high-level physical violence nearly three-quarters (16) of the staff interviewed in these 5 homes thought these incidents were severe, either in respect to the emotional impact on the young people or in regard to the physical severity of the violence. The remainder either disagreed that high-level physical violence occurred (3 staff in 2 homes) or whether the impact of the violence, both emotionally and physically, was significant (2 staff).

Only 1 establishment was situated in category three where the majority of staff interviewed (3 of 4) identified that high levels of physical violence had been present in the home throughout the last four weeks.

> Generally here we don't get too much physical stuff, just the normal sly slap or thump but sometimes it does flare up... mainly due to kids rubbing each other up. We had a bad spate a bit ago when two lads set on another and eventually beat him up really badly, nearly put him in hospital in fact, it was quite shocking for some of the less experienced staff here. (Senior Residential Social Worker, male)

Peer violence in the past year

By analysing violence over a longer time frame we were able to illuminate how both the nature and presence of physical violence changed over time in some homes whilst in others remained relatively constant. Whitaker *et al.* (1998) have highlighted the cyclical nature of residential care, with patterns of behaviour and problems varying over time.

In eight homes rated as category one during the past month, having had at most sporadic low-level physical violence, staff in only three stated that this had been the situation consistently over the past twelve months. In the remaining five homes, staff reported very disparate levels of physical violence throughout the previous year and beyond. In 3, the staff reported that within the past 12 months they routinely experienced high levels of physical violence between young people. Staff in the other two homes stated that sporadic outbreaks of high-level violence were not uncommon. Thus, for these homes, the 'snapshot' period of relative calm experienced recently, was, although not necessarily unique, a welcome interlude.

For 4 of the 5 homes situated in the middle range on recent estimates, the picture in the past month reflected the general picture over the past 12 months, and longer. Only staff from one home reported that the level of violence was usually significantly higher than depicted at the time of the fieldwork. Staff in the single home with a high level of violence in the recent month identified that this had been the situation for a number of months previously.

Thus, when viewed over a longer term, the distribution of homes alters between the three categories. Over the past year, three homes had experienced at most periodic low-level violence (category one), six homes reported sustained low-level physical violence with sporadic incidents of high-level incidents (category two) and five homes reported high-level violence that had occurred if not constantly, then at least frequently over the past twelve months (category three).

When we asked about this shift in the nature and level of physical violence between the snapshot and the longer term picture, two main explanations seemed to emerge. First, that some homes had recently made a concerted effort, including the removal of some children, to create a culture and structure where physical violence was no longer seen as the 'norm' by young people or tolerated by staff. Second, the mix of residents at the time of the fieldwork was not a representative reflection of the young people they usually worked with. These issues will be discussed in greater detail but are important to signpost at this stage.

Physical non-contact violence

Within all the homes staff recognised the possibility of non-contact violence occurring between young people. Staff in 13 homes described instances of non-contact violence occurring over the past year, and beyond. In eight homes all of the staff interviewed stated that incidents involving non-contact violence had occurred, or were still occurring within the current group of young people. Most of these staff felt, to varying degrees, that this form of violence posed significant issues in relation to the well-being of the young people in their care. In five homes staff were more divided on the prevalence of non-contact violence, both at the time of the study and in relation to the past 12 months. Thus, although the majority of staff (13) interviewed in these homes spoke about the problems relating to this aspect of violence, nine stated that they had no experience of this behaviour. In only one home were all staff in agreement that this form of violence did not occur, although all those interviewed felt they were aware of the possibility. Nearly all the staff who spoke about non-contact violence described it in terms of bullying, being high-level and divided into three main forms: control mechanisms, material violence and verbal threats. As with physical violence, these assessments of the impact of non-contact violence as being high level matched closely the young people's own judgements.

Control mechanisms

According to staff interpretations, the most common non-contact manner in which young people exerted control over one another was through the use of covert signals, for example a look, a stare, the flick of a head, tone of voice, how or where someone sits or unnecessary invasion of body space, such as walking too close to someone. For many staff, the above actions take on meaning only once they are understood as being indicative of unequal power relations between the young people concerned. Staff viewed these actions as a covert or subtle sign between young people to demarcate power differentials whereby the recipient is 'reminded' of their subservient position. As one worker stated, it is only when placed in this context that what may seem a relatively ordinary act takes on a very different meaning.

> If you didn't really look you'd think everything was OK, normal. But when you stood back a bit you could see that all wasn't well...just how all the kids acted when she (another young person) came in the room...like how she always got the best seat, watched what she wanted on TV. Nobody would argue with her...but we never saw anything obvious happen...nothing physical...just her being in the room was threat enough to scare the rest of em...it made it very difficult to stop...how can you sanction against a look? (Senior Residential Social Worker, female)

Interviewer: Is it always obvious what is happening between young people?

Worker: Absolutely not, sometimes it's not obvious at all...sometimes it's just a flick of the head directing somebody else to do something, or to remind someone about what might happen. Or they're just standing there making the other kids feel insecure just by their presence. That's the more devious and more difficult one to prove (than physical violence).

(Residential Social Worker, male)

The majority of staff stated that the effect of non-contact violence could be very significant, as the impact on the young person was often far greater than the single incident observed at the time. However, the subtlety of the signs alongside the 'ordinariness' of the act can make this form of violence very difficult to intercept, especially if the victim is unwilling to complain or name the person/s responsible.

Material violence

Staff also commonly identified material violence against a person's property and belongings. Often this form of violence occurred within the young person's bedroom. Many staff identified that for residents, as for young people generally, bedrooms are the only relatively private space they have available. Thus, for violence to penetrate this area can be particularly invasive, signalling to the young person that they have nowhere which is safe. Staff provided us with numerous examples of this form of behaviour, the most frequently stated included: putting substances in beds or on clothes including, toilet cleaner, after-shave, perfume, shaving foam, washing up liquid, toothpaste, used sanitary towels and tampons; cutting up clothes, photographs, letters; 'trashing' rooms; putting water in electrical appliances; burning belongings; urinating and defecating in beds, bags, shoes, on family photos and other personal items.

> Often they'll trash each others' bedrooms. I suppose they know how precious their rooms are, their only bit of privacy and for that to be violated can be really heart-breaking. We had a girl have her room done, usual sort of things, shampoo everywhere, broken jewellery...but they also took her diary and used all the private things she had written in it against her. We advise kids not to keep anything in their rooms now...it's terrible really 'cause I don't know how I'd feel if I couldn't have my personal belongings around me. (Residential Social Worker, female)

> I've seen horrendous bullying over the years, although I do think that training has helped us all become more aware of bullying and how bad it can be for the kids, so things are getting better...but it does still happen. Like here this lad went to bed and they'd all weed on his bed and put dog dirt in it...really disgusting. (Manager, female)

Verbal threats

This form of attack often relies on the threat of physical assault, which does not necessarily need to be carried out for it to intimidate or scare a young person (Stanko 1985). However, about half of the young people involved in perpetrating this form of violence had, according to staff, also been involved in some form of physical violence within the home, although not necessarily directed at the young people they were threatening. Hence, although the recipient of the threats may not have directly experienced physical violence, they were generally aware that the threat may indeed have some currency behind it. About a third of the staff interviewed recognised that the threat of violence, the accompanying uncertainty surrounding whether and when it would be carried out, may be just as difficult for a young person to deal with as the physical assault itself.

> Often I feel that the verbal stuff that goes on is worse than the physical. I'm not talking about getting stabbed or hospitalised, not that end of it, but I think having to live with the constant threat of being beaten up can be as frightening as actually getting it over and finished with...it's the constant uncertainty of when it might occur that can be just as bad for the kids to deal with. (Residential Social Worker, male)

Bullying

Staff, like young people, used the term 'bullying' as a normal description of peer violence, saw it as taking a variety of forms, and as being an abuse of power. Bullying was seen by the majority of staff as constituting high-level violence due to the unequal power relationship involved. Similarly, when staff talked about bullying they generally referred to actions involving physical and/or non-contact violence, and rarely to sexual violence.

Staff generally felt that physical bullying or 'hands-on bullying' as one termed it, was largely restricted to boys. Occasionally examples of girls as both perpetrators and victims of physical bullying were provided but these seem to be relatively rare. Girls were much more likely to be seen as being involved in non-contact forms of bullying. Physical bullying was the most frequently stated reason for young people being moved. Some staff questioned the rationale of this, feeling it may have reflected management concerns rather than evaluations of harm.

> I don't like having to say this but in my experience unless a kid's got bruises to show (from the bullying) social services won't intervene...I don't think they recognise the level of harm involved in bullying unless it's physical. (Residential Worker, female)

> No resident to my knowledge has ever lost their placement here due to bullying that wasn't physical....if you get beaten up bad enough and often enough something will get done, but if it's not physical then we're left to sort it out on our own. (Senior Residential Worker, male)

In 5 homes bullying was seen by staff as a problem at the time of the fieldwork, and in 11 homes staff identified that an incident of bullying had occurred within the past 12 months. In three-quarters of these 11 homes, at least one of these instances of bullying had been deemed serious enough to require formal action to be taken, in the form of an external investigation, which in 5 cases resulted in the removal of the perpetrator.

Looking at the number of young people involved in bullying within each home over the past year we find very disparate situations. In three homes, to the staff's knowledge, only one incident involving a single bully had occurred. Staff in six homes reported between two to three significant incidents of bullying involving different young people. And four homes stated that bullying had been (and often still was) an issue surrounding a number of young people. In only one home did all staff feel that no bullying had occurred.

In our overall assessment of violence within the 14 homes, we have omitted bullying as a category for reasons of repetition. As bullying denotes a wide range of behaviours, including physical, non-contact and verbal forms of violence, these acts have been included within these specific categories for analysis rather than under the generalised heading of bullying.

Sexual violence

Overall, we found that staff in all the homes had experienced an incident involving sexual violence, or 'inappropriate' behaviour between young people, within the past year. Focusing initially on what participants termed 'serious' sexual violence, 12 of the homes had experienced at least one incident within the last year resulting in some form of intervention. Of these, 6 homes reported more than one such incident within the last 12 months (between two and four). Overall, this resulted in 20 serious incidents of sexual violence occurring. Serious incidents included rape (4) or attempted rape (2), buggery (4), indecent assault (7) and touching a young person's sexual body parts against their will (3).

Staff accounts of incidents they experienced indicate that the majority of 'serious' occurrences were perpetrated by males on females, and involved young people of a similar age. In a minority of incidents both the perpetrator and the victim were males. Only in one home could staff recall an incident where a female had perpetrated sexual violence in this category. Most incidents involved individuals, but in five cases more than one young person had either been directly involved in the violence or was present as a bystander. In all these 'group' incidents the perpetrators were male, except in the above example which involved two girls. Only one incident, where three boys had raped two girls, involved more than a single victim.

The majority of 'serious' incidents discussed by participants had occurred on children's home premises, mainly in either the victims' or the perpetrators' bedroom. Three-quarters of incidents happened after 8 p.m. and before 11 p.m. Thus, in the majority of cases, staff were still working when the sexual violence occurred (homes usually have staff sleeping-in overnight).

Unlike physical violence, staff did not generally locate incidents of sexual violence in relation to wider power dynamics between the young people concerned. They did identify that nearly half of the instigators of the sexual violence had been involved in other forms of peer violence, especially physical and non-contact violence. This wider violence was not, though, generally targetted at the same young person who had been sexually assaulted, and none of the female victims had, according to staff, been physically assaulted prior to the sexual attacks.

Most often, staff stated they felt the sexual violence was a one-off incident, although in three cases long-term examples of sexual abuse were discussed. These all surrounded boy-to-boy abuse (female victims were often viewed as being more willing to seek help in relation to sexual violence than males) and lasted between two weeks and an estimated three months.

> Worker: We had a really bad case here of sexual abuse between an older boy and two youngsters here. We think it'd been going on for at least a month before we eventually realised what was happening.
> Interviewer: How did you realise?
> Worker: One of the younger boys started to show signs of distress, started wetting his bed, not wanting to be left alone with other kids in the home, having temper tantrums that sort of thing, really out of character. So we thought, hold on something's not right here. Eventually he did say that (name of boy) had been coming in his room at night and doing stuff to him. He never said exactly what but as soon as we got rid of (name of boy) his behaviour stared reverting back to normal. We think he may have also abused another boy here as well. The investigation's still going on but we've now got alarms on all the bedroom doors so it can't happen again.
> (Senior Residential Social Worker, male)

Surrounding these 'serious incidents' involving sexual violence were many more 'suspicious' or 'border-line' incidents.

> It's a very tricky area...they're at an age where they're going to be curious about the opposite sex, so it's like where do we draw the line between appropriate and natural behaviour, sort of behind the bike sheds sort of thing and what's not appropriate. I can name two girls here who I believe are being pressured to do more than they feel is willing, they don't directly say anything but when you read between the lines they're not happy but feel they don't have any choice if they want to keep their boyfriends. (Manager, female)

> He's very dominating in the home and I know from talking with other young women here that he acts inappropriately...pushing himself against them that sort of thing...I'm very concerned about his present

relationship with another female resident. She's not come to me with anything specific but I wonder how much say she has over what's happening...She's been (sexually) abused in the past and I doubt if she feels she has much control but it's difficult 'cause she won't even admit to us she's seeing him because if we knew officially we'd have to move one of them. (Residential Social Worker, female)

It's very difficult to say (if it was abuse) 'cause he...I think he partly enjoyed the experience but it was a case of he may not have chosen her, he may have chosen somebody else for his first time. It was one of those questions is it or isn't it inappropriate? She was a very powerful young woman, and very aggressive, though I don't believe she directly threatened him more than coerced him. At the end when we found out he said he just went along with it because he felt he couldn't say no. (Senior Residential Social Worker, male)

Slightly more of these borderline incidents involved girls as perpetrators, although they were still in the minority. There also seemed to be fewer group incidents here compared to the 'serious' incidents. Staff often spoke about the difficulty of determining when behaviour could be defined as constituting abuse. This was made especially difficult when young people were unwilling to talk to staff. Many staff stated that they had suspicions about potentially sexually exploitative 'relationships' or incidents between young people, but had no concrete evidence upon which to base their beliefs. Overall, many staff were struggling with what constitutes 'inappropriate' behaviour and what was 'normal' experimentation, although many realised that this could be very individualistic. Consequently, due to a range of reasons, including the young people's previous experiences of sexual abuse, what one young person sees as inappropriate, another may not. Thus, staff faced complex dilemmas over the need to respond to what they (often uncertainly) determined was inappropriate behaviour, in situations where the young people involved did not always share this assessment. Sufficient to state that this area was the most contentious for all staff and one where staff felt insecure, uncertain and in need of wider understanding of the area of sexuality generally. Farmer and Pollock (1998) reached the same conclusion.

Issues surrounding sexual violence and abuse between young people are obviously extremely sensitive. In four of the homes we visited, staff identified that some of the young people we interviewed had been involved in sexual violence, either as victims or perpetrators, but the young people concerned did not discuss this with us. Consequently staff accounts indicate that young people may experience greater levels of sexual victimisation, or more often carry out sexually aggressive acts, than the young people's accounts suggested. Similarly, although probably for different reasons, staff may also feel reluctant to discuss such issues with an external party. In fact sexual violence was the only area that some staff refused to discuss with us.

This may also reflect a desire to protect their establishment's reputation. All these staff were at residential social worker level, and no senior staff or managers refused to talk about this issue. However, overall, we found more discrepancy between staff's accounts on this subject than any other. This may possibly reflect an actual lack of information regarding incidents, although this seems doubtful as often records indicated that many of these (serious) incidents had resulted in at least an internal inquiry and sometimes a full-scale child protection investigation. We can, therefore, only surmise that some staff provided us with a highly selected account of their experiences regarding sexual violence. Having stated this, we found that most senior staff, and especially managers, were very comprehensive in their answers, even though for some this meant discussing 'mistakes' for which many felt some level of responsibility. Thus, due to the silence of some staff and the incomplete picture presented by others, we may be providing an under-representation of the level of sexual violence within the homes we visited.

Verbal attacks and insults

Perhaps unsurprisingly, nearly all staff identified that they had observed some form of verbal attacks amongst the young people with whom they worked. Many staff felt that verbal attacks, in the form of swearing and name-calling, were a common presence in residential life, and that this verbal backdrop did not have a significant effect on the young people. Although, on a few occasions, even toughened researchers found certain terms disquieting, especially when directed towards themselves.

However, not all staff felt this common currency of swearing and 'routine' insults was acceptable. Thirteen of the 71 interviewed stated that this situation was unhealthy and detrimental to young people's development. This was generally explained in relation to the worker's own family settings, staff often remarking that they would not allow their children to use such language. Unfortunately, many staff felt that they were fighting a losing battle and that, although continually challenging the use of such language, this had little positive effect.

In nine of the 14 homes, staff identified that verbal attacks occurred that constituted high-level violence as defined by our previous categorisation. Compared to physical and non-contact forms of violence, there appeared to be less agreement between staff within each home about the impact and therefore the seriousness of this form of attack. Overall, two-thirds of staff in the nine homes (30 of 44) assessed the behaviour as having at least some effect on the young person involved, although evaluations of the seriousness of this impact varied considerably within homes. Furthermore, these assessments often related to the physical retaliation that generally accompanied high-level verbal attacks. Thus, staff's concern often focused on the physical aspect of retaliation rather than the actual effect of the verbal attack itself. This reflected staff's concern with ensuring the physical safety of the young people in their care.

Three forms of verbal attacks were perceived by staff as having the most impact on young people: familial, sexual and racial.

Verbal attacks concerning families

Fifteen staff (9 women and 6 men) in seven homes identified verbal insults to young people's families as constituting a significant problem in its own right. Of these, six evaluated this as having a greater impact on young people than any other form of behaviour, excluding high-level physical and sexual violence. Staff generally identified two types of familial verbal violence; general and specific.

General insults involved detrimental sexualised comments being made about a young person's mother (generically known as 'mother cussing'), another female relative or occasionally their girlfriends. Usually, the content of the abuse referred to their level of sexual activity or sometimes their sexual orientation. These insults rarely, if ever, included male family members.

A few staff identified more specific insults based on prior knowledge about a young person's history or family situation. Often this information had been divulged by the young person and subsequently used against them at a later date.

> Often they just want to make friends (when they first arrive) so they talk about their past and they get loads of encouragement and tell a bit too much and the other kids are thinking 'hey this is great, great ammunition'... I've seen it over and over again with vulnerable kids... And then they'll have it thrown back in their faces for the rest of their stay... and you think, why did you tell them that? (Residential Social Worker, female)

Verbal attacks concerning sexuality

Fourteen staff in seven homes (mostly different staff from those who mentioned familial abuse) identified sexual verbal violence being a problem within their establishment, which had at least some effect on the young people involved. Nine women and five men identified this with ten stating that in their experience it was more widely used between girls than by boys. The impact of sexualised verbal assaults was recognised by many of these staff, although five did state young people were not overly concerned. This form of verbal attack was seen as being mainly used between girls in relation to generalised slanders on a girl's sexual reputation.

However, sometimes personal information was used against other young people, especially if the young person was known to have been involved in selling sex for money, having a number of different sexual partners or in some instances had been sexually abused. More staff identified the impact this form of personalised sexual attack may have on a young person's well-being than if it concerned the wider peer group.

Verbal attacks concerning race

Twelve staff, seven female and five male, identified racist verbal assaults occurring between young people in their homes within the last year. But we found that racist abuse was directed more routinely at *staff* than at other children, with 31 adult participants, from both majority white and minority ethnic groups, stating they had been subjected to this. Sixteen staff in nine homes identified that they had never heard a young person be racist to another, and this concurs with young people's reported experience. The issue of racist violence and assaults is covered in more depth throughout the following chapters.

Developing a continuum of violence

Development of this analysis to provide a more theoretical understanding of the overall impact of violence within the 14 different residential settings, drew on Kelly's (1987) definition of violence as a continuum of physical, emotional, verbal and sexual abuses of power at individual and group levels. A continuum can incorporate a range of violent behaviours from isolated flashes of physical violence to systematic prolonged verbal attacks. Our study maps both the type of violence and its impact upon young people, making it possible to explore the relationships between the different types.

Basing the assessment of levels of violence in homes on *impact* rather than on the nature of the violent act itself also separated the cause and effect of violence. Achieving a complete model for understanding violence meant bringing together participants' assessments irrespective of the type of violence to which they are referring, and combining types of violence which had previously been separated out for analysis. In practice we found that different forms of violence were frequently interlinked. This was especially true of high impact physical violence, which was rarely found to exist for prolonged periods separated from the wider context of other forms of high-level violence.

Using young people's evaluations as the primary data, but taking into account staff's assessments, homes were assessed on a continuum of violence ranging from 'low' to 'high' impact (see Figure 2.1). 'High impact' was determined when the majority of young people's evaluations within a single home depicted violence as a consistent and dominant aspect of their residential experience, which impacted negatively on their well-being. If all evaluations of violence were restricted to low-level forms, or at the most very isolated instances of high impact violence, homes were assessed as 'low impact'.

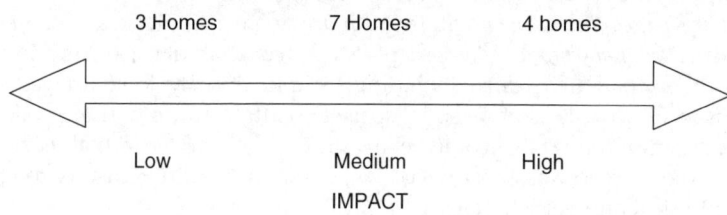

Figure 2.1 Diagrammatic representation of the violence continuum

The middle range of the continuum included homes where there was sporadic violence which most young people described as damaging to their well-being, but this did not constitute their overriding experience of residential life, and those in which a small group of young people appeared to have a particularly high level of negative experience which was different from that of most of their fellow residents. To ensure the validity of this approach, two researchers rated each home independently. This produced a high level of consistency with each positioning the 14 homes in a broadly similar pattern on the continuum.

On this model, four homes were located within the high range of violence. These consisted of two private, one voluntary and one local authority facility. Seven of the homes were placed in the middle range of the continuum where violence was present, and did impact on those living in the homes, but was not viewed by the young people as their dominant experience of care. These were all local authority homes. Three homes in our sample experienced very low levels of violence. These consisted of one private and two local authority homes; in one of these, participants could not identify any significant high-level violent incident occurring within the period of analysis. Although, therefore, we did find variations between different service providers, we also found variations within sectors. For example, although two private homes were positioned in the high violence category, another private establishment had rarely experienced any form of high impact violence over the previous 12 months. The possible organisational and structural factors which may help to explain these findings are explored in Chapter 6. However, before considering these structural factors, we need first to explore the meanings that different participants ascribed to their experiences of violence and how these understandings influenced participants' evaluations of the impact of different forms of behaviour.

Summary points

- Using young people's accounts, a categorisation of violence was developed which took into account the nature of the attack and the seriousness of

impact described by young people. This included:
- *Physical contact violence*: all forms involving direct physical assault.
- *Physical non-contact violence*: physical acts that harmed emotionally rather than physically, including intimidation by looks or gestures, forceful invasions of personal space and attacks on personal property.
- *Sexual violence*: unwelcome behaviour experienced as both abusive and sexual, which was experienced in a qualitatively different way to other physical and verbal attacks.
- *Verbal attacks*: spoken words hurting or intending to hurt, which predominantly took the form of name-calling concerning gender, sexuality, ethnicity, family and appearance.

- Most young people reported experiencing *physical contact violence* in residential care, as recipients, perpetrators or witnesses. The young people all described incidents taking place in their current home, with 21 also describing incidents from previous homes. Just under half experienced *physical non-contact violence*, usually involving destruction of personal property, threats of physical injury and control mechanisms which affected a young person's movement or imposed the aggressor's will upon them.
- Reports of *sexual violence* were low. Girls were more likely to report sexual violence and the most serious cases were experienced by girls, and the majority were from boys to girls. All were coercive, involving unwanted touching, sexual intimidation and one case of rape in a previous home.
- Nearly all young people experienced *verbal attacks*. Girls were more likely to use sexuality as a form of verbal insult; boys more prone to use family background, in particular 'mother cussing'. A number of young people identified verbal insults to their sexuality or their family as having greater impact than physical violence; a challenge to normative assumptions about the nature of violence.
- Staff accounts showed many similarities to those of young people but also indicated major differences in the frames of reference. Staff considered non-contact physical violence the most difficult to identify and deal with due to its hidden nature.
- Using young people's and staff's accounts, a model was developed in which three homes were located at the low end of the violence continuum, four were seen as homes with high levels of high impact violence, and seven were in a middle range.

3
Young People's Perspectives on Violence

Interviewer: If a young person was coming into the home for the first time, what do you think they should be aware of?
Lauren: I dunno...about the way other kids are and about the rules...what to do and what not to do, 'cause kids have their own rules. We have our own rules.
(Lauren, aged 14)

Chapter 2 went some way to map and categorise the frequency and impact of different forms of peer violence, as well as their interrelationship. Conceptualising violence in this way is helpful in enabling an analysis which can capture the diversity of young people's own accounts and experiences, particularly given the multifaceted and complex status of 'violent' behaviours. By adapting Kelly's (1987) concept of violence as a continuum, and using our categorisations of physical contact violence, physical non-contact violence, verbal attacks and sexual violence, and grounding our conceptualisation in young people's own accounts, certain patterns and relationships could be identified. These applied particularly to the meanings, definitions, evaluations and justifications of various forms of violence. Chapter 2 identified the following themes:

- *Normalisation of violence*: Findings suggest that the same type of violence (e.g. verbal insult) could impact upon young people in qualitatively different ways depending upon their previous experiences, the culture of violence in the home and their gender, age or peer group status. Participants' own concepts of violence varied considerably.
- *Peer group dynamics*: Much of young people's accounts of high impact violence was embedded in wider peer group dynamics and power relations.
- *Gendered nature of violence*: Particular types of violence were gender-specific. High-level verbal attacks for boys took the form of mother-cussing, and for girls derogatory sexualised attacks. Property attacks were reported to have a greater impact for girls. Sexual violence was

experienced mainly as a female phenomenon and physical violence was more severe for boys.
- *Justification*: According to young people, all forms of violence usually had some form of justification and rationale.

'We have our own rules': children's cultures and the normalisation of violence

Young people's cultures have been relatively neglected and under-theorised in the literature on children's homes. This is often due to a narrow definition of culture with its presumption that there needs to be a stable and static peer group for the development of shared cultural norms. This excludes young people in children's homes because of the fluidity and movement of young people between children's homes and other types of care such as foster care. A small number of studies, however, have commented that one of the reasons stated by young people for going missing from children's homes was the powerful peer group culture (Wade *et al.* 1998) and others have evidence that the culture of violence is a persistent feature of residential life (Morris and Wheatley 1994). Following Geertz's (1973) general approach to culture and more recent accounts of children's cultures within the 'new' sociology of childhood (see James *et al.* 1998), children's culture is no longer solely viewed as a distinct or separate children's world with its own lore. Rather, it is seen to be produced by the contexts in which children live out their everyday lives. James *et al.* (1998) characterise children's culture as:

> a form of social action contextualised by the many different ways in which children choose to engage with the social institutions and structures that shape the form and process of their everyday lives. (p. 88)

In relation to the current study, violence was the particular form of social action under investigation, and the children's home, with its own formal and informal regulations and structures, was the institution in which young people's actions, behaviours and cultural norms were contextualised. We found that tapping into and understanding young people's peer group cultures is central to the way violence is mediated and experienced by young people. As the quote at the beginning of this chapter illustrates, 'kids have their own rules'. Indeed, many young people in the study were aware of specific micro and macro cultural codes and practices in relation to their behaviour and conduct within the peer group. Most of these pivoted around modes of acceptable and unacceptable behaviour, in the words of one young man, 'what to do, what not to do'. We refer to *micro-cultural codes* as a way of theorising violence within each individual home's local peer group culture. *Macro-cultural codes* are a way of theorising wider peer group cultures and dynamics that cut across all children's homes and children's lives. Examples of this are their perceptions and constructions of ethnicity, gender (masculinities and femininities) and age (young/old or child/adult). The division is conceptual, and in reality the macro and the micro intersect and shape each other. The following sections illustrate the ways in which the micro- and the macro-cultural codes within and between peer groups led, with constant exposure over time, to the normalisation and desensitisation of different forms of violence and violent behaviours. We also explore how the process of normalisation and subsequent desensitisation varied between and within children's homes. Some young people's normalisation of violence was highly personalised and specific to their past experiences of violence, others were related to a shared yet hierarchical peer group culture on first entering a home.

'Seven months living here, you just get used to it': the importance of context

While there seemed to be a shared or common culture of low-level verbal insults in the form of swearing in all but two of the children's homes, the meaning and subsequent impact of violence could not be divorced from the local context in which it was produced and understood by young people. This was particularly the case over the existence or severity of violence within each home at the time of the fieldwork, which in turn led to the normalisation of violent behaviours. The cultures of violence within each home were often apparent from our first visits in which we negotiated access. In one home, two of the researchers were immediately confronted with verbal and non-verbal forms of intimidation, such as spitting and swearing, and were eventually locked in a vacant bedroom for approximately half an hour, while a group of residents ran screaming and shouting around the different floors of the children's home (see Barter and Renold 2002). In another home we encountered residents who were all sitting quietly and calmly in the TV room and when 'dinner' was called they each walked to their place at the dinner table, showed us to our seats and chatted about their day at school and future social activities that night. The contrast was stark indeed. Young people themselves were also acutely aware of the culture of violence within each home, to the extent that the culture of some homes was transmitted, not on direct exposure to the peer group, but solely via the circulation of gossip and rumour. One young person, for example, learnt of the abusive culture in the home he was shortly to be admitted to via his social worker.

Interviewer:	So what was it like when you first came here then?
Richard:	... my social worker said I'd get bullied.
Interviewer:	Your social worker told you you'd get bullied?
Richard:	He said children will take advantage of you and I come in here.

(Richard, aged 14)

The present study has attempted to position homes along a continuum of different forms of violence based upon impact, from low- to high-level violence. This provided an overall exploratory framework to identify in which homes the culture of violence was stronger than others and the institutional factors that may influence such cultures (such as control over admissions, high staff turnover, single-sex). However, although such variables were possible associates of high- or low-level violence, often the meaning that young people attached to living in a home with high or low levels of violence differed. For example, where 'violent' reputations of some homes instilled fear in young people, they could also be revered precisely because of their history of housing young people with challenging and violent behaviours, as the following extract illustrates:

> Everyone's all right in here...all the other ones in the other home were just all pure dick-heads, but they was younger. All the girls in here are all right and the lads as well, mmm it's a pretty good home this, 'cause when you come in this home, you have to be pretty mature to come in this home 'cause it's an hard home to be in, you know 'cause it's got a reputation this home for like...you know if like people are annoying, they'll threaten to send them to (this home). (Mandy, aged 13)

Cultures of violence within the home, however, did seem to impact directly upon young people's definition and experience of harm, to the extent that particular forms of violence could vary in qualitatively different ways depending upon the level of violence within the home. In a home categorised as exhibiting low-level violence, for example, pushing someone was considered to have a similar impact to being threatened with a knife in a home categorised as exhibiting high-level violence. Hence, exposure over time to violence led some young people to become desensitised to its impact:

> Interviewer: Would you like it to be less violent?
> Neil: I don't mind.
> Interviewer: It doesn't bother you now?
> Neil: No, it doesn't bother me...if I had first come in (to the home) then I would probably like it changed like, asked for the bully to be stopped. But, but now I just get used to it. Seven months living here, you get used to it.
> (Neil, aged 15)

Similarly, as shown earlier, the term 'bullying' was used by young people in a variety of ways including to denote persistent systematic physical acts of violence as well as isolated incidents of being wronged by another child.

One boy commented when asked what he meant by the term 'bullying':

> Ermm...punching, hitting people, swearing, not swearing I mean verbal abuse...there's hundreds of kinds of bullying, you've got physical abuse, verbal abuse, too many kinds...there's many kinds of bullying. (Chris, aged 14)

What became evident in the early stages of the project was that understanding the contextual nature of violence was necessary if we were to assess the meaning and impact that different forms of violence had for young people. It became increasingly evident that young people's perceptions of violence were highly contingent upon their place and role within the peer group and there was an emerging relationship between perception of harm, severity of violence and stability of peer group culture.

'Hi, I'm Ramon and I run this place': 'pecking orders' and peer group hierarchies

Previous research has described this aspect of residential life, though with varying perspectives on its power and significance. It has often been associated with larger institutions for boys, though some recent research on mixed children's homes has also touched on it (Sinclair and Gibbs 1998). The existence of 'top dog' networks was initially highlighted in the Castle Hill report (Brannan *et al.* 1993). Parkin and Green (1997) state in their study of residential life that 'top dog' networks existed in many of their homes where one or two children exercised considerable power and influence over others by actual or perceived physical strength and manipulation. They added that this enabled these young people to bolster their reputations, enhance or diminish those of others and have influence with the staff.

A consistent theme in our study was the centrality of the peer group dynamic in young people's accounts of how the cultures of violence were normalised. Given that the 'peer group culture partly emerges out of the temporal demands laid on children and young people by the institutional structures through which their growing up is regulated and controlled' (James *et al.* 1998:77), it could be argued that the residential component of the children's home placed an extra pressure upon the peer group. They would often have no choice but to be in close physical proximity with young people whom they may or may not know, over long periods of time. It thus came as little surprise that the peer group was often fraught with tension and that, embedded in young people's accounts of residential peer group cultures, was a constant reference to hierarchical peer group dynamics. In all but one of the residential homes, young people described this phenomenon as being present in their home at the time of the fieldwork. This described peer culture in terms of there being dominant members of the peer group who, via various forms of oppression and control, could impose their will upon other members of the peer group. However, young people had a larger repertoire, including, 'the boss', 'the ruler', 'top kid' or 'the leader'. As one girl described it:

> You have to have a leader...and like everybody knows who it is but doesn't say you know, doesn't let on, and like all the other kids get pushed around. (Amanda, aged 14)

Young people framed their descriptions in terms of domination and subordination and many could not only identify who was at the top of the hierarchy, and other relative subordinate positions within the hierarchy, but also who was next in line for the top position once it became vacant. However, there was no clear or consistent profile of those who were likely to be positioned at the top of the hierarchy. And while age, maturity, status (being, in their words, 'hard' or 'cool'), height, physical stature or strength, intelligence, manipulative powers, criminal record or experience and length of stay in the home, were all characteristics of those positioned as 'top dog', none were prerequisites. In one home catering for boys between the ages of 11–16, for example, the next young person to ascend to the top of the hierarchy was a 12-year-old boy. In another home, two relatively slight 15-year-old girls were controlling the peer group, which included a 16-year-old male and an older and bigger young woman. Rather, it was the ability to manipulate and control the rest of the peer group, whether it be through individual physical force or by more subtler means (threats, intimidation), that marked the 'leaders' from the 'pack' as one girl described it. Thus, it was not simply a matter of bruising your way to the top, but a complex process which often combined the deployment or threat of physical force with a range of manipulative negotiation skills:

> Well, Mark thought he was big and hard and thought all the kids were weak and 'cause he was like older like and well slightly older, he thought that no-one would even notice and he got battered up so many times for it. (Martin, aged 14)

The process of 'positioning', that is being assigned or assigning oneself to a place in the 'pecking order', was a common feature of admission. Usually, this transition occurred when a resident towards the top of the hierarchy left the home, leaving a vacancy for another member to occupy; or when a new resident entered the home, needing to find his or her place within the hierarchy. Many of these transitions took the form of a struggle of wills, described by the workers as 'acting out'. At these moments, young people would talk about 'standing their ground', 'protecting their patch', or 'standing up for themselves'. If new residents did not resist or 'fight back' in some way to the initial positioning process, they would often incur verbal and sometimes physical attacks and intimidation. Furthermore, if new residents disclosed to staff what was happening to them they would almost automatically be placed at the bottom of the hierarchy and be labelled as 'weak' or 'soft', in contrast to those who endured attacks or 'stood up for themselves' by fighting them off. Conforming or challenging the will of the group and its leader often seemed the only way to graduate from being placed at the bottom of the hierarchy, to the top or near the top. Young people's accounts of the process of attaining a stable peer group were markedly different. They described how the peer group structure needed constant maintenance and their relative position within the peer group hierarchy involved continuous covert practices (although to varying degrees) of domination and subordination.

'He rules the place and bullies everyone': bullying as a 'natural' and inevitable peer group dynamic?

Interviewer: So when you first came here he was...?
Ross: He reckoned he was big and hard and owned the place.
Interviewer: Did the other kids think he was top dog as well?
Ross: Yeah 'cause he kept bullying them and stuff.

(Ross, aged 14)

There was only one home in which young people reported stable and a relatively equal distribution of power relations. Indeed, talk of safety and feeling safe correlated strongly with stable and non-hierarchical peer group dynamics:

> There's never really been any bullying in this house. Like you hear a lot like there's bullying in children's homes and stuff, but everyone's sort of equal here... there's no head dog in this house, do you know what I mean, everyone treats each other like they'd like to be treated. (Christine, aged 14)

Over half of those who discussed their experiences of hierarchical peer group dynamics framed their accounts within discourses of 'bullying'. Bullying was often referred to in this context as an abuse of power, as the following quotes go some way to illustrate:

> Rob, he's the eldest, 'cause he's not here everything seems to go so easy, but when Rob's here, because he's the eldest he thinks he rules the place and he bullies everyone. He's always hitting me... (Colin, aged 13)

Interviewer: I know that one of the boys was causing grief... could you tell me about that?

Ross: He was just bullying everyone...the younger ones as well ...the little ones you know like Neil and that...all the little ones he was bullying and shit...beating them up, taking their money, scaring them...stuff like that...

Interviewer: What sort of things did he do to scare them?

Ross: Real weird stuff...like mind stuff you know telling them they couldn't do this or that or he'd beat the shit out of them that night...like not to eat or say he's going to get one of them so they'd be scared all day not knowing when he would do it...he just liked making people scared of him made him feel big suppose doing that sort of shit.

Interviewer: Do you know how long he was doing this?

Ross: About three months, quite a long time he did it for, 'cause they daren't do anything cause...I think a lad before him had done the same to this kid and then he was chucked out and he started on the others thinking he was the boss.

(Ross, aged 14)

Only one girl viewed hierarchical peer group dynamics, and the bullying tactics used to maintain the structure, as a natural phenomenon. Overall, young people regarded the hierarchies as something inevitable, which had to be endured given the context of life in a children's home. They were viewed as a wholly negative part of residential experience, with nearly all young people perceiving them as fundamentally harmful and abusive. Their accounts were indeed a long way from interpreting hierarchies as beneficial or perceiving them as a natural part of peer relations or growing up. However, there were differences in the ways in which peer group hierarchies were maintained, particularly in relation to the levels of bullying and types of violence deployed. For example in one home, one boy manipulated and tyrannised the whole peer group (younger boys and girls) with physical, psychological, verbal and sexual violence, over a period of three months, unbeknown to staff. In another home, two girls ruthlessly and in an intimidatory manner placed all but one other girl into subservient positions using threats and psychological coercion. A third home saw a group of girls subordinating a new resident by vandalising her belongings and threatening similar action if she resisted conforming to their rules. All three examples reveal, either through a single dominant individual or through combining dominant forces, how the peer group is manipulated and controlled via oppression and subordination, whether it is through physical force or intimidation.

Young people's responses indicated that some residential workers were complicit in reinforcing the hierarchical structure, and some young people's position as 'top dog'. Staff's use of peer group hierarchies is explored in more depth in Chapter 4.

The masculinisation of physical violence

> Interviewer: And what was it, when you first came in here, what was your first day like?
>
> Tim: It was scary, not scary if you know what I mean, like I was scared because like there's so many big boys and they're just big, puffed up, all hard and I was very worried.
>
> (Tim, aged 12)

Violence has long been recognised as a 'reference point for the production of boys and men' (Hearn 1998:7) and associated with 'normalised' forms of masculinity. Yet while such behaviours are universally condemned they are simultaneously legitimised through a language of 'boys will be boys' (Miedzian 1992). The residential setting is no exception. The gender regimes operating inside the home echo much of the literature on other institutions such as the school or the prison (see Mills 2001) and the masculinisation of violence within wider society (Connell 1995, Home Office 2000), which suggests that the majority of violent behaviours and incidents are perpetrated by boys and young men. Indeed, the majority of violence engaged in by boys, both as 'receivers' and 'doers', was physical violence and much of the physical violence was normalised by boys as just 'what boys do'. This is conceptualised as *display violence*, that is where boys and young men engaged in low level forms of physical violence, not necessarily to inflict pain, but as a means of constructing a particular type of masculinity. Boys' accounts of their involvement in physical violence were mainly framed in terms of their expression and projection of a 'tough' or 'hard' masculinity. To this end, many incidents were conducted in full view and knowledge of staff, with young men aware that workers would intervene to prevent any serious physical harm. This provided for safe instigation of violence, in which boys could position themselves as aggressors, thereby confirming their masculinity to others:

> Most kids want the staff to be there because when they kick off they are going to get restrained and it makes them look like they've just beaten him up. So I could walk to a really big kid, go and hit him and as soon as they've restrained me he can't touch me, so it will make me look like I've just, can you see what I mean. (Robby, aged 14)

However, while many boys' experiences of physical violence were normalised and ingrained within wider notions of what it means to be male or masculine, girls' accounts of physical violence were, not surprisingly, markedly different.

Challenging and transgressing passive femininities: girls and physical violence

While girls' accounts of physical violence were not normalised or routinised as part of their everyday lives, individual identities and social relationships, girls also used physical contact violence, predominantly between themselves. Some girls even used the discourses of cultivating and projecting a hard exterior to others through the deployment of physical violence as a means of protecting themselves, particularly in homes where the peer group dynamic appeared unstable or was especially hierarchical. Sometimes, girls' use of physical violence with each other seemed to imbue them with a sense of power, particularly when directed at other weaker boys in the home, as they set out directly to challenge traditional passive notions of girlhood and femininity and access more masculine notions of power:

> Amy: Sometimes I can get really mad and start a fight 'cause they get on your nerves...like Connor (resident)...did you see all those scratches on his face?
> Interviewer: Yes, I saw them this morning.
> Amy: I did them (laughs and punches the air victoriously)...I think he was embarrassed that I'm a girl and 'cause he's small for his age.
>
> (Amy, aged 13)

The sexualisation of female violence

Dominant notions of femininity were, however, maintained in the constant conflation of femininity and sexuality in young women's reports of their experiences of violence and verbal attacks. Indeed, and not surprisingly, types of violence which damaged young women the most were those in which a girl's sexuality or sexual reputation was questioned, which as the following two extracts illustrate could occur through verbal abuse and intimidation:

> Interviewer: If someone wanted to hurt someone's feelings, are there certain names that are more hurtful than others?
> Fiona: Yeah...like whore, slag, lesbian, things like that.
>
> (Fiona, aged 13)

Another example of the ways in which violence for women was sexualised, although less common, was when a girl's body was sexually violated either directly (via sexual violence or harassment) or indirectly (via sexual intimidation or threats) by male residents. However, like so many reports of female sexual harassment and sexual intimidation, their experiences were undermined, as a form of sexual harassment, through a language of uncontrollable masculinities and insatiable sex drives. For example, when one young woman was asked if the male resident who grabbed her breasts would have gone further, she replied:

> Yeah, he would've done more yeah... the boy was a highly sexed man. (Melissa, aged 16)

Some girls, however, were able to draw upon aggressive femininities and thus challenge widely held perceptions of girls as passive victims by fighting back and confronting boys who sexually intimidated or harassed girls. Either collectively or individually, many of the girls experiencing or witnessing the sexual harassment or intimidation, took it upon themselves to either confront or retaliate in some way. Indeed, most young people advocated some form of retaliation. Similarly, many of these accounts are highly gendered, particularly in relation to the masculinisation of revenge.

'I never hit him before he hits me': violence as social justice

Most young people, when subjected to any form of violence, advocated some form of retaliation. When they discussed their involvement in violent activity they almost always framed their accounts within discourses of justification, as the title quote above illustrates. With the majority of young people providing logical rationales for their actions, it made the usual classification of recipient and perpetrator more complex. Over half of the young people, when recounting their involvement in violent scenarios, acted as both perpetrator and recipient. Only a small minority of young people described their involvement in violence in terms of internal causes such as loss of temper, thus adopting a different means of absolving themselves from the consequences of their actions. Very few young people were able to avoid situations of conflict by walking away, ignoring taunts or jibes or getting staff to intervene. Those that did only managed to do so either when behaviours had little impact upon them, or they were unable or too afraid to fight back. For the majority of residents, retaliation was perceived as a form of social justice.

Justification narratives and the eradication of personal responsibility

The consensus that violence begets violence seemed to be embedded within the social codes of the young people in the study. Closer analysis of the justification narratives revealed that they were often less about defence and more about retaliation which were, as the quotes below illustrate, produced within a language of revenge, prevention, protection of honour or status within the home, engaged in as a last resort, or when the young person thought that recipients somehow deserved it. Those who viewed retaliatory violence as a legitimate response believed strongly in their own sense of reciprocal justice. However, there did seem to be two distinct types of retaliation, categorised here as *spontaneous* and *planned* retaliation narratives.

Spontaneous retaliation narratives

All low-level and some high-level violence necessitated some form of spontaneous retaliation. Young people reported that this usually involved responding with the same type (physical with physical, verbal with verbal etc.) and impact (e.g. low-level with low-level) of violence, although boys were more likely to respond with physical violence to verbal attacks. These included retaliation as a form of

Protection

> When people just try, you know, to push me and that I won't take it, I'll just go straight in there just to protect myself. (Fergus, aged 15)

Just deserts

> Interviewer: So does she pick on you like she does on the other kids?
> Amy: No, she knows not to.
> Interviewer: Why's that, do you think?
> Amy: Because that, because last time she tried, she picked on me, she tried to pick on me and she got what she deserves. I kicked her and I punched her and I smacked her in the face.
> (Amy, aged 13)

Last resort

> Yes the day I was going on holiday she tried to, she started annoying me and I told her to leave me alone and when I went to go upstairs she followed me, she came to my room, sat down so I told her to get up. Then she ran down the stairs screaming that I was going to kill her or something. I didn't say anything to her, then I went back up the stairs and I was running up, she grabbed hold of my legs and tried to pull me down so I just started strangling her, I'd had enough. (Jesse, aged 16)

Loss of control

> Andy: Well, like I was pissing around when I just tripped him up and he goes flying up to me, thinking oh yeah I'm a hard man, grabs me around my neck and when somebody grabs my neck, I don't care who it is, I just go berserk on him.
> Interviewer: Right, so you find it hard when that happens to you, to control how you react?

Andy: Yes it ain't nobody else's fault, it's just like it's this thing I can't control any more.

(Andy, aged 13)

When retaliation inflicted more serious, high impact forms of violence, justification narratives were usually framed within discourses of prevention – that is preventing similar situations of conflict from arising and preventing themselves from being subordinated in the future, by re-securing their dominant status within the peer group hierarchy:

Interviewer: Do you think if you didn't fight back they'd keep on at you?
Peter: Yeah, that's, that's why I do it and since then I've stuck up for myself and no one bothers me at all... they know where they stand.

(Peter, aged 15)

Planned retaliation narratives

Planned retaliations were less common, and mainly involved inflicting high-level forms of violence, usually group attacks upon individuals. The most common theme in the reported accounts of planned retaliations was the notion of revenge within a wider framework of social justice:

Interviewer: This happened to you (boy stealing his cigarettes)?
Claude: Yeah.
Interviewer: What did you do?
Claude: Got them back... tied a piece of rope round their neck and kept on pulling it until they gave me my fags back... and they actually did.
Interviewer: And that worked?
Claude: Yeah, it was actually a good method.

(Claude, age 14)

Interviewer: When fights happen, if someone has been nasty to you do you actually plan a time when staff aren't going to be around so that you can do something to someone else.
Steven: Yes, like my friends say revenge is best served cold.
Interviewer: Revenge is...?
Steven: Revenge is best served cold. What it means, is that you got to plan it before you do it, because it's like if you just go into it wobbly and you don't know what you're doing and you just crack him one and hurt him really badly, you'll be happy but then you could get nicked, but what I'm trying to say is right, if you plan it easily enough like to just run

up to him and crack him in the face and run off and go out or something so staff think, oh no he's just messing around again.

(Steven, aged 13)

The more serious forms of planned revenge attacks took place in homes which had high levels of surveillance. This finding could be partly explained by the fact that increased surveillance left young people few opportunities to engage in spontaneous retaliation, but also the fact that homes which had high levels of surveillance admitted more young people with challenging behaviours.

'I will survive': discourses of power and survival in girls' justification narratives

Young women's retaliation strategies involved responding with similar types of violence as those to which they themselves were subjected. Only one young woman reported responding to a verbal attack with physical violence. This finding was in stark contrast to boys' accounts in which all reported retaliations to verbal violence involved a counter physical attack. While boys' physical retaliation to verbal violence is discussed below in detail, some explanation is needed for girls' responding like with like. One interpretation could be that girls are all too aware of the pain that can be caused through verbal attacks and insults (particularly through sexualised forms of abuse, as discussed above). They may feel that responding to verbal attacks with a physical assault would not inflict as much emotional damage. An alternative interpretation is that, unlike boys, girls' embodiment of their gender identity is less related to the projection and maintenance of a tough exterior.

The only form of violence which rarely involved direct retaliation was sexual violence and sexual harassment which involved physical assault. This was particularly evident in cases of high impact sexual violence (such as rape and sexual assault). In these incidents, young women usually sought support from their female peers, although in one case of sexual assault, fellow female residents took it upon themselves physically to attack the young man in question:

Interviewer: So nothing has happened like that here to other girls?
Julie: No, not that I know, no...oh one, one boy did try it on with one of the girls, but he didn't have a very good time after...
Interviewer: What happened?
Julie: We just distressed him for doing it, that's what I'm saying, it just doesn't happen, 'cause once a boy does then.
Interviewer: When did that happen?

Julie:	When one of the people was in bed and he just went in there, I can't remember exactly what he did, but he did try something.
Interviewer:	And did she tell staff or another young person first?
Julie:	Young person first see that's...
Interviewer:	So when you found out what did you do?
Julie:	I just had a right go at him and everyone just jumped on his back and I don't think he'd ever do that again.

(Julie, aged 15)

There were two additional differences between boys' and girls' justification narratives: their attitudes towards retaliation and their position as recipients and/or perpetrators. First, girls were more likely to frame their accounts of retaliation, particularly planned or physical retaliation, as a last resort:

> 'cause every time when I've had a fight here when it's not been my fault but I've never, like, I would do anything I can to avoid a fight but then sometimes that's going to be the only way to resolve it. So you just do it and it will finish after that. (Jessie, aged 16)

Indeed, their descriptions of engaging in violent behaviours were, like the boys, normalised, but as part of their strategies of survival. This was particularly in relation to preventing the onset or continuance of bullying and maintaining or re-securing their hierarchical positioning within the peer group, rather than retaliating as part of their gender identity construction or maintenance.

> It's like the same thing I done to Sherry when she wrecked my room, she ripped my pictures, my favourite pictures and so I got her and I pushed her and I stamped on her, I was like, 'cause she stamped on them and she ripped them so I said, 'You don't like it when I stamp on you so don't stamp on my stuff and throw my stuff around.' (Amy, aged 13)

A further gender difference between young people involved their perception of themselves as either perpetrator or recipient or both. Girls, for example, were almost twice as likely to describe themselves as perpetrators than boys. Closer examination of their justification accounts suggested that perpetrating violence, whether physical, verbal or material, was often viewed in a positive light. Their actions appeared as a signifier of their power over other girls and boys, and within wider ideas of passive and weak femininities. Rarely did their accounts portray their actions as an abuse of unequal power relations. For boys, as the following section illustrates, being a perpetrator of violence had more ambiguous connotations and could simultaneously position them negatively and positively.

'Standing ground' and 'saving face': projecting, protecting and maintaining 'hard' masculinities

Boys were much more likely than girls to retaliate physically to any form of violence. Unsurprisingly given the masculinisation of violence, their (physical) retaliation accounts were embedded within wider discourses of what can be termed 'hard' hegemonic masculinities (Messner and Sabo 1990, Connell 1995). These justification accounts were also framed within a language of *personal rights* – that is, that they have the right to retaliate to violence, and what we have termed *uncontrollable masculinities*, with physical violence as the sole and accepted property of masculinity. Such essentialistic notions, as Mills states, serve to 'take the responsibility for violence away from the perpetrator' (2001:57). The following quotation illustrates the connection between violence, retaliation and the need to project and maintain 'hard' macho exteriors:

> Interviewer: Do you think there is more fighting and things in this unit than there was in the home you were at before?
>
> Donatus: No. Like I said, people just fight anywhere because they want to be big or want to try and look big and impress people or show people they can do this and that. Kids will just try and snap back just to look as though they won't take no crap.
>
> (Donatus, aged 15)

Proving their masculinity to others and mostly male co-residents could go some way to explaining the higher number of planned retaliations by boys than by girls. Indeed, the increased public surveillance in the residential setting, in which the peer group either at home or at school was ever present, may also shed some light on this finding. For many boys, particularly in single-sex homes, retaliation was not simply about revenge and prevention but was also one of the predominant routes to constructing and maintaining masculinity. This is further emphasised in one of the rare accounts of boys as perpetrators, justifying their behaviour in terms of peer group hierarchy maintenance.

> Stuart: Yeah he tried picking on everyone.
> Interviewer: Oh did he?
> Stuart: Yeah.
> Interviewer: And why do you think he was doing that?
> Stuart: Because he thought he was like trying to test us all out... like hard man, he wanted to be the boss so he had to fight us all, but I'm not going to put up with that so I kicked the shit out of him and he didn't come near me after that.
>
> (Stuart, aged 15)

Masculinities were often under threat, not only by the more dominant femininities displayed by some of the girls, but by the constant public surveillance and policing from other boys (and girls) in the home. With a predominant part of masculinity constructed around the gendered and heterosexualised notion of female protection (Frosh *et al.* 2002), 'mother cussing' seemed to be one of the strongest challenges to a boy's masculinity. So powerful was this form of verbal abuse amongst boys in the residential setting that in all reported cases, it provoked a physical, and in the boys' accounts, an entirely legitimate form of retaliation.

> No one would ever say anything about my mum because I would get up and hit them so hard. (Andy, aged 13)
>
> When he was cussing me he was going, 'oh your mum's this and that' and I was getting really wound up about it so we ended up fighting. (Neil, aged 15)
>
> If someone called my mum a twat or something, I would flip out at them, I wouldn't care and I wouldn't stop until they were on the floor. (Patrick, aged 12)

However, not all physical retaliations were so unambiguously justified or constructed as legitimate forms of response. Many boys, unlike most of their female counterparts, avoided positioning themselves solely as perpetrators of violence. This was achieved by describing themselves as the victim of an unequal distribution of power relations within the group. Put another way, they strongly disassociated themselves from being labelled as 'bullies'.

> No one targets anyone for no reason, I mean that don't happen. I mean that's bullying. (Chris, aged 14)
>
> One day I was, I was going to fight him because he started shouting and saying just like, being rude to me, and I was just about to punch him, but I thought, 'No, he's smaller than me' and I'll be...as like one of the bullies, 'cause I gripped him, but I didn't and I said 'No' I let go of him and I said, no I don't want to bully him, because then I'll get called a bully in the house. (Nick, aged 16)

As the above extracts illustrate, being a bully involved capitalising on an unequal distribution of power (be it size, intelligence etc.) and attributing yourself with power by subordinating other weaker members of the group. It was thus almost always perceived negatively, with many boys highlighting the falseness of creating dominance in this way. To this end, boys' accounts of themselves as perpetrators had to be carefully constructed, even though the more serious planned retaliation involved the very maintenance of peer group hierarchies and unequal power relations that they deplore in others. Indeed, the lengths to which both boys and girls went to justify and rationalise their engagement in various forms of violence, has significant implications for staff in terms of reactive and proactive intervention, as we shall see later.

'He acts like a two-year-old': age and immaturity as catalysts for violence

A quarter of young people commented on how the age of a resident and the age gaps between residents acted as catalysts for low-level and some high-level forms of violence. Below are reports of how younger residents living with older residents are labelled as 'irritants', particularly in terms of first, 'winding-up' older residents, but also destabilising peer group dynamics and hierarchy.

> She was bullying us...bullying us 'cause she was winding us up on purpose to make us hit her so she could go and tell staff and get us in trouble for it...She would really get on our nerves...she shouldn't have been put here 'cause she was too young and we don't want to put up with that kind of stupid behaviour. (Melissa, aged 16)

Closer analysis of young people's accounts suggested that it was not necessarily the chronological age of co-residents but their perceived immaturity. Some of the younger boys were not seen as irritants and were thus not bullied, while some older boys and girls were so perceived, and were thus subject to various forms of bullying and intimidation:

> (He was bullied) because he acts like a little two-year-old, he's 16, he's older than me, and he acts like a two-year-old, then everyone left and it was just him. I was away, all the incidents happen when I am away, because if I see anything they know I will just charge in and like...whereas him, he doesn't know where to stop. One time there was a little kid here, he was only 14, and the kid just strangled him and his nose started bleeding and he got kicked out and went to (another home). So if I was there to see that I would have done him twice as bad you know. (Nick, aged 16)

Some young people's accounts illustrated how residents, seen by their peers as 'immature', were for some reason not conforming to the informal codes and subordinate position within the peer group hierarchy. Rather they were blatantly challenging the hierarchical structure by provoking (either physically or verbally) those young people positioned high up, regardless of whether or not they could win the fight or come out on top.

Some young people could ignore such outbursts because they had some sympathy or understanding of the young person's background, past abuse, behavioural or learning difficulty.

Because one time when I was watching TV and he done that (pulls his trousers down) and I ran into the old computer room and if I wanted to I could have hit him in the face about 50 times, but I didn't I just turned my fist about that far away from his face and he was just scared. There was no point in hitting him because he is younger than me and it won't hit any sense into him. (Male, aged 14)

Ross:	Yeah, normally it's done in jest (name-calling) but Brian, when I first moved in, he used to be 'fuck your mum this' and 'fuck your mum that', and everyone used to batter him.
Interviewer:	Was that like a really bad thing?
Ross:	Yeah.
Interviewer:	So now how do you do it, do you just ignore the younger ones?
Ross:	Yeah, keep myself to myself. I'm out of the way.

(Ross, aged 14)

Other young people reported difficulties in ignoring such challenges. Rather, they took it upon themselves, either individually or collectively to 'keep them in line' and reposition them subordinately within the peer group hierarchy using whatever means necessary.

We got in a fight and I hit her 'cause she was coming up to my face and saying things about my mother so I hit her and I got in trouble but she was the one causing the trouble and she doesn't get told off. We're told to ignore what she does but how can you ignore someone who's right in your face winding you up and saying stuff?... But they knew what she was like 'cause she had to leave the last home 'cause all the residents said they were going to beat her up, so they had to move her but she shouldn't have got sent here 'cause she's too young to live with us... she's just a little bitch and it's not fair on the rest of us having to put up with it... you wouldn't like to live with her would you?... so if I hit her it's her fault 'cause she asks for it all the time. (Jessie, aged 16)

Indeed, it was almost as if the disregard which these less mature residents had for the peer group hierarchy made visible its often fragile and constructed nature, thus provoking others to retaliate and reassert their dominance. This explanation may account for the high number of justification narratives which cited immaturity as a catalyst for the instigation and perpetuation of violence.

Summary points

- The homes taking part in the research had manifest differences in the nature and levels of violent behaviour, among the young people and towards others. However there was a consistent theme of the importance of the hierarchy or 'pecking order'. The young people gave sophisticated accounts of the hierarchy in their children's homes, outlining the relative subordinate positions within it, and identifying not only who was at the top of the hierarchy but also who was the heir apparent who would inherit the top position once it became vacant.

- Perception of hierarchy among young people was strongly linked to gender, and it was a common feature that hierarchies were seen as inevitable by young people but not as 'natural'.
- The use of the term 'bullying' was common among the young people and usually referred to an abuse of power.
- Studies of young people's behaviour in many contexts have described the masculinisation of physical violence, in which violence is represented as normal for boys. This perception was reflected in the attitudes of the young people in the present study. In contrast, physical violence for girls was not 'normalised' but was used both defensively and as a deliberate challenge to male power in the group of young people.
- For young women, the sexualisation of violence was very significant. While they often confronted sexual aggression from boys, they also 'normalised' it by regarding it as a natural part of male sexuality.
- The normalisation of violence was also reflected in the way in which young people conceptualised it as social justice. While bullying others was seen as an abuse of power, violence used in self-defence, or as a response to assault or insult from others was seen as justified, and was not described as 'bullying'.
- Triggers for violence which were most likely to be seen as justifying retaliation, included insult to the young person's mother or family, sexual insults, and behaviour by very young or immature residents aimed at 'winding-up' other young people.

4
Staff Perspectives on Violence

> Boys aren't generally as vindictive and nasty as girls. I mean, boys have their squabbles, they have a go at one another, but then the next day they're fine with each other, but girls don't. They hold grudges and you'd think it's all quietened down and someone will do something really sly and nasty...they hold grudges, boys have a much easier time of it, it's a case of doing the manly thing, it's a row and then a pat on the back and it's all forgotten, but with girls it's much more devious and long-lasting.
> (Senior Residential Social Worker, female)

> (Young people) have to find the one who'll rule the roost, peer pressure is the greatest thing for kids at this age, it lets them know where they stand.
> (Residential Social Worker, male)

In this chapter we examine staff perspectives on violence. We decided to present staff accounts separately from young people's for a range of reasons. Foremost was the importance of ensuring that both young people's and staff's explanations should be viewed within their particular child and professional understandings and explanations. Consequently, at certain points in the following chapter readers may have a sense of déjà vu, as in some instances, young people and professionals identified similar micro- and macro-processes for the development of violence. However, the definitions and understandings that were attributed to these processes differed markedly, both between groups and between homes. Both the similarities and the differences are of central importance if we wish to understand how meanings impact on young people's experiences of violence and verbal attacks, and how professional cultures and practices interact with these complex processes.

By this theoretical separation we do not mean to imply that these differing perspectives have no influence on one another. As Alexiadou (2001) states, the development of shared definitions of meaning are created within institutions by the continual social interactions between staff and clients. This process is defined by Berger and Luckman (1966:72) as 'institutionalisation' and represents an essential element in understanding how residential processes and structures are formed and experienced. Institutionalisation, therefore, provides a theoretical framework for understanding how behaviours and practices develop in organisational contexts. Both of these central features of residential life – child/professional interactions and institutional dynamics – are discussed in Chapter 6.

Within staff accounts five key themes emerged, which framed professional understandings of violence and verbal attacks: peer group hierarchies; the gendered nature of violence and verbal attacks; social relations (racism); age; and, lastly, young people's background. Several of these correspond to those which arose in young people's accounts, although the meanings ascribed to them differ.

'They all know their little places': hierarchical peer group dynamics

One of the most important explanations by staff of the normalisation of unequal power relationships between young people in residential homes concerned hierarchical peer group dynamics, uniformly referred to by staff as the 'pecking order'. In all except one home in the present study at least half, and often nearly all, the adults interviewed described this phenomenon as being present in their home at the time of fieldwork. Furthermore, the majority of them stated that the 'pecking order' was a constant aspect of residential life, with staff who had experience of other residential settings stating that it was common to those as well. Overwhelmingly, staff within our study perceived this ordering of status as being normal or at least inevitable. For the majority of staff, this was an enduring aspect of peer relations in a very wide range of residential settings. Although many felt that the residential context exacerbated the significance of the pecking order in the lives of young people, others felt that the hierarchical structuring of peer relations was a common aspect of children's social relationships in general. Indeed, the process involved was viewed by some as being beneficial to children's life experience, as one of the quotes at the beginning of the chapter demonstrates. In some cases, the structuring of relationships in this manner was not only synonymous with children's cultures but was viewed as a common feature of all social relations.

> Everyone's fighting for the top dog place, to be the main kid or at least not to be at the bottom of the ladder. It's just how kids are when they're together, how they organise themselves naturally, as it were. (Residential Social Worker, female)

> It's a form of character building, everybody's vying for the top spot to be the top dog, it's the same everywhere, even work places, everyone wants to be at the top, don't they? (Deputy Manager, male)

Only 5 of the 71 staff interviewed acknowledged that hierarchical peer dynamics may be a direct misuse of power and domination. These staff disputed its perceived normality, although often this was explained in terms of the artificiality of the residential setting.

> I worry about what the pecking order means for kids. Does it mean they're intimidated into their position? I expect children at the bottom see it very differently to those at the top, or indeed to how some staff see it. (Senior Residential Social Worker, female)

> I don't think it's a common feature of normal relationships (between children) but this is not a normal environment. (Residential Social Worker, male)

One manager of a home for younger children perceptively questioned whether definitions based on adult interpretations of children's hierarchical cultures reflected children's own experiences.

> Adults often, I think, see it as a normal aspect of growing up. However, I feel that young people may see it differently. Top dog may to them mean the biggest bully, asserting their power over them. I do not feel this is either a normal or, at least, not a healthy situation to allow to develop so we try to discourage this view of it here. (Manager, male)

The majority of staff interviewed in 13 of the residential homes could clearly identify where they believed individual children and young people were positioned within this hierarchy, generally producing highly consistent accounts of this ranking. In nine homes very strict delineations were identified by staff; in four the ordering was more diffuse. However, all staff could generally name who was situated at the apex of the hierarchy at the time of fieldwork, universally referred to as the 'top dog'. Other positions in the hierarchy described by staff included 'deputy dog', 'under dogs', 'lap dogs' and 'worker dogs'. All describe subservient positions young people are perceived as holding within this social structure. Some staff demonstrated their belief that young people were also clearly aware, not only of their relative position within the peer hierarchy, but of who was the 'top dog' at any one time. A residential worker in one home described how one 'top dog' would shout 'Who's the daddy? I'm the daddy!' to proclaim his status. Not only were staff within individual homes able to identify consistently who they felt was the current 'top dog' but which young person was due to inherit this position once it became vacant.

> They have to sort the pecking order out each time a new kid comes in from top dog down to the bottom boy. You can see who's where and who's in line for the best positions once the top kid goes. (Deputy Manager, female)

> In any (residential) home the pecking order needs to be established and needs to be clear, they (young people) sort it out between themselves. (Senior Residential Social Worker, male)
>
> They all just naturally slot into their little places, it's incredible... you can see who is next in line. He will be a great top dog 'cause he's so clever and gets on well with staff. (Residential Social Worker, female)

In this quote not only is this worker able to identify who will ascend to the prime position within the hierarchy, perceiving this process as natural and inevitable, but also clearly favours this young person for the job due to his usefulness for staff interactions with the resident group.

'What makes a good top dog?' Staff evaluations of ascendancy

A wide range of factors was associated with ascendancy within the peer hierarchy including age, maturity, physical strength, length of stay, intelligence, criminal activities and respect from staff. It was also routinely stated that status within the peer rankings was not necessarily associated with age, physical strength or gender. Indeed, the 'top dog' in waiting described above was one of the youngest boys in the house and definitely not the most physically threatening. The most commonly stated criterion required for the 'top dog job' according to staff was intelligence, more specifically the ability to manipulate peers and situations for their own benefit.

> All the girls go to school or college, so they see themselves as more superior than the boys, 'cause mostly they're excluded, thus they're top of the hierarchy. They differentiate themselves from the boys who are seen as much lower down in the pecking order. (Deputy Manager, female)
>
> He's bright (the top dog) and uses it to make sure he gets what he wants, through manipulating the other residents to do exactly what he wants them to do. (Residential Social Worker, male)

However, intelligence alone was rarely viewed as enough to secure the top positions, this had to be accompanied by a strong personality and some degree of 'street credentials'. A range of specific factors was associated with the 'top position' including having the 'biggest mouth', 'most nerve', 'best lies', 'most celebrated career in crime' (real or perceived), 'most dominant personality', 'most intimidating attitude' and 'highest street credentials'.

> It's not the most physically imposing kid, but the brightest one, who can lead the kids into wanting to side with them yet still being scared of them by creating an air of fear and invincibility. (Manager, male)

Thus according to staff, different qualities and characteristics come into play in determining where a young person will be located within the hierarchy.

Consequently, although positions within the strata were not necessarily achieved through the deployment of violence, in practice they often were:

> Peer pressure is primarily based on intimidation. Top dogs are like predators, they're street-wise, they've gone through the system and they do the hunting surrounded by their pack, as it were. They establish a power base by creating a street ethos based on intimidation within the unit itself. (Residential Social Worker, male)

> The higher you go up the pecking order the more you do to others what has been done to you, so the victim then becomes the bully. (Manager, female)

Indeed, when we matched where young people were said to be positioned within the hierarchy with young people's own accounts of peer dynamics, we found a high correspondence between accounts of victimisation and intimidation and subservient positions within the peer group hierarchy. Interestingly, many staff initially introduced the concept of the 'pecking order' in their general discussion of intimidation and bullying within residential homes. Although staff did not overtly conceptualise peer group hierarchies as always detrimental, and many viewed them as normal, they were nearly always associated, at least indirectly, with the misuse of power. The view of the worker given below for example, describing two young women who share the top spot in one of the homes, denies that they used intimidation but were still 'a force to be reckoned with'. Many of the 'lower-status' girls in that home did not see their behaviour quite in this light (see Chapter 3: p. 64).

> (You) always get someone who rules the roost. Like at the moment it's two girls, but they don't use bullying as such or intimidation, but they are a force to be reckoned with. (Residential Social Worker, female)

> All young people use different means of showing off, a bit of verbal, possibly a little push or something...It's just a competition to sort out their places. So in that sense, they're just protecting their own...laugh at it really, just let them get on with it and it's all sorted out in a couple of days. (Residential Social Worker, female)

> Peer pressure is very strong for teenagers, especially in relation to the pecking order...It's not violence exactly, not abuse, it's difficult to label, often they don't know what they are doing, it's (a) sort of control over another young person which can be positive or negative. (Residential Social Worker, male)

> Well the next one in line would be Wayne but then he's been bullied and he would say he was against bullying totally. He's got very definite opinions on it and whether he would move into that slot or not I'm not

sure, as he's reluctant to do that to others. (Residential Social Worker, male)

'We're quite aware of their little power games': changing populations and realignment

Some young people accompanied their manipulation and intimidation of peers with physical violence and, in a number of examples, high impact physical violence was routinely used, mostly, although not exclusively, by young men. In the instances when staff were aware of the use of this form of physical violence they routinely intervened, often stating that the dynamics had 'got out of hand'. This conceptualisation allows the perceived normality of the peer hierarchy to remain unchallenged whilst at the same time enables staff to identify that individual young people occasionally used unacceptable means to either challenge or reinforce their superior positions within the peer culture.

> Sometimes the kids just take it too far... then the dynamics have got out of control and we have to intervene, otherwise we'd be condoning violence wouldn't we? Just need to let them know where the boundaries are and that we're aware of their little power games. (Residential Social Worker, female)

> She ruled through her gangster boyfriend. She'd get him onto the others if they crossed her. We kept an eye on it 'cause it could easily get out of hand. (Manager, female)

Staff often stated that flash points for physical and non-contact violence within the 'pecking order' occurred upon a new admission or when a young person towards the top of the hierarchy left, leaving a space for one of the lower status participants to fill. Staff identified that, at these times, the internal stability of the group collapsed due to transitions in power and fractures in social relations. This caused a variety of 'acting out behaviour', where young people often 'acted out of character' in the attempt to portray a hard exterior.

> The admission of just one new young person can affect the whole group. Good dynamics can crumble and young people panic, get frightened and do things out of their characters, they try and act tough. 'I'm tough too so leave me alone'... It's just a survival strategy, but not a very positive one. (Manager, female)

This acting out was most prominent upon a new admission, when such behaviour routinely extended towards staff as well as other young people, resulting in dramatic changes in the home's dynamics. Some staff identified that this caused additional problems, especially if this was the young person's first experience of residential care, due to their perception of this transitional phase as being representative of typical peer–staff relations. According to staff, this process often resulted in shifting alliances within the peer groups, leading to feelings of broken loyalties and jealousy, and leaving children and young people feeling threatened and insecure about the changes occurring. One worker felt that the anxiety a new admission created for young people surrounded the invasion of their space and the additional competition for attention this would entail, and thus in a sense they were 'protecting their patch'. Staff identified that, although different 'initiation ceremonies' were used by young people in this period of flux (for example pretending that it was obligatory to bath together or removing a young person's belongings), it was not until the 'new social order' was clearly established that the peer group 'settled down'. This process generally took between a couple of days to a few weeks. It sometimes involved a decline in the level of intervention by staff, as young people were viewed as 'having to find their place'. Once this had been clearly established the 'status quo' would be regained. In homes that had regular changes in admissions, realignment could be a constant process. According to staff, these dramatic changes in the hierarchy occurred most severely when emergency admissions were placed in designated longer term units. Then the new hierarchical positions could affect children for a number of months or, even in some cases, years.

In some instances, no one single individual was able to 'fit the top spot', due to the lack of any overriding or dominant personality within the home at that time. In this unsettled situation, small power struggles constantly erupted with *'young people all continually flexing their proverbial muscles at one another'* leading to constant *'squabbles and power games'* within the group. These unsettled peer relations caused additional problems of control for staff and were universally seen only to stabilise when the hierarchy could be re-established, generally through the dynamics being altered through a new admission.

Fourteen staff from several different homes felt that the peer group hierarchies were highly gendered, enabling two separate structures for boys and girls to be present in an individual home. Consequently some staff argued that by having a large single sex peer group, the dynamics were magnified for those at the 'bottom of the pile', as they had more young people in positions of power over them. Nevertheless, in other homes, workers identified mixed gender peer hierarchies where girls as well as boys could hold high status positions. However, the actual mechanisms by which ascendancy was achieved were often viewed as being highly gendered, with boys being seen by staff as relying on more physical or overt strategies, whilst girls were viewed as using manipulation and 'intelligence'. These differences will be explored in greater detail later in this chapter.

Staff routinely identified differences between 'good' and 'bad' 'top dogs'. These judgements were influenced by whether the young person was supportive of staff roles and culture, or embedded in negative (generally meaning highly violent or offending) youth subcultures. It is unsurprising, given the criteria required to achieve the uppermost positions, that the latter was seen as the most common strategy used by young people. A number of examples were provided by staff of what they considered to be more positive peer group leaders. The assessment of a 'good top dog' depended on their usefulness to staff in their interactions with the wider peer group. The most commonly repeated illustration of this was staff's use of the 'top dog' to pass on selected information to the wider group and, thus, provide a valuable mechanism for controlling and influencing other young people. We can see in the first of the quotes below how staff's conceptualisations of the peer hierarchies are normalised and, thus, desensitised through the denial of intimidation. At the same time, the unequal relationships inherent in the peer structure are acknowledged and deemed acceptable and beneficial, both to young people and to staff.

> The leader in the house... she dictates to young people. They listen to her and take her point of view seriously and she'll feed back to staff in a good way. I think it's good to have a leader when you're young. It's not really any sort of intimidation, but she likes her bit of power and others listen to her which is very useful. (Manager, male)
>
> Normal situation, normal moans and groans between young people that's all... (the) peer group leader teaches other young people what they can and can't do. (Deputy Manager, female)
>
> You get good and bad top dogs, the one at the moment is there due to his age and he's good 'cause he keeps the others in line, stops bullying and tells us what's happening. (Senior Residential Social Worker, male)

Furthermore, some staff felt that the social isolation many young people experienced due to the lack of external peer friendships meant that they were often over-reliant on the residential setting, which subsequently intensified the importance of the peer dynamics in the lives of these young people.

> Our kids don't have many external friends so they are very reliant on this setting for all their peer interactions... That serves to intensify the situation, blows it's importance in their lives out of proportion 'cause they're always in it... That's not very healthy and can lead to increased levels of competition between the kids and violence. (Residential Social Worker, male)

In only one home did staff state that no peer group hierarchy existed between young people, and that they would not allow such a structure to develop, believing it was ultimately based on an unacceptable misuse of power.

We don't allow peer pressure here. All the kids are in the same boat, all here to help each other... Pecking orders are always based on some form of inequality and that is something we don't allow in this home. (Senior Residential Social Worker, female)

Gender and violence

The second most commonly presented factor surrounding peer behaviour concerned staff's perceptions of the impact of gender. Over two-thirds of staff interviewed (29 male and 21 female) mentioned gender, generally in relation to three main areas: the normalisation of violence within certain forms of masculinity, the differential forms of domination used by boys and girls, and the use of sexuality by girls.

'Boys will be boys as they say': the normalisation of physical violence through 'divergent masculinities'

Boys and young men were often described by staff as being 'simple', 'one-dimensional' and 'straightforward'. In turn, their use of violence was also portrayed in these terms. Boys were widely believed to rely upon physical rather than non-contact forms of violence. The most commonly presented scenario concerned male on male violence, centring upon a specific argument, resulting in a fight which was quickly forgotten by both parties. In this context, boys' violence is presented as an unsophisticated, although honest, method of conflict resolution. Furthermore, some aspects of low impact, and less frequently high impact, physical violence were validated by staff in relation to boys' emerging masculinity and, as such, viewed as a developmental practice employed in their progression to adulthood.

> A lot of bravado really, it's just boys finding out about themselves really. It's just part of growing up isn't it. Nothing more. (Residential Social Worker, female)
>
> Most of it (physical violence) is just boys trying to be men... I expect I was just the same at their age, it's how most teenage lads act, especially round here. (Residential Social Worker, male)

Thus, physical violence, in the form of one-to-one fights with another equal male opponent, was seen as a normal although uncontrolled aspect of male development. A minority of staff (mainly at senior level) provided a more complex analysis of the situation, equating this form of masculinity with the deprived environments from which young males originated. These staff argued that, due to the limited opportunities available to these boys, the only way they could reinforce their own reputations and feelings of self-worth was through the use of violence and intimidation. This reflects established conceptualisations surrounding masculinity and violence. Gilmore

(1990: 224), for example, argues that 'the data shows a strong connection between the social organisation of production and the intensity of the male image... the harsher the environment and the scarcer the resources, the more manhood is stressed as an inspiration and a goal'. In other words, a lack of economic and social resources has the consequence of rendering issues of power, and therefore their sense of masculinity problematic. For some, physical toughness and violence become major vehicles for the assertion of their masculinity in the absence of any other available avenues (Newburn and Stanko 1994).

> It's due to their home situations mostly. Mostly our lads are from deprived areas where there's high unemployment and the way to portray yourself in these situations is through being tough, not letting others walk over you... There's little else to look forward to for many, except having some street cred through their ability to be the hardest on the street. The worst thing you can do is look weak. (Manager, male)

However, in the present study, some staff stated that for a minority of boys, this had been compounded by their additional exposure to highly misogynistic environments, resulting in deeply entrenched negative attitudes towards females.

> Some kids treat women and girls horrendously. They have learnt to hate women, see them as irrelevant and something they can just abuse... it's down to how their mothers and sisters are treated at home and they just take these negative values on. (Deputy Manager, male)

In direct contrast, girls were generally viewed by staff to be more mature, complex and stronger in character than their male counterparts. Accordingly, they were often perceived as being more perplexing to understand and, therefore, more difficult to work with, due to this multilayering of their personalities.

> Boys are more easy to work with than girls, with boys you get through one layer and that's it, with girls there's just multiple layers to get through. (Residential Social Worker, male)

'Bitching', 'cunning creatures' and 'cat fights': girls, physical violence and verbal attacks

Girls' and young women's aggression was seen as being predominantly through verbal attacks or non-contact violence. Physical violence was rarely ascribed to girls. Examples of the terminology used by staff to describe girls' use of verbal attack and non-contact violence included: 'bitchy', 'nasty', 'manipulative', 'vindictive', 'malicious', 'spiteful', 'vicious', 'scheming', 'cunning creatures', 'calculating', 'revengeful', 'holding grudges', 'liars' and 'festering'.

> Girls rarely come to blows. It's more a war of attrition with them, they just keep pecking away at another person's self-esteem. (Residential Social Worker, male)

> Well, boys as a whole are much more straightforward in their actions 'You've made me angry and I'm going to thump you', whereas with girls it's 'You've made me angry, I'm gonna go and pour something on your clothes, or tell tales about you'. Girls are much more manipulative, I think, and deal with things differently. On the whole with boys, once it's sorted, it's sorted, but with girls it can last for ever...I know these are huge generalisations but they are true. (Deputy Manager, female)

In this context, girls were viewed as exaggerating problems, holding grudges, prolonging feuds for extended periods of time and being unwilling to seek closure on conflicts with others, especially with other girls. Girls were seen as being more covert in their methods, using more subtle and planned means of harm, which often extended to 'ensure' other young people colluded with them. They were viewed as 'operating behind the scenes' in a 'scheming', 'underhand' and 'manipulative' manner, designed to attack others' (mostly other girls') sense of self-esteem, self-worth and security. Many felt that the impact of girls' favoured methods of attack was more detrimental than that used by boys, had longer-lasting effects in terms of emotional impact and, at the same time, were perceived as being more difficult to observe and influence.

> Boys tend to physically square-up to each other and get it over with. Girls are far more devious, wind others up in a more verbal way. They're more cunning and manipulative in their ways, they know just how to really wound someone. (Senior Residential Social Worker, male)

> Boys are wham bang in your face, a bit of physical bravado, a bit of a crescendo and it's all sorted. Girls, however, fester...they go on and on, bitching, niggling, snide comments, hours and hours of it...They're generally much more hurtful and hold grudges for much longer than their male equivalents. (Deputy Manager, female)

When girls were seen as using physical violence, often the impact of this was minimised through terms such as 'bitching matches' and 'cat fights'. Whereas boys' use of physical violence was situated in wider constructions of masculinities, girls' use was predominantly viewed as transcending feminine gender roles, with girls who engaged in these forms of violence being described as 'butch' or 'hard'. The use of this form of violence by girls was also primarily viewed as resulting from their past experiences of family violence, something only related to boys in the context of extreme misogynistic behaviour or high-level violence. Schaffner (1998, 1999) describes the way that girls were often viewed by workers as having more developmental problems than their male counterparts for perpetrating similar levels of physical violence, and this was also evident in the present study.

> I think, generally, that for girls to use physical forms of violence they have to be more damaged themselves, do you know. Like boys, it's sort of natural isn't it... but for girls to physically attack another person I think it shows they need help. (Residential Social Worker, female)

In addition, a small minority of staff felt that girls' use of physical violence reflected wider changes in society, and especially what has been termed by the media and 'PR' companies as 'girl power', where traditional male characteristics of aggression, retaliation, independence and competitiveness are being adopted by young women (Hanna 1999).

> I think it's society as well and standing up for your rights. Girls are coming a long way in that, the girl power sort of thing. They're not going to be sat on, they're not going to do this, that and the other if they don't want... Sometimes I think that although that's what they've learnt, they haven't actually got the skills for it to be done in a proper way and I think that's when it gets abusive. (Senior Residential Social Worker, female)

'Boys just don't stand a chance': girls' use of sexuality

A related area introduced by 28 staff, both male and female, concerned young women's use of their sexuality, including sexual exploitation, as a mechanism for controlling boys. Rationalisations surrounding this perceived misuse of power reflect polarised views of male simplicity and female manipulation.

> The girls here are definitely the main people... they use their female wiles to get the boys to do exactly what they want and the boys just comply... Sometimes they do flex their muscles and do the manly bit and try and boss the girls a bit, but this doesn't really last very long. (Residential Social Worker, female)
>
> Poor boys... they've got testosterone flying around, raging hormones like they're on heat all the time and they're, therefore, very easily led astray by the girls who can use this to gain a lot of power over them. (Residential Social Worker, male)
>
> Girls manipulate boys through using their sexuality, they get them running around after them, it's horrible to watch and it encourages

more macho behaviour, 'cause they try and impress which causes more problems for them, and the girls are just doing it for a laugh. It's all deception, 'cause really they're not interested in them. (Senior Residential Social Worker, male)

Boys are not only positioned as being victims of their hormone-driven uncontrolled sexuality, but are also prey to female sexual duplicity. Boys are seen as being less developed and, therefore, unable to control or understand their sexuality; whilst girls, and especially those percived by staff as promiscuous, are viewed as harnessing their sexual powers to gain control over boys. This use of female sexuality was also viewed by some of these staff as increasing the use of physical violence. Girls' sexual manipulation encouraged competition between the boys, which resulted in increased 'macho' behaviour including physical violence. Ultimately, this resulted in staff intervention and sanctions for the boys, whilst the 'instigators' (meaning the girls) 'remained at large'.

The girls just do dreadful baiting of the boys and the boys do whatever they're told to do... Inevitably, they get in(to) trouble... even when they haven't thought of doing it themselves, and it's not fair 'cause the girls are far more guilty, setting the lads up in that way, but they pay the price, including criminal records, and the girls who have done all the behind the scenes encouragement get away scot-free. (Residential Social Worker, female)

One female worker described how the 'Venus syndrome' manifested itself within residential settings. She stated that, irrespective of how physically attractive a young woman was, she would be the 'most popular thing since sliced bread' with the boys, and joked that the only way to manage the situation would be with bromide. Although staff stated that boys do seem to get 'fed up' with this female manipulation and seek to regain control they inevitably, according to one female worker, '*settle down once more happy with their lot*'.

However, a very few (5) female staff held an opposing view of female sexuality. These staff stressed the importance of empowering girls in relation to their sexuality through messages of independence, choice, self-reliance and resistance to traditional gender relations. Central to these messages was the need for girls to separate themselves from male control, and especially from older boyfriends, who were often viewed as representing a significant threat to their well-being.

We try to get the girls to look at their relationships with these lads, to see what they are getting out of them and what their so called boyfriends get, which is often sex whenever they want it, and the girls get very little.

> Often they are very damaging to their self-esteem 'cause they are just being controlled by these men. (Senior Residential Social Worker, female)

This reflects Hanney's (1996) work on the treatment of girls within the US juvenile justice system, where individual staff asserted the importance of female autonomy in relation to men, and especially boyfriends, who were uniformly viewed as being responsible for the girls' criminal activities. According to Hanney, these staff were calling into question the validity of the heterosexual contract. However, this challenge was generally viewed as an unwelcome attack by the girls themselves who, lacking access to any other form of social power, placed great weight on the one area of social privilege (heterosexuality) they could control. These findings warn us against applying a one-dimensional theory of institutionalised gender relations where a singular set of male-dominated gender norms is imposed on clients, for it is clear that these individual staff viewed themselves as being separate from this system. Unfortunately, these staff may also represent a minority in the United Kingdom. An earlier exploratory study by Carlen (1987) found that young women in residential care complained that they had been denied the opportunity to develop any aspects of control over their lives, especially over their own sexuality.

In the present study, alongside the dominant negative female representations, some staff placed a different interpretation of how the presence of girls in mixed homes changed the residential peer group dynamics. In these assessments, staff felt that boys benefited from a mixed-sex establishment as they 'try and act maturer' to impress the girls. Thus, female presence was seen as improving male behaviour and therefore reducing the presence of male physical violence. O'Neill (2001) identified similar views regarding young people in secure accommodation.

Overall just under a third of staff interviewed (22) commented on girls being more difficult to work with than boys; the remaining staff did not differentiate by gender. A minority of staff (8) from different homes stated that they would not like to work with girls or that given the choice, they would work only with boys. More female than male members of staff stated this. In contrast, no staff stated they preferred working with girls. In addition, staff in the two male-only units, which regularly accommodated young sexual offenders, stated that in this context having a mixed group would be dangerous for the girls and provide major supervisory problems. Only one participant (a manager) stated that girls' and young women's particular needs within residential care were not always recognised or prioritised.

> I feel that the interests of a lot of young women in residential settings are neglected because the boys are seen as the problem, and the girls just get forgotten. It's not a new problem, it goes back a hundred

years, it's a legacy of (residential) care being set up primarily for boys and consequently the girls' needs are just sidelined. (Manager, female)

Indeed, this omission has not been restricted to practice. Except for a few notable exceptions (e.g. Ackland 1982, Carlen 1987, Farmer and Pollock 1998, O'Neill 2001) residential research had generally ignored the issue of gender.

'Racist stuff just isn't allowed here': racial violence

The impact of wider social relations of inequality was generally absent from staff assessments of violence, except in one important area, that of racism. Racism as a motivation for peer violence was raised by only a minority of staff. This was not because staff did not see racist violence as significant, in fact the converse was true, as it received the most swift and consistent staff response. The overwhelming majority of staff interviewed (62) stated that racial violence would have a far greater impact on a young person than if the act had no racial element. All homes stated that racism would not be tolerated and that any occurrence was taken very seriously.

> I think (residents) are all very clear from our reaction to anything racist that we will not tolerate it, that it is unacceptable, and on the whole we don't have much racist abuse here 'cause we're very strict about it. (Residential Social Worker, female)

A small minority of staff challenged the ascendancy which they felt racism had achieved in both residential policy and practice, and questioned whether this had been attained at the expense of acknowledging and prioritising other forms of oppression.

> No it's just that this is a sore point with me because I'll try and be careful how I put this... everyone seems to jump on the racist bandwagon and according to a lot of people the only oppression is racism. They don't get that there's homophobia and all the rest of it and they only pick up on racism which annoys me. There are other forms of oppression that are just as bad but for some reason we seem only to highlight the racist issue. (Residential Social Worker, male)

For six staff this blanket response to the use of racism was viewed as being rather 'heavy-handed'. They felt that some children and young people, especially younger ones, may engage in racist name-calling in some contexts but that this use of racist language did not mean they actually held racist beliefs. Previous work has also shown that children's belief systems and their subsequent actions are not necessarily always synonymous (Troyna and Hatcher 1992, Barter 1999).

> It (racism) seems to be more of a problem for the adults than it is for the kids 'cause the kids they might make silly remarks, you know like children do, but...I'm sure they don't mean a thing. Sometimes staff overreact when the kid doesn't mean nothing by it really...It doesn't mean they're racist or anything. (Residential Social Worker, male)

However, the effect of being a victim or witnessing such racist abuse may not be so contextualised (Sibbitt 1997). Generally staff felt that young people viewed the use of racism within the peer group negatively, and were as likely as staff to reprimand a young person for racist behaviour or views. Nevertheless, staff identified that they had worked with young people who held very entrenched racist views, which were generally attributed to racism within their families and local neighbourhoods. Efforts to change these rigid attitudes had generally been unsuccessful.

> If the child comes from a very racist family it can be very difficult to challenge their racism...We have had kids here who constantly go on about 'those blacks'. One young man would just talk openly about blacks and niggers and stuff like that and it was just repeated from home, but we couldn't get him to stop...Often you can't do anything if it's so deep-set. (Residential Social Worker, male)

Staff did not think that there were gender differences in racism, although younger children were seen as more likely to produce contradictory statements regarding their beliefs and subsequent behaviour. However, certain minority ethnic groups, especially asylum seekers and South Asian males were, according to staff, most at risk of racism both from white and other minority young people.

> Oh, they were completely racist towards the Kosovan kids, completely, really bad, really horrible to them. They thought they shouldn't have been over here eating all our food and doing this and that. (Deputy Manager, female)
>
> The group that stands out here are young Asian people, and Afro-Caribbean kids are as likely as white young people to instigate the racist bullying towards the young Asians. (Deputy Manager, female)

In addition, many staff, and particularly those from minority ethnic groups, reported that they had themselves been victims of racist abuse from young people, often the same young people who expressed anti-racist views. Consequently, although many young people stated that they were opposed to racist behaviour, this was somewhat dependent upon whether the victim, for whatever reason, was perceived as being an insider or an outsider in the peer group, with the latter being more likely to face racist abuse. For example, it may be that certain groups are not ascribed the 'street credentials' attributed to other ethnic groups in the wider youth cultures in which many of the young people engaged.

This phenomenon has previously been described by Majors (1989) as 'cool pose' in which African Caribbean males embody an 'aggressive assertion of masculinity' which 'emphatically says "white men, this is my turf. You can't match me here"' (1989: 84). Sewell (1997) asserts that this 'cool pose' positions African Caribbean boys as superior to their white/Asian counterparts in sexual attractiveness, style and hardness 'they are heroes of a street fashion culture that dominates... (but also) experience a disproportionate amount of punishment in our schools' ... (thus they are both) 'the darling of popular youth sub-cultures and the sinner in the classroom' (1997: 9). Paradoxically these boys are both feared, respected and discriminated against. However, the 'performance' (Butler 1990, 1997) of this 'supermasculine' image (Tizard and Phoenix 2002) imposes severe costs, including the need to suppress emotional expressiveness, and motivation to learn, due to an anti-school stance. Ultimately, many African Caribbean young males will come under severe peer pressure to embody or at least pretend to embody these 'cool pose' characteristics.

Some commentators suggest that this differentiation may be especially exaggerated in relation to South Asian boys and men, as racist constructs often position them as effeminate, weak and passive (Back 1994, Mac an Ghaill 1994). It may be that these stereotypes act to exclude this group from the dominant form of masculinity present within some residential homes and, thus, position them as outsiders to the peer group structure. Unfortunately, little theoretical base exists to explain why girls may also experience similar patterns of discrimination within peer cultures. It seems to be assumed that simply by association they are bestowed or denied the 'street credentials' associated with their male counterparts.

'The youngsters just hit whilst the older lot are more subtle about it all': age and violence

Age was seen as another important factor by 25 staff (15 male and 10 female) in relation to the nature and frequency of violence and attacks within homes. Closer analysis revealed that staff in different homes produced very disparate accounts. After gender, the most commonly agreed factor amongst staff concerned how children and young people of different ages used distinct forms of violence. Younger children were more likely to use physical violence and be less inclined to hide it from staff. Older residents were more prone to using covert physical violence and non-contact forms of violence. For example, staff in two boys' residential units catering for different age ranges stated that, whilst the older boys tended to use intimidation backed up with covert physical violence, the younger boys relied more on overt physical violence. In some instances, younger boys were able to bully their older but 'weaker' counterparts, which they would do using very overt methods and, consequently, reinforce their standing within their peer group through their observed domination of an older peer.

> Generally the older lads bully the younger ones...but it also happens the other way round, but then the younger ones don't bother to really hide it 'cause they're proud of themselves to be able to bully someone who's older...The older ones are definitely more likely to hide it. (Residential Social Worker, male)

In relation to the mix of ages within homes and the effect this has upon violence, experiences were varied and contradictory. It is now widely accepted that children under 12 should not be placed in residential care if a foster placement is available. However, specific circumstances (often a high degree of 'challenging' behaviour) may mean a residential placement is sought. Many homes operated, at least in policy, by rules which meant that younger children and older young people should not be placed in the same unit. Nevertheless, we found that in 6 such homes, in the year prior to fieldwork, 9 children under 12 had been or still were accommodated alongside older peers, against the formal objectives of the establishment. In a further three homes, young people who were older than the prescribed age limit had been accommodated with younger children. These situations produced contradictory views between homes about the impact of these mixed age ranges on the nature and degree of violence.

The most commonly identified situation, not unexpectedly, surrounded the bullying, intimidation and exploitation of younger children by their older counterparts. Staff in seven homes stated this either was now, or had been, a problem. Staff generally felt that, in these circumstances, the explanation for the exploitation of these children was solely that they were younger and therefore less powerful and easily manipulated. It seemed to make little difference in relation to the targeting of younger children if they were isolated in the home or in the majority, although this may have significant effects on the emotional impact of the violence, especially for an isolated younger child.

> When we have mixed age-groups then the younger kids definitely come off worst for bullying...the older ones will pick on them, order them around...bullying really. (Senior Residential Social Worker, female)

> The young kids tend to be an easy target for the older ones. They can get them to do things for them, go to the shops, things like that...We have

to keep a very tight eye on things when we've got mixed ages. (Residential Social Worker, male)

It's the pecking order thing again, the younger kids do get picked on by the older ones, and sometimes this does include bullying. There's no point pretending it doesn't. (Senior Residential Social Worker, female)

In other homes, staff identified that problems arose in relation to the setting of age-related rules. For instance, in one home the different bedtimes of younger children and teenagers created a flashpoint for conflict and violence. Younger children would try to avoid going to bed by playing-up, which impinged on what the older residents viewed as their time with staff, thus causing hostility which quickly turned into physical violence. However, some younger children were seen as being vulnerable not simply by virtue of their chronological age but due to their level of immaturity. For example, wanting to join in with older peers resulting in the disruption of the activity, through trying to emulate the behaviour of their older counterparts, or trying to engage in situations where their lack of maturity meant that they did not comprehend the wider implications of their own and others' actions.

You can't tell a 12-year-old off for provoking a 16-year-old with mental health problems, 'cause he was just acting like a 12-year-old does, but not all kids have what I would define as a normal tolerance level and they retort too quickly with physical violence even against a much younger kid. (Deputy Manager, male)

In a number of instances, younger children were viewed as purposely trying to 'wind-up' the older ones, often with great consistency and skill. Many staff viewed the younger child's behaviour as an attempt to secure attention, either from the staff or the young people concerned. In 1 home the referral of a 12-year-old girl to a mixed older adolescent unit caused major disruptions. The girl had previously been moved from another home for her own protection in response to serious threats from her peers. Her effect on the new home was immediate, and soon all the other young people were up in arms in response to her continued confrontational behaviour. This included spitting in their faces, invading their personal space, stealing their belongings, disrupting their leisure time, lying and making up stories, and repeated verbal attacks. She carried this out with great determination in nearly all her interactions with her older peers, irrespective of whether staff were present or not. Her behaviour seemed to be exclusively aimed at ensuring she was the centre of attention for the staff and young people. This resulted in retaliatory behaviour by many of the young people concerned, including the use of threats and attempts at actual physical violence. One young woman was so concerned about the effect this girl was having upon the others, and the possibility that they may have to leave if they resorted to severe physical violence, that she took it on herself to supervise the girl's activities, up to the point where she sat outside her room at night to ensure that she was left alone.

Older residents were generally advised by staff to ignore the behaviour, and told that they should be able to rise above such childish attempts at conflict, due to their greater maturity. However, many of the older residents were unable to follow the advice, and often in the face of continuous provocation, resorted to using physical violence against the child in question. This subsequently led to staff intervention and the older resident being reprimanded, which fuelled feelings of injustice.

> The younger kids do tend to wind-up the older ones, sometimes on purpose... One of our kids used to do this constantly, and in the end the older ones were lashing out at him physically, which had no effect as any interaction was okay as long as he was the fulcrum of attention. Staff were like 'good he deserves it', but at the end of the day he was a lot younger than the others and they should have known better. (Residential Social Worker, male)

Although the majority of staff viewed the mixing of ages within homes as problematic, some participants felt this situation was beneficial to the residential experience of young people. The advantages seem to concern two issues, being able to separate a large group by age and better peer support for younger children.

> I think having a mixed-age group tends to work better. You can do different things with each so you don't have one huge group, but they separate naturally which makes control much more easy. (Residential Social Worker, female)

> With a mix of ages the older ones tend to go out a lot with their boy- or girlfriends, which leaves the younger kids in the home where they can get a bit more one-to-one attention, which works out well. (Senior Residential Social Worker, female)

Thus age is seen as a natural divider amongst children which works to the homes' advantage by reducing competitiveness and conflict as the different ages will want to do different things, thus separating the group. Second, having a mixed-age range was seen as providing the younger children with better avenues for peer support systems, especially in terms of having young women in the home. For example, in a home for younger children, a 13-year-old girl was the oldest resident there by three years. Although in some ways she appeared developmentally immature for her age, she provided the other children, and especially the girls, with an important additional support system they could access. Indeed, if the girl had been moved to the local adolescent unit she would have been an easy target for intimidation by the other young people, something both she and the staff in the home were aware of. Therefore, although chronological age is an important factor, sometimes there may be other considerations.

> I think it all depends on the personality of the child, how mature they are in themselves rather than their actual age. Developmentally, we get kids that are well below their chronological age and that can cause problems, but it's not really taken into consideration when they are placed here. (Residential Social Worker, female)

However, although these are important insights, overwhelmingly staff did feel that having a mix of ages within homes increased the risk of violence, and significantly increased the risk of victimisation of younger residents.

'They've never been shown how to behave properly at home, so they just use violence to get through life': young people's backgrounds and understandings of violence

In their discussions of violence between young people in their care, staff made little reference to young people's backgrounds. This was also reflected in many of their vignette responses, where as we shall see few participants introduced familial or background factors in their evaluations of the young person's behaviour, either as 'perpetrators' or 'victims'.

Only one-third of adult participants, and proportionally more senior staff than junior staff (half compared to a quarter), explained background factors as important in their understanding of children's involvement in violence and their responses to victimisation. The most common use of children's backgrounds in staff's explanations concerned young people's inability to manage stressful situations. A number of staff felt that due to their past experiences, many of the young people in their care were less likely to have developed effective coping strategies to deal with internal conflicts and worries. Consequently, they used violence as a way of externalising these pressures.

> Problems around violence manifest early, they're not focused on, and then they come into care, and as soon as a problem arises they can't deal with, they resort to violence as a way of trying to deal with it and we're left to try and work through it with them... They (social services) take the kid away but do nothing to heal the damage. (Residential Social Worker, male)

> It's just the trivial matters that set them off, because of their backgrounds. Some have seen violence in the home, that's why some of them are so

> violent, because they know no better, they've seen Dad knock Mum about and think that's the thing to do. (Residential Social Worker, female)
>
> Some young people can cope and learn new ways to cope, others just find a way to survive that might have worked before, including violence, and just stick to that one way and are unable to find other ways to deal with their problems. (Senior Residential Social Worker, male)

The majority of those who used background factors to explain children's and young people's engagement in violence saw them as perpetrators rather than as victims. As we have already seen in relation to girls' physical violence, children's past experiences of victimisation in their families were used to explain their current use of violence in the residential homes. In this context, young people's loss of power in their family lives was viewed as the reason they now sought to exert control over other young people. Thus, through their harmful familial experiences they had come to view themselves as being 'powerless'; 'lacking in respect', 'self worth' and 'control'; and experiencing feelings of 'fear and isolation'. Their subsequent use of violence was therefore felt by staff to be a negative coping strategy employed by some young people in their efforts to achieve some level of control over their lives and gain the 'respect' of others. Staff often felt that these young people would violently react to quite 'trivial' triggers which 'normal adolescents wouldn't even bother about'.

> They just blow... really trivial things can set them off. Things that normal boys would just laugh at can be a case of hospitalisation here. (Residential Social Worker, male)

Less often, staff related a young person's vulnerability to victimisation to their previous experiences of familial abuse or violence. The exception to this was found among eight senior staff, who thought that girls' sexual risk-taking behaviour resulted from previous experiences of sexual abuse. Unfortunately, the understanding shown by some senior staff was not reflected in general working practices. We found little evidence that staff considered the possibility that promiscuous or risk-taking behaviour may be an indication of previous abuse. In fact, male promiscuity received little if any comment, whilst girls' promiscuous behaviour was generally condemned as an inappropriate transition of gender roles.

Farmer and Pollock (1998) highlighted a lack of concern regarding young people's sexual behaviour in their study on sexually abusing and abused children in substitute care. We also encountered situations whilst on fieldwork where we felt a young person's safety could have been jeopardised. For example, in one home a 14-year-old girl had just moved into her new placement (out of her local area). Having been in the home for four days, she had arranged a 'date' with a man across the street who was in his late twenties, and spent much of that day talking about this. She spent a considerable amount of time getting ready for her meeting, with encouragement from the staff who gently teased her about the evening ahead. It appeared to us that the staff were trying to bolster her feelings of self-esteem. However, to support a 14-year-old's wish to meet with an older man potentially placed a vulnerable girl in a very dangerous situation.

Some staff shared with us their concerns regarding what they saw as the neglect of developmental issues in understanding young people's violent behaviours.

> I feel that staff here don't really look behind the negative behaviour at the deep rooted causes... It's just 'that was bad so now you're on a sanction', but that's not getting to the root of the problem so nothing will change for that young person... I find that aspect of this work very frustrating. (Residential Social Worker, female)

> (The) most difficult aspect of this job is trying to understand their backgrounds, what they've been though and how that affects them now... abuse, loss, all need to be taken into account. Unfortunately, lots of staff just treat behaviour as either good or bad, but don't consider their backgrounds... Staff tend to just personalise it and see the young person as bad rather than a child in need. (Residential Social Worker, female)

Indeed, some staff felt that the lack of recognition went further and meant that children's wider needs and problems were left unmet, both by residential staff and social services more generally.

> Most of the young people here don't know how to behave with each other, they're just fighting all the time. They don't sort out their problems they just abuse each other, physically, verbally. They don't possess the necessary skills and nobody's ever tried to help them and they come here and still nobody really helps them, us or social services, 'cause we don't have the skills and social services won't pay for proper help. (Residential Social Worker, female)

Although we did find individual staff who sought to explore with young people the relationship between their current behaviour and their past experiences, these were pockets of good practice rather than routine occurrences. Often attempts at establishing this level of work was hampered by the short-term nature of the young person's placement and the crisis management in which some homes found themselves perpetually involved. This is discussed later.

A number of staff said that young people put themselves at risk of victimisation by telling other residents the reasons they were living in residential care. Staff stated that they routinely warned young people about the risk of sharing personal details with their peers, especially when they first arrived. However, many also recognised that peer pressure often led young people to discuss their experiences, especially when trying to establish themselves in the peer group.

> Kids sort of like to try and make friends when they get here and often tell other kids everything about why they're here. One boy told the whole group something very personal about the abuse he and his sister had suffered at home and, like, the kids just thought 'this is great ammunition' and they just used it against him constantly. (Senior Residential Social Worker, female)

> Everyone's always very interested in each others' backgrounds and why they're in care. If a new resident doesn't say anything about themselves the others can get very suspicious about what they've done to be put here. (Residential Social Worker, female)

Finally, 12 staff felt very strongly that the behaviour of the children and young people they worked alongside was no different to that of children in any other settings and that their backgrounds had no impact on their current behaviour.

> I don't think there is any difference in relation to the behaviour of young people in here to other situations. It's the same sort of behaviour as you get in schools, playgrounds and on the street, I don't think this is any more or less violent than anywhere else. (Residential Social Worker, male)

> A lot goes on, a lot of kids get slapped, but a lot get slapped outside. It's part of growing-up if you're from a rough part of town, it's just how you deal with things. I reckon what we deal with is just normal rough and tumble. (Residential Social Worker, male)

Summary points

- In most homes staff accepted the 'pecking order' as a normal aspect of peer relations, generally and in the resident context. Staff were able to identify young people's position in the hierarchy, and say who was next in line for 'top dog' position. Distinctions were made between good and bad top dogs, according to the methods used for maintaining dominance and the purposes for which power was used. Staff generally viewed intelligence as more important than physical size or strength for young people maintaining top dog position.
- New admissions to the home were seen as causing upheavals in the hierarchy, particularly when a 'top dog' left the group. Homes which had

frequent short-term admissions and a shifting population could have continuous pressures of this kind, while unplanned emergency admissions to homes which otherwise had long-term stable groups of young people could also cause problems.
- Boys' use of physical violence was often viewed by staff as a normal (although sometimes uncontrolled) aspect of their emerging masculinity. In contrast, girls were perceived as using more covert methods of harm, generally involving attacks on other young people's property, or verbal attacks.
- In comparison, we found that in another context – racist behaviour – staff did routinely challenge wider relations of inequality.
- Age and maturity were viewed by staff as influencing the nature of conflict and conflict resolution between young people. Although most homes had policies of not mixing younger and older residents in the same home or group, in practice this often happened due to pressure on placements.
- Children's backgrounds were largely absent from staff's explanations for peer violence, even though many young people living in residential care will have experienced, chaotic, and at worst abusive, familial situations.

5
Shared and Different Understandings of Violence

> They might be bullying her 'cause she might be different... she might dress different, talk different or look different... everyone's different, but they might think she's too different... They're bullies... She'll feel really scared and not want to be there, she'll probably run away.
> (Gail, aged 14)

> So what if she's been bullied? She's probably a really irritating stupid little slag and they're pissed off with her... it's her fault, isn't it?
> (Ray, aged 15)

> She's more or less enticing him, thought he had an open invitation, showing his frustration by grabbing her breast – her clothes give the wrong impression, invite attention, really, I feel he's been set up due to the mixed messages she's sending out.
> (Senior Residential Social Worker, female)

The use of vignettes

Chapter 1 outlined the design and use of vignettes to explore young people's and staff's understanding of violence. In qualitative research vignettes have been increasingly employed to explore cultural norms derived from participants' attitudes to, and beliefs about, a specific situation. They also highlight ethical frameworks and moral codes. The most obvious criticism of this technique concerns the difference between belief and action; what people believe they would do in a given situation is not necessarily how they would actually behave. However, some writers have argued for a different theoretical perspective (see Douglas 1971, Finch 1989). Finch, for example, suggests that it is not always necessary to be concerned about the inconsistency between beliefs and actions. Thus it is perfectly possible for an individual to agree to a particular social norm, but at the same time believe that it is not relevant in particular circumstances, or that it does not apply for particular reasons. Therefore, it is not the action that the individual says s/he would take in a particular situation that is of interest, for this will always be situationally specific, but the process of meanings and interpretations used in reaching the outcome that is of central concern. Vignettes provide a very useful tool to illuminate and tap into these complex processes.

Ultimately, no research tool can completely capture the complexity of social life; however, by adopting a multi-method approach, researchers can build on the individual strengths of different techniques. We used semi-structured interviews to investigate with young people their personal experiences of violence, and vignettes to explore their more abstract reasoning and belief systems.

Four vignettes were used. Each was based on young people's real experiences and represented a range of physical, sexual and verbal attacks of differing severity and context. Each vignette had a series of stages, shown to interviewees one at a time, and each had probes which were used to follow up issues covered in the vignette. The vignettes were:

Stockwell Road: represented male to male physical violence of increasing severity, in retaliation to psychological provocation. Staff response was to ignore the fight.

Lawson Drive: represented male to female sexual violence (touching sexual body part) including previous non-disclosure. Staff response was to talk individually to both parties.

Forest Way: represented female to female unprovoked verbal attacks and group isolation leading to extortion and threats of violence involving a third party. Staff response was to talk individually to all parties and warn the instigators of the possible consequences if they continued.

Swallow Road: represented male to male intimidation, with a possible sexual element and non-disclosure to staff. Staff response was to reassure the victim.

All of the staff responses in the vignettes deliberately depicted less interventionist aspects of professional practice. This was to reduce the possibility that staff might agree with a higher level of intervention than they really felt was appropriate, for fear of appearing to minimise the issues involved.

Not all vignettes were systematically used with all participants (see Table 5.1). This was mainly due to the flexible format the research interaction took, which enabled participants a greater degree of freedom to determine for themselves the balance between revealing their personal experiences of violence, and restricting discussions to the vignette scenarios. In addition, shortage of time often meant that not all the vignettes could be used. This was especially true for staff.

Table 5.1 Vignette sample

Vignette	Total sample	Young people			Staff			RSW	Senior	Manager
		Total	M	F	Total	M	F			
Stockwell Road	60	43	28	15	17	10	7	14	2	1
Lawson Drive	53	32	14	18	21	7	14	9	8	4
Forest Way	52	37	16	21	15	8	7	8	4	3
Swallow Road	40	24	16	8	16	9	7	7	5	4

Physical attack – vignette A

1st stage

Nicky often messes around 'winding' other residents up, playing jokes on them so that he gets on their nerves. Nicky has been doing this all day to Sammy, tripping him up and embarrassing him in front of the other kids. Later that day Sammy finds out that Nicky has stolen his fags and taken them out with him. Sammy waits for Nicky to get back that night. Outside the home Sammy demands his fags back but Nicky says he's smoked them all and starts to laugh. Sammy pushes Nicky backwards a couple of times and Nicky falls down and hits his head.

2nd stage

When Nicky is on the ground Sammy kicks and punches him on the arm. Nicky tells Sammy to stop because he's hurting him, after a couple more kicks Sammy stops.

3rd stage

James, a member of staff, comes out just at the end and sees the boys fighting but doesn't do anything to break it up. Afterwards when Sammy asks James why he didn't stop the fight James says that if Nicky winds other young people up he will have to face the consequences.

1st stage responses

Young people (43)

- 24 young people thought that the 'pushing' response in story was a justified use of violence, and 19 thought it was unjustified.

Staff (17)
- 9 staff thought that the 'pushing' was unacceptable, 5 thought it was acceptable and 3 described it as 'typical'.

Rejection of retaliatory physical violence

Just under half of young people stated that the use of physical violence in the first part of the vignette was unjustified. All young people in this group viewed the physical violence as being very much worse than the emotional harm caused by the non-contact provocation. Consequently these young people rejected the use of physical violence when the provocation was psychological. Many stated that they felt the use of physical violence was rarely justified even if the provocation was physical or verbal in nature. They were much more likely to say that the correct course of action was to inform staff and allow them to deal with the situation. Furthermore, many felt that the use of physical retaliation required a greater degree of punishment (sanctions) from adults than did the psychological provocation, highlighting young people's belief in the importance of social rules governing the use of physical violence.

> He had no right to have pushed him. He should have gone to the staff to sort it out, not take it into his own hands... shouldn't go around hitting even if they are trying to wind you up, 'cause that's just as bad... He should get done by the police for assault. (Goran, aged 14)
>
> He's acting in a mean way by pushing him, should have asked him nicely for his fags back, but he's been nasty to him so he'll get worst trouble now ... shouldn't use fighting to get your own back 'cause that's worst. (Sarah, aged 13)

Many of these young people came from children's homes at the lower end of the continuum of violence described earlier. In these particular homes, the social rules concerning non-violence were deeply ingrained, not only in adult working practices but also in the young people's own cultures. However, five came from homes located towards the higher end of the violence continuum, although in these settings they represented the minority view.

In common with the above young people, the staff who discussed this vignette usually condemned both the provocation and the use of retaliatory physical violence. Over half stated that physical violence was an unacceptable response to any form of provocation. In contrast, eight staff felt that the 'pushing' was acceptable, or at least a normal response, given the provocation. All these staff stated that this was a common situation in their homes, where many young people viewed the use of violence as an acceptable response to being provoked either verbally or physically.

It's a normal reaction. It's natural if someone's been on your case all day to lash out and put them in their place... It's not a legitimate response to everything, but in this case a push is about OK. (Residential Social Worker, male)

Retaliatory violence as social justice

Young people who viewed the use of physical retaliation as justified almost exclusively came from children's homes which were towards the higher end of the violence continuum. Only a minority came from homes where violence was minimal, and in these settings theirs' was the isolated standpoint. No gender distinction was found with proportionally half of all young women and young men agreeing with the retaliatory act.

> He deserves to get pushed. I'd do the same 'cause he's got to learn he can't just nick stuff off other kids, so I think that's about right. (Goran, aged 13)
>
> I'd have done just the same, only I'd have really smacked him 'cause he thinks he's hard, winding others up. So I'd show him, he deserves it. (Colin, aged 15)
>
> Good, he stuck up for himself, like here I can't stand to be wound up, and that'll teach him... make him learn. So it's fair enough, he deserved all he got. (Jesse, aged 16)

These young people placed greater emphasis on the immorality of the psychological provocation than on the use of retaliatory physical violence (Astor 1994). For these young people 'fighting back' was perceived as a form of social justice. Most of these young people not only felt the response was justified, they also stated that they would have reacted in the same way given the provocation. However for many this was not simply abstract reasoning. Numerous concrete examples were provided detailing their experiences of both giving and (to a lesser extent) receiving such retaliations. In these discussions many emphasised the necessity of publicly replying in such a manner not simply to stop the provocation but also (and possible more importantly) to indicate openly to others that they were not a person to 'mess with'. Interestingly, young men's responses on the use of such violence was often celebratory, enshrined in perceptions of 'masculinities' (Connell 1987, Newburn and Stanko 1994). Young women more often depicted the use of violence more pragmatically, generally in terms of survival. Nevertheless, both groups emphasised the importance of gaining respect through their willingness to employ violence in conflict situations (Batchelor *et al.* 2001) and thus maintain a 'credible threat of violence in their day to day lives' to borrow a phase from Daly and Wilson (1988: 128).

I wouldn't have pushed him just for doing that 'cause he'll get in more trouble with staff...but you've got to show you can stand up for yourself else you'll just get picked on all the time...If others know you'll smack 'em they'll respect you more and you'll get left alone. (Ross, aged 14)

He showed him that he won't get pushed around by bullies, so now everyone will know that. (Megan, aged 15)

For these young people the use of physical retaliation produced no moral discord. In many of these young people's assessments, physical retribution was the expected and necessary outcome. Consequently, the use of physical retaliation to either verbal or physical provocation was viewed as an established rule in these young people's social worlds. This perceived consensus surrounding the consequences of provocation reinforced their claims of social justice: 'he knew what he'd get so it's his fault'. Compared to the young people who condemned the use of violence, those who viewed it as a legitimate reaction were less likely to recognise social rules against the use of physical violence and more likely to place greater weight on their own sense of reciprocal justice (Astor 1994).

> **2nd stage – vignette A**
> When Nicky is on the ground Sammy kicks and punches him on the arm. Nicky tells Sammy to stop because he's hurting him, after a couple more kicks Sammy stops.

2nd stage responses

Young people (43)
- Only 18 young people thought Nicky should have told staff.
- 24 thought that Nicky deserved being 'kicked on the ground', although 11 of these thought it should not have continued as much as it did.
- 19 thought the kicking was wrong.

Staff (17)
- 16 staff felt that the kicking was unacceptable.

Breaking the rules of justified retaliation

Once the violence had progressed to the boy being kicked whilst on the ground, some young people's assessments of the situation changed. Although all the young people who had previously viewed the initial physical retaliation as acceptable still held this premise, just under half (11) now accompanied this view with some reservations. In respect to gender breakdown, just under one half of all young women and one-third of young men still unconditionally agreed with the physical violence, whilst two young women, but one-third of the young men, now only partially agreed.

For these 11 young people, the severity of the physical violence at this stage was deemed to be too severe for the provocation; generally described as 'OTT' (over the top). In their opinion the retaliator had now become the aggressor and, consequently, in their assessments social justice had ceased to be the presiding force behind the physical violence.

In addition, for some young people the legitimacy of the retaliation was also closely linked to perceptions of 'fair fight' protocols. A central component of this dictated that once your 'opponent' was unable to defend him- or herself the fight must cease, at least until they were able to continue. Kicking someone who was down (meaning on the ground) breached these rules. As one young person explained:

> That's a bit tight, he shouldn't have kicked him when down – deserves a bit but only a fight proper. (Bronwyn, aged 14)
>
> My Dad always taught me that you should fight proper and not kick someone when they're on the ground, only when they're standing. He should have let him get up and then smacked him again. (Adrian, aged 17)

Consequently, many young people stated that the consensus surrounding the use of retaliatory physical violence was regulated by two constructs: the retaliation had to be viewed as commensurate to the provocation and fair fight protocols must prevail. However, 13 young people stated that the level of physical retaliation was justified. In many of these young people's evaluations, the violence depicted was viewed as a normal and routine aspect of everyday social interaction. Previous research suggests that children who experience familial violence may come to view violence as an acceptable behaviour (Straus and Hotaling 1980, Olweus 1987). Astor (1994) further argues that violent children may place greater focus on the psychological provocation due to their childhood experience of violence. Although we did not ask young people directly about their previous experience of violence outside the residential context, in their discussions with us many of the above young people revealed childhoods and social worlds marked by physical violence. In contrast, the young people who rejected the use of violence provided far fewer examples and were often shocked at the use of physical violence in the story. (However, due to the non-systematic nature of data collection this suggestion must be tentative.)

> **3rd stage – vignette A**
>
> James, a member of staff, comes out just at the end and sees the boys fighting but doesn't do anything to break it up. Afterwards when Sammy asks James why he didn't stop the fight, James says that if Nicky winds other young people up he will have to face the consequences.

3rd stage responses

Young people (43)

- Of the young people 19 disagreed, 7 agreed and 17 had mixed views over the staff reaction of ignoring the fight.

Staff (17)

- No staff agreed with James's behaviour and none thought it represented normal practice in homes.
- Only 1 member of staff said that workers may sometimes turn a blind eye to physical violence.
- 10 staff questioned how it had been allowed to get this far, 8 thought that James should face disciplinary proceedings.

Unsurprisingly, those young people who rejected the use of physical violence also unanimously rejected the story of James's non-intervention in the fight. In fact, one-third felt that the staff member should face disciplinary proceedings and should no longer be allowed to work with young people.

> No, he'd lose his job here 'cause we'd make a complaint if that happened here and staff didn't intervene... He shouldn't work with kids if he's not going to protect them, no matter what they've done to deserve it... don't matter, he's wrong and should be kicked out. (Lisa, aged 16)
>
> Wrong, really wrong, he might have had a knife and killed the other kid, he should be fired from his job and shouldn't be allowed to get another job forever. (Rachel, aged 12)

This view was overwhelmingly reflected in staff evaluations. Many focused on the general lack of supervision in the children's home in the story, and wanted to know how the situation had been allowed to get this far. All condemned the worker's response and most expressed shock that the worker had not acted to protect the young people concerned. Half stated that the staff member should face formal disciplinary procedures.

> Where are the staff? I can't imagine a home being run like that. I would be alarmed to say the least if any of my staff acted in that manner, and to be honest I doubt whether I'd want them on my team, and I expect the rest of my staff would feel exactly the same. (Manager, female)
>
> It's unbelievable, I know it's true 'cause you said at the beginning (that the vignettes were all based on actual incidents) but to do that is so unprofessional, it's just wrong. Forget about it being in residential you'd stop kids wherever from fighting wouldn't you? I'm really shocked that nobody noticed what was happening anyway, and then to allow that to happen, I just pray that that staff member got disciplined for that. (Residential Social Worker, male)

Staff as protectors and guardians of young people's welfare

It may be anticipated that those young people who viewed reciprocal violence as legitimate would also view the worker's non-intervention as acceptable, especially as the worker's explanation in the scenario reflected young people's own cultural frameworks governing social justice. In practice, young people's rationalisations were more complex. Five young people who stated that they believed the violence was justified felt that staff should nevertheless automatically intervene to stop all physical violence, irrespective of the reasons it occurred or the severity of the incident.

For a greater number (12), the ambiguity present in their answers demonstrated young people's moral dilemma of viewing the physical retaliation as legitimate, but concurrently believing that this legitimacy should not determine professional intervention. Most of these young people initially stated they agreed with the lack of intervention on social justice grounds, but on further consideration of the possible consequences of setting such a precedent, changed their opinion.

> Yeah, I reckon that's right what that staff did, 'cause he shouldn't have nicked his fags and he deserves it... but no because, like, normal staff wouldn't just leave him to get beaten up like that, 'cause it's their job to stop it. So no, thinking about it, I think staff should stop it even if he deserved it. (Cole, aged 13)

Central to all these evaluations was young people's concern with personal protection and safety. The role of staff was overwhelmingly perceived as being guardians of young people's welfare irrespective of the context in which the violence occurred. Staff were, therefore, positioned as being outside young people's own cultural frameworks concerning social justice. Ultimately, these young people were asserting that, in this particular context, their own value systems should not influence professional practice. Nevertheless, many did feel that the sanctions imposed on young people who use physical violence in retaliation should be more lenient due to the provocation involved.

I sort of agree and then again don't agree. It's hard 'cause I think he should have hit him, but I think staff should take that into consideration when sanctioning them both and not give a real heavy sanction 'cause he hit him. (Jesse, aged 16)

Only seven young people agreed with James's behaviour in the vignette. These were nearly all males (6) and all self-proclaimed users of retaliatory violence on a regular basis.

Heavy ... yeah, I want that staff to come work here. (Ramon, aged 12)

Yeah, I think that's a fair answer, the staff's got a point 'cause they should let us sort it out, and he should face the consequences so I think he's right to leave it. (Phil, aged 12)

Reassuringly, nearly all young people and staff stated that James's behaviour would not happen in their children's homes, although as we will see later, pockets of staff inconsistency in responding to violence were reported by some.

Psychological attack – vignette B

1st stage

Sarah was sometimes called names by two other girls, Jane and Julie, who lived in the same children's home. Jane and Julie would tease her about how she looked and what she dressed like. Then they started calling Sarah names like slag, bitch and lezzie. Although the other young people in the home didn't join in with Jane and Julie, some did stop being friendly to her and started ignoring her when they were having meals and watching TV and so on. (At this stage a question was asked about whether and how the situation would differ if the verbal abuse was based on racism rather than sexuality.)

2nd stage

After this had gone on for a couple of weeks Jane and Julie started to 'push' Sarah around and threatening to 'get' Sarah if she didn't give them cigarettes and lend them her tapes and so on, which she never got back. They also told Sarah that one of their boyfriends, who had a reputation for being violent, would get her if she ever told.

3rd stage

Sarah was very upset about what was happening but didn't feel she could talk to anybody about it as she didn't have any friends in the

(continued)

home and felt too scared to tell staff. Eventually Sarah ran away to her old foster parents who contacted the children's home to try and work out what should be done. After the staff in the home had spoken to Julie and Jane about threatening other young people and the possible consequences of them acting in this way, Sarah agreed to return. Sarah's foster parents contacted her after a couple of weeks to see how she was and if the threatening behaviour had stopped. Sarah said that Julie and Jane had called her a wimp for telling tales and still called her names but they had not threatened her since she got back, mostly they ignored her as did some of the other young people, although a few have started to talk to her more now.

1st stage responses

Young people (37)

- The majority of young people (32) stated that verbal attack based on sexuality was a common occurrence amongst young women.
- Most young people (26) viewed the young women's behaviour in the first part of the story as constituting bullying.
- Fourteen young people thought the bullying was due to jealousy and eight felt it was because she was different in some way.
- Sixteen thought she would feel upset.
- More than half (20) of the young people thought racist verbal attacks were worse than those based on gender or sexuality.

Staff (15)

- 8 thought the initial situation was serious, 5 a cause for concern and 2 staff said it was nothing to worry about.
- 10 staff thought Sarah would be very upset and 8 thought she would probably withdraw into herself, 4 felt she may become violent or commit self-harm.
- 7 staff felt the 'bullying' was either due to jealousy or perceptions of difference, 3 felt it was solely due to the bullies' own problems and 2 due to the victims' sexualised behaviour. 3 staff gave a wide range of possible reasons incorporating several of the above.
- Staff response to the initial stage included talking individually to all the parties concerned (6), individual and group meeting with the wider resident group (5), just group meetings (2) and observation alone (2).
- The majority of staff (12) stated they would have noticed that something was wrong before it had reached this first stage.
- Almost half of the staff (7) felt that verbal attacks based on racism were worse than other forms of verbal attacks, 5 stated it made no difference.

The majority of young people stated that verbal attacks based on sexualised insults were a common aspect of young people's, and especially young women's, social worlds, a similar conclusion to that reached in other studies of adolescent girls (Lees 1986, 1993, Sharpe 1994, Holland *et al.* 1998). In their study of girls and violence in Scotland, Batchelor *et al.* (2001) stated that verbal attack was the most common form of violence against girls, with girls 'attributing a superior and in-depth knowledge of the intricacies of "slagging" to other girls' (p. 129). Only the word 'lezzie' (lesbian) was singled out for further comment in response to our vignette. This was predominantly due to the perceived unacceptability of challenging a teenage girl's heterosexual status. In direct contrast, a very small number of young people (4), stated that the use of this term was offensive as it was based on homophobia. However, when we moved on to discuss the wider context in which the verbal attacks occurred, young people's evaluations of the situation altered considerably.

Abuse of power – bullying

Most (26) of the young people defined the 2 girls' behaviour at the beginning of the vignette as constituting bullying. They felt that the recipient had not provoked the incidents in any way and that she was being unfairly victimised. Due to the unprovoked and repeated nature of the verbal attacks, these young people unanimously condemned the behaviour. Most stated that they believed bullying could severely affect a young person's well-being, leading to feelings of misery, despair and loneliness. Additionally, in many of the young people's assessments, the unfairness of the situation was further compounded by the fact that the victim had been targeted by more than one assailant.

> She's probably just easy to pick on, she's probably not done nothing wrong to those girls. She might be a bit quiet or not very strong...but they're just being horrible and they're cowards anyway, 'cause it takes two of them to bully her. (Patrick, aged 16)

> That's unfair and not very nice. They're insecure and it makes them feel better to pick on Sarah, I feel sorry for Sarah 'cause she'll feel scared and lonely and having two to bully you must be really bad I think. (Melissa, aged 16)

Only seven young people (four young women and three young men) felt that the responsibility for the behaviour lay with the 'victim'. In nearly all these accounts the girl in the story was viewed as having done something which warranted such a reaction.

> She might stink...she might have done something to them, like robbed one of their fellas or something...or say, like, she's going out with them

on activities and she's looking a mess...stink or look dead scruffy...or she's probably a slag with all the boys so she probably deserves it. (Mia, aged 15)

She's done something to them...probably wound them up on purpose in some way, so it's her fault...She deserves being called names if that's what she's done. (Ray, aged 15)

These seven young people supported the instigator's actions in terms of social justice, although in this instant without any supportive evidence from the vignette. Often, these young people both condemned the victim for not 'sticking up for herself' and used this non-retaliation as evidence of her guilt. This perceived weakness further strengthened their presumptions surrounding the girl's 'deserving victim' status (Richardson and May 1999, Stanko 2000). Only one young man both defined the behaviour as constituting bullying and also found it to be acceptable, stating it was an inevitable aspect of peer relations. All of the above seven young people were identified by both fellow residents and staff as routinely using intimidation and bullying in their peer interactions.

However, other young people (6) were also identified by staff as being responsible for bullying who, nevertheless, provided us with very plausible answers to the vignette about why bullying was wrong (often referring to the misuse of power involved) and the harm it caused. These young people rarely identified their involvement in bullying to us. Instead they explained their 'bullying' actions as linked to social justice. But upon examination their accounts often contained discrepancies, which suggests that staff's perceptions of their actions were justified. This reinforces O'Neill's (2001) premise that to understand fully the dynamic processes present within institutional settings, it is important to explore both staff's and residents' accounts of everyday life.

'Ganging up' against individuals

Most young people and staff agreed that the group's main reason for isolating the victim was due to them being scared of the instigators and fearing that, if they did not comply, they might be picked on next. Many young people, however, felt that the group's response was unacceptable and would make the victim feel very much worse. Proportionally more young women than young men felt this would be especially hurtful, particularly as she had previously been friendly with the young people. This reflects other research findings which show that young males and females use friendship networks differently. Girls' relationships are often characterised as highly intimate and supportive (Berndt 1986, Belle 1989, Rutter et al. 1998), whilst boys are often prevented from showing their feelings with other boys due to the need to sustain a 'cool' image (Frydenberg 1997). The area of peer friendships is a neglected area in previous studies of the care system. It is often presumed that, due to the rapid turnover in children's homes, it may be difficult for young people to build very close and trusting relationships with other peers (Whitaker et al. 1998). However, Sinclair and Gibbs (1998) found that just over half of young people said that they had a particular friend or group of friends with whom they went around at the residential home, although one-third of them were prepared to say that they did not. In our discussions with young people many (although mostly young women) stated they had developed relatively close friendships with other (generally female) residents.

When asked how they would respond to this situation, the most frequently stated reply from young people was that they would inform staff (15), although some argued that this was due to the girl having no peer support in the home. Eleven claimed they would retaliate with some form of physical violence. Other responses included ignoring the bullies (4), do nothing (3), asked to be moved (2) and did not know (2). More young men provided answers where they either dealt directly with the situation themselves or ignored the behaviour, whereas young women were slightly more likely to seek external advice and assistance. This mirrors an earlier finding from Fuller et al. (2000), who explored the complexities of adolescent worries and problems, including those of young people living in residential care. They found that, overall, young people in residential care preferred trying to solve problems themselves compared to those living with their families, and that this coping strategy was particularly marked for young men.

When asked how they felt staff would react to such a situation, most young people were unsure, although two-thirds stated that staff did not allow bullying in their placements. Reflecting many young people's evaluations, eight members of staff felt that the situation at this stage was serious and that the 'victim' would be experiencing considerable distress, which needed to be acted upon immediately. However, five staff felt that, although the situation was of concern, they did not feel it was particularly serious and two stated it was not significant. Concerning positive intervention, six suggested that they would talk to all those concerned individually to try to determine what was happening and why. Five said they would talk both individually to those directly involved and with the resident group as a whole. Two staff felt they would just talk with the group generally about bullying and a further two stated that they would only observe at this stage. None of the staff believed that any external managers or social work staff would need to be informed at this stage.

2nd stage – vignette B

After this had gone on for a couple of weeks Jane and Julie started to 'push' Sarah around and threatening to 'get' Sarah if she didn't give them cigarettes and lend them her tapes and so on, which she never got back. They also told Sarah that one of their boyfriends, who had a reputation for being violent, would get her if she ever told.

2nd stage responses
Young people (37)
- The most frequently volunteered response was to inform staff (13) followed by retaliating with physical violence (9).

Staff (15)
- Upon the behaviour progressing to include extortion and threats, 8 staff said that they would now initiate child protection procedures including the police and 7 stated they would continue to deal with the situation within the home.

Third party involvement in violence

Once the behaviour progressed to include extortion and threats of violence from a third party, both young people's and staff's evaluations of the situation changed very much. Most young people felt that the use of threats by a third party was unacceptable, many felt the girl would now be terrified and feel very isolated.

> Threatening a girl with your boyfriend, that's not fucking right, is it?... No man who was a man would hit a girl... They (Jane and Julie) are just cowards if they can't do it themselves... She'd be shit scared I'd guess. (Bronwyn, aged 14)

Although young people's condemnation of the situation was thus compounded by the escalation in behaviour, young people seemed more unsure about how they would respond, with fewer stating they would now inform staff due to the possibility of reprisals. Five young men stated that they would retaliate with increased levels of physical violence or get 'friends in to deal with them'. Other answers included telling external family or friends (3), or running away (4). Many (15) either did not know what they would do or did not wish to comment.

3rd stage – Forest Way

Sarah was very upset about what was happening but didn't feel she could talk to anybody about it as she didn't have any friends in the home and felt too scared to tell staff. Eventually Sarah ran away to her old foster parents who contacted the children's home to try and work out what should be done. After the staff in the home had spoken to Julie and Jane about threatening other young people and the possible consequences of them acting in this way, Sarah agreed to return. Sarah's
(continued)

> foster parents contacted her after a couple of weeks to see how she was and if the threatening behaviour had stopped. Sarah said that Julie and Jane had called her a wimp for telling tales and still called her names but they had not threatened her since she got back, mostly they ignored her as did some of the other young people, although a few have started to talk to her more now.

3rd stage responses
Young people (37)
- Many young people did not know how staff should or would respond, 12 young people agreed with the vignette response and 8 stated it was inadequate.
- The majority of young people (25) stated staff did not allow bullying to occur in their children's homes.

Staff (15)
- Overall, 12 staff thought the vignette response was inadequate, only 2 felt it was sufficient.

Reflecting their uncertainty about how they would respond, some young people (16) were also unsure about how they felt staff should intervene in such a situation. Twelve young people agreed with staff's response in the vignette but nine felt it was inadequate. These young people generally felt it would be futile in stopping the behaviour and stated that more interventionist practices were needed, up to and including the permanent removal of one or both of the bullies from the placement.

Staff were more concrete in their assessments of the inadequacy of the response depicted in the vignette. Almost all of these staff (12) felt that the worker's response was completely inadequate, two felt it was 'about right' and one worker did not know. When we asked how they would have responded to such a situation, very wide discrepancies concerning individual practice emerged. Half of the staff (8) (including three managers and a senior worker) stated that the behaviour now constituted a child protection issue and that an assessment would need to be undertaken. In addition, five of these staff felt that the police would need to be informed that threats of violence involving a third party had been made. In contrast, the remaining seven staff (including three seniors) felt that it would be sufficient to deal with the problem through individual meetings with all the parties involved alongside increased monitoring. In their opinion, no external managers nor social work staff would need to be informed at this stage. This disparity in practice may go some way to explain why young people found it so difficult to determine how they felt staff would respond in their own homes.

Reasons for bullying

The most frequently stated reason provided by young people for the victimisation was that the 'bullies' were jealous of the girl in some way. Numerous motives were volunteered, including 'she may be prettier', 'be more intelligent', 'get on better with staff', 'have nicer clothes' and 'have a better boyfriend'. Eight young people felt it may be because she was different from the other young people, possible suggestions included the way she dressed, spoke or behaved. Only two young people felt that the 'bullies' would not need a reason. None of the young people felt that the verbal attacks were based on any direct personal knowledge of the victim. Instead, most participants viewed such insults as common forms of generic verbal attacks used against females (Lees 1986, Holland et al. 1998, Batchelor et al. 2001). All young people felt that if personal knowledge had been used this would be more hurtful (Batchelor et al. 2001).

Most of these young people viewed the perpetrators of this 'illegitimate' violence as either 'bad' or 'evil', reflecting a common (although mistaken [Stanko 2000]) view that violence can be attributed solely to individual motivation. In contrast, some staff were slightly more likely to place the young people's actions in wider social relationships and contexts. Senior staff generally placed greater emphasis on the young persons' background in their explanations, especially possible experiences of past abuse and the associated feelings of powerlessness. However, junior staff more often relied on individual motivations, reflecting young people's own conceptualisations.

> They want power over others, they don't need a reason. It's probably a pattern of behaviour they've both learnt previously and it's hard for them to break. I would want to find out why they felt they needed to behave like this, what's happened to them in their pasts to make them feel the need to control and intimidate others. (Manager, female)
>
> They're using Sarah 'cause they've got something they're trying to cover up... It's a diversion from something that's maybe hurting them and they're directing that hurt on to Sarah. You'd need to look at what happened in their backgrounds to make them feel this way. (Residential Social Worker, female)
>
> She might be prettier, got better clothes, or more liked, or they (Jane and Julie) might just be nasty, some kids are just like that. (Residential Social Worker, male)
>
> They (Jane and Julie) are just being childish, or not very nice. (Residential Social Worker, male)

Perceptions of racist attacks

In the above vignette, we explored with young people and staff if they viewed racist name calling any differently to insults about sexuality. Overall,

19 young people stated that they felt that racist abuse would have a greater impact on a person than sexualised verbal attacks. Five felt the effect would be similar, although this was dependent on the specific context in which the attacks took place, and three stated that it would be different irrespective of the context. Similarly most staff stated that racist attack was always very much more hurtful than sexualised verbal insult, and five felt it was no different.

Interviewer:	If they were to use racist names would that make any difference?
Young Man:	No, but if it was racist she needs to get them done by the police.
Interviewer:	So if someone here said something racist to another young person would that be seen as needing to get the police involved?
Young Man:	I would... 'cause it's not the same like those other names they're just what you expect but racist stuff that's different it's... like it's just 'cause you're black so I suppose I do think it's worse more upsetting than being just called a slag.

(Dan, aged 15)

Racism gets staff off their arses to do a lot more 'cause it's different – their colour – dead upsetting, especially if they had a normal life and not used to insults. (Fiona, aged 13)

Interviewer:	And would it make any difference to Sarah if the names they were using were racist?
Gail:	Yeah they'd be dead upsetting to her.
Interviewer:	More so than sexual comments?
Gail:	Well it depends what's gone on in her background, 'cause if she's like not had a normal life (meaning in this instance previous experiences of sexual abuse) and that then, it depends what sort of environment she's come from.

(Gail, aged 14)

As the last extract indicates, when other mediating factors were introduced by the participant, such as issues of past abuse, the impact of sexual insults is then viewed as being as equally serious as racist ones. In addition, although one of the above participants states that racism is 'not nice' she also later admitted to sometimes using racist insults. Previous research has shown that it is not unusual for children and young people to hold contradictory views on racism: to have anti-racist beliefs while still using racist insults in particular circumstances (Troyna and Hatcher 1992, Barter 1999). Again, this brings into focus the conceptual distinction between belief and action, highlighting the need to explore in what contexts and under what circumstances different interpretations and meanings are applied. Furthermore, young people's own rationalisation of why racism is unacceptable do not necessarily fit with adult or professional interpretations.

Interviewer:	If they were calling Sarah racist names would that make any difference?
Martine:	Oh yeah ... it's ... it's 'cause really, if you think about it, say, if you have a black person and a white person. That black person is the same as a white person 'cause under their six layers of black skin they're white ... I've seen it on TV ... It's nothing different with 'em they've still got feelings ... and everything they're just the same as us but on top they're a different colour. I can't stand it (racism) me.

(Martine, aged 13)

Male on female sexual attack – vignette C

1st stage

Helen comes downstairs to have breakfast in her 'nightie'. Mary, a member of staff says 'Helen, I don't think that's a very suitable thing to wear at the breakfast table, can you get your dressing gown.' Helen replies that 'There's nothing wrong with it, I'm not going upstairs for that, I'll go when I've had some breakfast.' Mary lets Helen stay downstairs to have her breakfast. At the table Helen gets a lot of attention from the boys, which she doesn't seem to mind, and is particularly 'flirty' with John, another resident. Helen leaves the table and so does John. They both go to the hallway where John pretends to bump into her and starts messing around play fighting. Helen then goes upstairs to her room. A minute or so later John follows Helen upstairs and waits outside her room and then enters without knocking. Helen is getting changed and tells John to get out. John asks why and Helen pushes past John to get out of the room. John grabs Helen's breast as she goes past him.

2nd stage

Helen goes to staff and says that John went into her room without permission and that he touched her. She says that he has done this before and that she does not like it.

3rd stage

Staff told John not to go into people's rooms and spoke to Helen about dressing and acting in such an inappropriate way and warned her of the trouble she might get herself in.

1st stage responses

Young people (32)

- 19 young people thought the boy's actions constituted sexual harassment (young people's own terminology) and 12 thought it inappropriate behaviour.
- 13 young people thought the girl was responsible for the violence due to 'leading him on'.
- Only 3 young women thought she should be able to wear what she wants.

Staff (21)

- 8 thought his behaviour constituted sexual harassment and 8 thought it sexually inappropriate, 4 thought it normal adolescent behaviour.
- 7 thought the girl held no responsibility for the boy's actions, 9 placed considerable weight upon the girl's actions and 5 felt the girl was to blame.
- Most stated the girl should be made to change into something more discreet.
- In relation to the first stage, 8 staff stated they would talk individually to both parties and 12 stated they would initiate a child protection investigation.

Female responsibility for male sexual violence

A central component in both young people's and staff's evaluations of the above situation concerned the degree of responsibility attributed to the girl's actions in explaining the boy's sexual violence. Overall about half (27) of all participants viewed the girl's flirtatious behaviour as being directly responsible for the boy's subsequent actions. Proportionally more young women (10) than young men (3), and proportionally more staff than young people (67%/40%), felt that the girl held substantial responsibility for the boy's actions. In relation to seniority, proportionally more junior staff held this view than did senior staff or managers. Although most of these participants felt the boy's behaviour was not acceptable, neither did they feel that he was necessarily completely responsible for his actions, due to the provocative nature of the girl's behaviour; generally referred to as being 'led on'.

> She led him on by play fighting, so it's partly her fault 'cause of dressing like that... she was being like provocative and he got the wrong idea so you can't blame him. (Fiona, aged 13)
>
> The boy's an idiot, but she shouldn't be putting herself about like that. She shouldn't give that impression and not expect to get that sort of

attention back. He's not completely justified, but she's equally to blame, they both played a part. (Melissa, aged 16)

Just normal boys' behaviour. If a girl acts like she does, she's a tease and she's lucky he didn't do more. (Grant, aged 11)

She did seem annoyed but, basically, she was at fault for coming down in her night-dress and acting in that way, because she's drawing attention to herself and leading him on...It's not fair to blame only him, 'cause he'd think he was in with her and he'd be confused about such mixed messages. (Residential Social Worker, female)

The boy's been led on to think the girl is interested, sexually, in him, so it's understandable he felt he had the go ahead...the girl's putting herself in a vulnerable position, but the boy is acting inappropriately even though she has to take the blame. (Residential Social Worker, female)

The quotes illustrate how the concept of provocation is highly gendered, as women and girls are far more likely than men and boys to be blamed for making themselves vulnerable to violence (Richardson and May 1999). Consequently, as Kelly (1988) stresses, there is a greater expectation on women to protect themselves from violent attack through modification of *their* behaviour in social contexts. This 'common sense' gendered understanding of perpetrator actions, whereby the victim's behaviour may be perceived as a mitigating factor in 'justifying' various forms of male violence towards women, especially when the violence is sexual, has been widely documented (Dobash and Dobash 1992, Godenzi 1994). Epstein and Johnson (1998) state that it is well established in feminist research that women both represent and are responsible for sexuality in the larger society but, paradoxically, have no control over male sexuality. The fact that in our study three times more young women than young men emphasised the girl's culpability indicates the degree to which young women internalise these messages.

However a further 19 young people and 7 staff explicitly stated that the girl's behaviour had no bearing on the boy's subsequent sexual attack. Many of the young people labelled the boy a *'pervert'*, thereby placing his actions outside the realms of 'normal' masculinity (Newburn and Stanko 1994a).

I think that's dirty and perverted...if a bird likes you then she'd tell you wouldn't she...if I saw that happen I'd knock his block off...he's a pervert. (Colin, aged 15)

That's sexual harassment, there's not an excuse for his behaviour. He shouldn't have done it full stop, and he should be moved out. (Robert, aged 14)

She's not responsible for his perverted behaviour...you should be able to wear what you want in your own home, he's acted like a prick, he had no right to touch her...I'd have killed him. (Linda, aged 15)

As far as I'm concerned, it doesn't matter how she's dressed or acted, nothing like that should ever happen...I'd be worried about what that young man thought about women for him to behave like that...I imagine she feels it all got out of control and now feels very violated. (Manager, female)

Some staff interpreted the scenario very differently. Two staff felt that the adolescent girl was simply exploring her sexuality and 'probably did not realise what effect she was having on the young man' (senior residential worker, female). At the other extreme, a manager suggested that the girl may have limited control over her sexuality due to previous experiences of sexual abuse. These very divergent explanations concerning the girl's behaviour were in the minority, as most staff did not offer any reasons surrounding why young people behaved as they did, except to place blame. Worryingly, only two staff mentioned the need to investigate if any other young women in the home were at risk. Most staff individualised the sexual incident and, thereby, disregarded the possibility for wider victimisation.

Nevertheless, nearly all participants felt that the girl should not have been allowed to continue her breakfast dressed only in her night-dress and should have been made to change into something more appropriate. Nearly all young people and staff stated this would have been the response in their home, with many staff providing numerous examples of having to deal with similar problems. A common element of these discussions generally concerned the need to 'protect' young men from becoming sexually aroused due to the 'unfair' strain this placed on their self-control mechanisms. This has been identified in previous research (Soothill and Walby 1991, Carabine 2000). Similarly O'Neill (2001), in her insightful study of secure units, emphasises how institutional practices for controlling sexuality were deeply gendered. Female dress, actions and relationships were under constant scrutiny and regulation, whilst young men's sexuality (even though many of them had been convicted of a sexual offence) remained unnoticed. In the lengthy discussions which surrounded this topic in the present research, not one participant mentioned the inappropriate appearance of males. This highlights participants' inconsistent perceptions of sexual provocation. Additionally it also calls into question earlier evaluations, for although 28 participants explicitly rejected any victim responsibility, nearly all these participants nevertheless implied in their wider discussions that a girl's appearance does, to some degree, affect a man's ability to control himself sexually and, therefore, needed regulation.

This gendered control over sexuality took many forms and was demonstrated in a wide range of working practices. For example, in one private children's home where staff had been quite adamant about the need to restrict girls' 'inappropriate' dress, a researcher nevertheless found herself surrounded by sexually explicit pictures of women whilst interviewing a young man in his bedroom.[1] At the same time, and without any realisation of the incongruity of the situation, the young man informed the researcher that he respected women and to view them as 'sex objects' (as he felt the boy in the vignette had done) was completely unacceptable. We do not wish to enter the debate surrounding the effects of pornography; allowing young men to display such images, even in their bedrooms, does seem to us, to say the least, questionable and somewhat contradictory in the face of staff's earlier assessments concerning appropriate female attire.

Perceptions of seriousness

Participants' evaluations of the seriousness of the incident varied. When these were looked at closely they fell into three distinct categories: sexual harassment; inappropriate sexual behaviour and normalised masculinity.

The term 'sexual harassment' was spontaneously used by a number of young people and staff to denote the very serious nature of the incident. When participants were asked what this term meant, most stated it indicated that a serious sexual assault had taken place. Also included in this category were all responses where the very grave nature of the act was emphasised and when the young man's actions were regarded with disgust. The second category contained all references where the behaviour was seen as inappropriate but of a less serious nature or where the impact was viewed as minimal or of limited concern. The third category contained all responses where the incident was deemed to be normal male conduct.

Proportionally slightly more young people than staff described the incident as constituting sexual harassment. These young people placed considerable emphasis on the immoral aspect of the boy's behaviour, often referring to the boy in the vignette as a 'pervert'. Many of the young people stated that if this had happened in their home, they would have 'beaten him up', an indication of the degree of hostility which was expressed by many of the young participants in their replies to this vignette.

> Pervert, I'd have beaten him up, she didn't invite him in ... if she were my friend I'd smash his face in. (Ramon, aged 12)
>
> He's perverted, dirty. I'd have knocked him out if he'd touched me like that. (Jae, aged 15)

---

[1] Although young people's bedrooms may not be the most appropriate place to undertake fieldwork, this was often the only available private space that could be used (see Barter and Renold, 2002 for a more detailed discussion of the challenges of undertaking fieldwork in this area).

About the same proportion of staff (8) and young people (12) viewed the behaviour as being inappropriate but not as severe as harassment. Participants in this category generally stressed that the behaviour was unacceptable although not particularly serious in nature.

> He's a bit of an idiot, he shouldn't abuse her personal space, shouldn't have touched her, but really it's not that bad, but he should still get told off and sanctioned for it. (Rob, aged 15)

> That's not acceptable behaviour, even if he did get the green light, or thought he did, she didn't give him permission to touch her like that... don't think it's that serious, but he did overstep the mark. (Senior Residential Social Worker, female)

Four staff (although no senior staff) felt that the young man's behaviour was normal or at least 'typical' of male behaviour.

> I think it's quite normal behaviour for young men... expected behaviour... she's probably more aware of what she's doing... it's not really his fault, but he's been a bit silly... I think it's the girl's responsibility as much as the boy's. (Residential Social Worker, female)

Only one young man stated that the girl was a '*slut*' and that she got what she deserved, which does imply he felt the boy's behaviour was acceptable.

When we compared the three levels of seriousness attributed to the sexual violence to evaluations of the girl's culpability a tentative pattern did emerge (see Table 5.2). Overall, participants who attributed no culpability to the girl's behaviour were proportionally more likely to view the sexual behaviour as more serious than those who believed the girl to be culpable for the boy's actions in some way. Indeed, all five participants who viewed the boy's actions as normal also attached the greatest degree of female responsibility. These findings indicate that evaluations of impact are often associated with assessments of gender-related provocation and protection.

Table 5.2 Perceptions of female culpability and the seriousness of sexual violence

	Boy's behaviour seen as		
	Harassment	Inappropriate	Normal
Young people think girl culpable	4	8	1
Staff think girl culpable	3	7	4
Total culpability	7	15	5
Young people think girl not culpable	15	4	0
Staff think girl not culpable	5	2	0
Total non-culpability	20	6	0

> **2nd stage – vignette C**
> Helen goes to staff and says that John went into her room without permission and that he touched her. She says that he has done this before and that she does not like it.

2nd stage responses

Young people (32)

- A majority (24) were clear that she would feel angry, upset and shocked at what happened.
- Nearly all young people (26) felt she did not tell staff initially due to being scared of not being believed or taken seriously, 4 felt it was because she was scared about the boy's reaction, and 2 gave alternative reasons.

Staff (21)

- Just over two-thirds of staff (15) said that she did not inform staff initially due to feeling she may not be believed, 5 provided alternative responses.

Most participants stated that the girl did not initially inform staff due to being worried that she would not be taken seriously or believed, or that she would be held responsible. Disconcertingly, some young people provided examples of their own experiences where disclosures of sexual violence had not received the level of professional response they expected.

Interviewer:	What did you do when he did that (just described 15-year old male resident 'grabbing' her bottom)?
Megan:	Told him to fuck off.
Interviewer:	Did you tell staff?
Megan:	I did but then I, they just thought I was lying... but the staff think that the girls make false accusations.
Interviewer:	That's what they said was it?
Megan:	That's what they think... 'cause when me and John and Jane was in the room, they give it, 'Oh John I know what would happen, Jane has made accusations before and Meg (interviewee) has made accusations before' and they would try to say that we just go round saying that boys are touching us up. And Ryan's a little bastard man, he'd touch everyone up.
Interviewer:	Did he just do it once?
Megan:	He done it all the time.
Interviewer:	And when you told him to fuck off?
Megan:	He just carried on... and then I just smashed his stereo up and then he just (stopped).

(Megan, aged 15)

Some residential staff (6) and very few young people (2) felt the girl may have had alternative reasons for not informing staff the first time. These included: 'planning to get her own back', 'making a false allegation to get the boy into trouble', and that 'she had started what she couldn't handle'. Wattam (1999) argues that many professionals simply assume that young people will want to confide in them. When this does not occur, they seek alternative explanations other than considering the possibility that young people lack trust in staff.

> **3rd stage – vignette C**
> Staff told John not to go into people's rooms and spoke to Helen about dressing and acting in such an inappropriate way and warned her of the trouble she might get herself in.

3rd stage responses

Young people (32)
- 16 young people disagreed with staff's response, with 12 feeling the police should be involved and five stating that John should be moved out.

Staff (21)
- At the second stage 6 stated they would talk to both parties only, 12 stated a child protection investigation was now warranted, 6 of these felt the police should be contacted.

Evaluations of professional response

Unsurprisingly, the seriousness of the incident was a central determining factor in participants' evaluations concerning the level of professional response required. Only 2 young people agreed with the staff's response in the vignette, 16 strongly disagreed, 12 of these felt the police should be called. A further 10 young people made comments indicating they were not happy with the response but did not expand on this any further, although all seemed to be indicating the response was not severe enough. Four provided no answer or did not know. That this was not an isolated incident did not much change young people's evaluations, although those who stated that they disagreed were more vehement in their response. All the young people who rejected any level of female culpability either disagreed with the staff response or indicated it was not sufficient. Many young people, in fact just under half, were unsure what would happen in their own residential homes if such a situation occurred. About a quarter felt that 'child protection would be called in' and 10 stated the boy would probably be 'thrown out'. However, most young people seemed unsure if the young man would be removed or what the possible outcome may be.

The analysis of staff's evaluations concerning the professional response in the vignette revealed sharp distinctions in the level of response deemed necessary, which in turn were linked to seniority and, to a slightly lesser extent, perceptions of female culpability. Over one-third of staff (9) felt that the vignette response of talking with both young people was adequate. These replies were often accompanied by comments about not wanting to label the young man a 'sexual deviant' for such a 'trivial' act. Twelve staff felt that the incident constituted a child protection issue; that the social services department and external managers should be informed; and that a conference was needed to discuss the incident, the young man's care plan and possible implications for him remaining. This group included all four managers and six senior staff members. Of these, four felt that the police should be automatically informed as a criminal act had been committed, although a further five stated that Helen should be advised of her right to call the police if she so wished.

When the information was provided that this was not the first time this boy had behaved in such a manner, staff's assessments of the situation changed slightly. Only five staff still agreed that the vignette response of talking to both young people was adequate.

Male on male sexual attack – vignette D

1st stage

Jay, who lives in Swallow Road Children's Home, is on the sofa watching TV in the sitting room on his own. Then Tony, who also lives in the home, walks in and stands in the corner watching TV. Jay does not like Tony very much and doesn't pay much attention to him. After a while Tony sits down quite close to Jay on the sofa. Tony touches Jay's leg.

2nd stage

Jay does not say anything or move away. Then Caroline, a member of staff, enters the room and sees Tony and Jay sitting together on the sofa. Tony jumps up when he sees Caroline and leaves the room saying he's going to get a drink from the kitchen. When he's gone Caroline asks Jay if everything's okay, Jay replied that nothing was wrong. Nothing further is said about the incident.

Some methodological considerations

Overall, the Swallow Road vignette was used very much less frequently with young people than any of the other scenarios. A number of factors may have contributed to this, including the subject area itself. The Swallow Road vignette was the only story that young people did not seem to relate to. This was especially true for adolescent young men, where monosyllabic responses often replaced the general flow of conversation achieved with the other scenarios. Many of the young men were unwilling to discuss issues relating to any aspect of male to male sexual contact.

Another factor which limited the usefulness of this vignette as a research technique concerned the lack of context contained in the story (Finch 1989). Consequently, many young people felt unable to elaborate on their initial comments due to the absence of background information on the characters; somewhat calling into question the adequacy of our piloting skills. Also, unlike the other scenarios, most young people stated that they had not encountered such a situation (or at least were not willing to disclose this to us), which meant that they had no personal experiences to draw upon, an important aspect of vignette methodology (Barter and Renold 2000). Consequently, either consciously or unconsciously, researchers often introduced this scenario later in the research interaction, which meant if time ran out (which it commonly did generally due to the physical space being needed for meetings, watching TV, eating or sleeping) the vignette was not used. The frequency of use with staff did not reflect this pattern, with nearly all the vignettes being equally employed.

1st stage – vignette D

Jay, who lives in Swallow Road Children's Home, is on the sofa watching TV in the sitting room on his own. Then Tony, who also lives in the home, walks in and stands in the corner watching TV. Jay does not like Tony very much and doesn't pay much attention to him. After a while Tony sits down quite close to Jay on the sofa. Tony touches Jay's leg.

1st stage responses

Young people (24)

- 21 young people felt the behaviour was sexual, 3 felt it constituted non-sexual intimidation.
- 6 young men and three young women felt that being touched on the leg by another boy warranted physical and verbal retaliation, 4 young people said they would inform staff.

Staff (16)

- 8 staff viewed the behaviour as intimidatory but not sexual, 4 thought it was sexually motivated, three were unsure if there was a sexual element and one worker stated it was about sexual identity.

Homophobic and non-sexual interpretations

Young people usually felt that a definite sexual element was present in the young man's actions, and only a few saw it as being solely intimidation. In comparison staff were more likely to see the behaviour as intimidatory but not sexual.

The most commonly reported response from young people (predominantly males) concerned declarations of immediate retaliation, mostly physical (8) and some verbal (4). These replies usually included homophobic insults (8), although framed in terms of social justice.

> I'd smack him, that's what I'd do, it isn't the right thing … the right thing is (to) leave him alone, but I'm not into what this guy's into, shouldn't do that sort of thing in the home. (Fergus, aged 13)
>
> Urgh! Gay … I'd smack him. (Linda, aged 15)

Four young people stated they would tell staff about the incident, with one young man stating his reason for doing so was that he would be scared what the boy may try next. Three young people said they would simply walk away and another three stated they would feel angry or 'odd' but provided no further elaboration. One young woman stated the 'victim' 'probably fancies him but is scared to admit it'.

> It'd make me feel odd, uncomfortable … I've nothing against them … gays … but I'd leave the room. (Adrian, aged 17)
>
> I'd feel scared, disgusted, humiliated … wonder why did he did that to me? I'd worry that maybe next time he'd try and do more. (Cole, aged 13)
>
> Gay and trying it on … I'd get up and say 'I'm not gay' and walk off … make me feel like shit … Don't mind gay people, but when they touch me that's different. (Ross, aged 14)

The majority of young people commented that they would feel uncomfortable, angry, scared or simply 'odd'. Nearly all of the girls stated this in relation to anyone (boy or girl) touching them in such a way whereas boys rarely stated this in connection to girls. Three young people interjected positive statements about homosexuality in their discussion on this vignette, in an attempt to counteract what they perceived would be the general homophobic responses of other young people.

2nd stage – vignette D

Jay does not say anything or move away. Then Caroline, a member of staff, enters the room and sees Tony and Jay sitting together on the sofa.

(continued)

> Tony jumps up when he sees Caroline and leaves the room saying he's going to get a drink from the kitchen. When he's gone Caroline asks Jay if everything's okay, Jay replied that nothing was wrong. Nothing further is said about the incident.

2nd stage responses

Young people (24)

- 10 young people thought that the boy didn't tell staff because he was either embarrassed, didn't want to get bullied or didn't want to get the boy into trouble.
- 5 young people thought that the worker should have done more.

Staff (16)

- 7 staff said they would have casual conversations with each boy but no more, 5 stated a possible child protection investigation may be warranted, and 4 thought the vignette response was adequate.
- Staff stated the boy did not tell because he felt uncomfortable with the situation (6), was scared (4) or felt powerless (2). 4 stated it was because there was nothing to tell.

Non-disclosure to staff

When young people were asked why they felt the young man had not informed staff about the incident, we received very diverse replies. The most common response was that he was being bullied and was thus scared of the possible consequences of telling (5). Three young women felt it was because he didn't want to get the other boy into trouble. Three young men stated that it was because he was embarrassed that it had happened to him. A further three thought that it was because he was attracted to the young man but thought these feelings were wrong, and one young woman felt they may have previously been in a relationship which was now over. Two remarked that he would be scared staff would not take him seriously, and two stated that it was because he was not bothered. Five did not know.

Most of the young people were unsure of what the staff response would or should be either in practice or in theory. Five young people were of the opinion that the staff should definitely have done more, however homophobic reasons were given by two of these young participants who said that the boy should be moved as homosexuals should not be allowed to live with other young people. The staff who commented on this vignette provided very divergent answers regarding suitable staff responses to the situation. Four residential staff stated they agreed with the vignette response. These staff said that the incident would not have raised any real concerns and they would have left it as a casual enquiry if the boy did not make a complaint. Just under half of the staff (7), including two managers and two senior staff, stated that they would have had more in-depth conversations with both parties and, if this did not satisfy their concerns, they would have to ensure that their behaviour together was more thoroughly supervised in the future. The remaining four members of staff, including one manager and one senior, felt a child protection investigation was warranted even without an allegation and with no further incidents occurring.

Having examined young people's and staff's responses to the four vignettes in detail, the final part of this chapter brings together some of the main themes that have emerged from this analysis. These themes are considered in relation to dominant discourses on violence identified by previous commentators. Furthermore, using the continuum of violence introduced in Chapter 2, we compare how different findings from the 14 homes relate to their position on the continuum. By undertaking this, we do not mean to imply that meanings and beliefs surrounding violence exist in isolation from other aspects of the residential context. In Chapter 6, we undertake a similar process in relation to institutional and organisational and structural factors.

Dominant discourses on violence

One of the most dominant discourses surrounding violence involves the linking of violent acts to individual motivation or individual pathology (Cameron and Fraser 1987, Young 1996). This concentration on violence as an individually motivated act serves to obscure and therefore disassociate it from the wider social context in which it occurs. Stanko (2000) argues that this approach has long outlived its usefulness, if not its popularity, in public thinking.

Linked to this individualistic framework are ideas about victim status. This has been conceptualised in previous work as a dichotomy, or a crude opposition, between 'innocent' and 'deserving' victims (Richardson and May 1999). In this line of thought certain individuals are viewed as less deserving of the victim status than others. Often these judgements surround whether the 'victim' willingly provoked or participated in the violence or failed to take 'appropriate' care. Stanko states that 'If people frequent places that are known to be dangerous or they do not follow exactly the rules for precaution then we implicitly hold them responsible for whatever happens to them' (1999: 49).

As we have already seen in our analysis, this is often strongly related to gender, as women in our society are more likely to be blamed for making themselves vulnerable to violence than are men (Dobash and Dobash 1992). In addition, individual victim characteristics are also related to perceptions of their victim status. Marginalised and stigmatised groups are unlikely to be constructed as innocent victims, demonstrated by Richardson and May (1999) in their work surrounding homophobic violence. This dichotomy may also be applied to the scandals concerning the institutional abuse of children by professionals, as discussed in our opening chapter. In these instances, children and young people deemed 'challenging', and therefore regarded as less deserving of the victim status, endured systematic sexual and physical assaults whilst the relevant authorities ignored the warning signs and children's own disclosures (Utting 1997, House of Commons 2002). This is similar to what Goffman (1990:12) called 'discrediting characteristics', which make individuals vulnerable to a social devaluation process whereby the whole person is reduced to a tainted and stigmatised category (Richardson 1996).

Both young people and junior staff regularly applied the above ideas to their understanding of violence. Individual motivation or pathology was often cited as the reason for the violence rather than wider social relations (except, interestingly, in respect to racism). This emphasis allowed both 'acceptable' and 'unacceptable' acts of violence to be disconnected from the social settings in which they occurred. In addition, conceptualisations about the 'innocent victim' – 'deserving victim' dichotomy were strongly evident in many young people's and residential staff's replies, although they were not necessarily associated with intervention in any straightforward manner. However, this dichotomy was linked in certain instances to impact, this being especially apparent in relation to female culpability and male sexual violence, although this did seem more marked in staff's evaluations than young people's. The gendering of violence was also visible in many young people's and staff's perceptions of how young men are expected to live, with the resulting normalisation of certain forms of male violence.

Some young people and staff rejected this crude victim dichotomy, although not necessarily the emphasis on individual motivation. This was most noticeable in relation to the use of retaliatory physical violence, where the portrayal of the victim as either deserving or undeserving was rejected in favour of generalised statements concerning the inappropriateness of physical violence as a legitimate response.

The professional explanation used mostly by senior staff or managers overcame some of the populist frameworks used by many of their junior colleagues. In these cases individual motivation was more often situated alongside the wider social context of the behaviour. Most often, these related to wider issues of poverty, powerlessness and abuse, and to a lesser extent gender relations, specifically challenging the central role of violence in certain forms of masculinity.

Most senior staff had gained formal social work qualifications or were embarking on them. Although it is not possible to directly link this wider conceptual framework to increased levels of qualifications or training (see Sinclair and Gibbs 1989), this may be one possible explanation for the distinct differentiation we encountered in relation to seniority. Unfortunately, although the central role of social relations was evident in many managers', and to a lesser extent senior staff's, understandings of violence, this had not routinely influenced other workers', or indeed residents', conceptualisations. This may to a great extent be linked to populist explanations of violence, which provide easily defined dichotomies for explaining, labelling and responding to violence. Ultimately, to challenge wider social relations is perhaps viewed as more complex than to label individual pathology. It may also appear futile, given the limitations of the residential context, where most young people will spend only a few months before moving back to their families or out into a community placement.

Even so, in one important area – racism – this challenge is exactly what had occurred. In this instance, most staff and many young people rejected the individualistic innocent/deserving victim dichotomy outright, placing racist violence solely within wider social relations of inequality (although a minority did question the supremacy this form of violence had gained over other social relations). This may reflect wider changes in how racism, and racist violence especially, are perceived, although the evidence to substantiate such a transformation in societal thinking is disputed. Obviously, as we have already emphasised, we need to distinguish between belief and action. For example, although nearly all young people rejected bullying we know from young people's accounts, and from the homes' daily log books, that some young participants either lied to us about their beliefs, or alternatively believed that bullying was wrong but still engaged in it. The same may well be true of racism. Unfortunately, as these young people did not disclose to us their involvement in these activities, we were unable to analyse these inconsistencies any further in discussion with them. Nevertheless, the impact of the residential context, and the commitment of many staff to challenging racist perceptions in homes, should not be underestimated. This is not to say that young people did not experience racist violence (they did) nor that all minority ethnic groups benefited equally from the rejection of the 'deserving victim' status (they did not). However, the impetus to challenge wider social relations rather than blame individual pathology was evident.

Linking meaning and experience

There appeared to be both distinct and consistent differences between participants' framing of violence depending where on the violence continuum their home was situated. As we shall see, there may be organisational explanations for this. However, here we will restrict our discussion to the different meanings or cultures the homes exhibited. Three main interrelated themes emerged from the analysis: attitudes towards violence as social justice; differing thresholds of impact; and differing thresholds of intervention.

Social justice

Young people's views about violence and social justice differed markedly depending where on the continuum their home was situated. The higher along the violence continuum the home was located, the greater the application of social justice explanations in legitimising violence as an acceptable response to provocation (either real or perceived). It did also appear (although numbers are small) that, in these homes, staff were also slightly more likely to see retaliatory violence as legitimate or at least 'typical'. In addition, the acceptance and celebration of this form of violence was a pervasive feature of young people's cultures in high violence establishments. This was in contrast to lower violence homes, where reference to social justice as a justification for violence was rare. Instead, we found that in these homes, the residential cultures of both young people and staff considered retaliatory violence, irrespective of the provocation, to be an unacceptable response.

In contrast we detected less of a discernible pattern between homes in relation to non-retaliatory violence, such as bullying. This form of violence was generally perceived by young people as being illegitimate due to the victim's 'innocent' status. However, the minority of young people who still considered the use of 'unprovoked' violence justified came from 'high violence' homes. We could detect no general pattern of belief in female culpability and male sexual violence in relation to positions on the continuum of homes.

Differing thresholds of impact

Our findings imply that differential thresholds of impact were applied depending on the level of violence homes experienced. Both staff and young people in homes with higher levels of violence more commonly applied higher thresholds than those who lived in homes where violence was less common. Possibly then, when residential homes are regularly exposed to violence, this may serve to desensitise those living and working there to its impact. Behaviour that may appear in one home as unacceptable may be perceived in another as normal. This has important implications for the protection of young people, as we will see in relation to intervention.

Differing threshold of intervention

Perhaps inevitably, differing perceptions of impact corresponded to differing levels of intervention found in homes. Consequently, homes which held relatively high impact thresholds also consistently demonstrated relatively high thresholds for intervention. When participants' interventionist responses to the vignettes were taken as a whole, we found that homes situated lower on the continuum consistently provided more interventionist responses earlier on in the scenarios than those homes where violence was more prominent. Although there were discrepancies in individual homes, often along seniority lines, this pattern did hold true across all forms of violence.

Summary points

- Young people's answers showed a very complex mix of values relating to the nature and seriousness of the attacks. Responses identified many of the themes described in earlier chapters. Answers showed that any level of attack was expected to work within clearly defined parameters of acceptability, governed by rules which protected codes of retaliatory justice, or set the limits of tolerable revenge.
- When assaults were at a relatively low level, many young people responded that they were justified and that staff should not be told. When events were more serious or risky young people saw clearly defined boundaries, beyond which severe sanctions, including police involvement or young people losing their placement, should come into play.
- The majority of young people were emphatic that staff would intervene to prevent physical violence, but not always in agreement that they would welcome that.
- Young people and staff both identified sexually provocative behaviour by girls as culpable in leading to sexual assaults from boys, and therefore held females responsible for male sexual violence.
- Staff showed a very clear consensus that they must intervene with actual or threatened physical violence, but showed much less consensus on the appropriate reaction to the sexual incidents. The incident concerning possible sexual touching by boys was nearly always identified as a sexual assault by the young people, and provoked strong homophobic reactions, whereas staff were very much less likely to see it as either sexual or serious.
- Once again the dominant discourses on violence concerned gender, and a decision on the status of the victim, whether they were innocent or deserving of retaliation and punishment.
- There was a consensus by young people and staff that racist insults and attacks were more damaging than those concerning sexuality, and answers again showed that racism was likely to be challenged in a more coherent way than other forms of violence and intimidation.
- Young people's responses showed clear links with the culture of the home in which they were living. Those who advocated violent retaliation, or who assumed victims deserved whatever was happening to them, came almost exclusively from homes where there were frequent descriptions of high impact violence from young people and staff.

6
Institutional and Organisational Factors Associated with Violence

> I'd definitely like to see a lot more information given to kids and a lot more say in what goes on in their own home, but with staff included in that, 'cause we find here that we've got management, then little bits of management underneath that, and then us and it's constantly a fighting battle, 'cause the management'll come in and make rules and they'll all go home and we're left to implement them, yet they don't ask our opinion.
> (Residential Social Worker, female)

Meeting the needs of children and young people in residential children's homes is widely acknowledged to be both a complex and demanding process (Department of Health 1998a). This challenging role can be further exacerbated by both institutional and organisational factors that are often out of the direct control of individual homes. In this chapter we consider how these factors were seen to influence the climates of violence and verbal attacks within the residential settings. First, the formal residential policy and practice guidelines relating to peer violence are examined, including the manner in which these are presented to young people, and young people's own awareness and assessments of their appropriateness. Leading on from this, the issue of children's rights in residential homes is considered in relation to institutional policy and practice developments surrounding violence. Following this, the organisational factors associated with issues of violence are documented. These are largely restricted to workers' own assessments, although young people did provide opinions on three areas: physical structure of buildings, function of homes and staffing. Last, the organisational and structural factors identified by participants are considered in relation to the position of homes on the violence continuum, originally presented in Chapter 2.

Policies and procedures

Over two-thirds of staff interviewed (48) raised the issue of formal policy and practice guidelines, although their reasons for doing so varied. Nearly all establishments had written policies and procedures governing different aspects of conduct within the homes. This seems an encouraging improvement on findings reported in the 1990s, when many homes did not have even Statements of Purpose, which are a statutory requirement (Berridge and Brodie 1998). Common features of these guidelines concerned the rights of young people to feel safe from intimidation, violence and exploitation from other children and young people. Many stressed that any form of intimidation and/or physical violence was unacceptable and would not be tolerated. The implications of such behaviour, including ultimately the need to move out of the home, were a common feature. Some homes had written sanctions governing what actions could and would be taken by staff in relation to intimidatory and violent behaviour from young people, including the use of physical restraint. The majority of homes included these in the young people's *moving-in pack* and all young people were spoken to by staff regarding these rules and expectations either prior to arrival or, if an emergency placement, when they joined. In three-quarters of homes young people were asked to sign an agreement to show they both understood the homes' rules and procedures and agreed to abide by them. However, in some cases workers felt this was rather a token exercise and that it held little meaning for many of the young people.

In some homes (4) policies and procedures relating to behaviour between young people were being updated. For example, in one home the bullying policy was being extended specifically to include 'emotional' and non-physical forms of bullying. Workers presented varying accounts of how useful they felt were the written procedures and policies. A common response was that, in reality, it was all 'common sense' and experience that governed working practices rather than formal procedures (Whitaker *et al.* 1998). Workers stated that, due to the very disparate nature of children's behaviour, written guidelines were unable to reflect this complexity and, consequently, many felt they were of little practical assistance. Another commonly voiced view was that when a situation arose it was not really possible to go and check what the 'correct' practice response was.

> It's more common sense really... you can't keep looking at policies all the time to make sure what you're doing is exactly what is written down. You have to go with your own intuition about how best to respond in each individual situation, policies can't give you that. (Senior Residential Social Worker, male)

> If a situation is developing, you can't just tell them to stop while you just check what it is you should do in line with policy... it's just not realistic, is it? (Residential Social Worker, female)

Another problem associated with the formal guidance concerned the degree of consultation residential workers had in the development of working guidelines. Workers in four homes felt that this lack of involvement meant that many formal procedures were impractical, mainly due to them being devised by external management rather than embedded in everyday practice.

> The problem here is that we're given rules and procedures from above that in practice are unrealistic and often unworkable... that doesn't make our job any easier and causes resentment 'cause we're not consulted really at any level about changes that directly affect us and the kids. (Senior Residential Social Worker, male)

Although many workers could recount the main principles contained in their homes' guidance documents, few were able to recall these in detail. Many stated that they would need to check the residential home's guidelines to answer our questions fully. In a minority of cases (9) workers felt unsure what formal polices were in place in relation to peer violence.

The most common complaint from workers (20) surrounded the residential homes' lack of guidance on the use of physical restraint. In most cases, workers introduced this in connection with worries about their increased vulnerability to having a complaint issued against them by a young person due to the lack of formally agreed guidelines. When viewed alongside the fact that a high minority of workers stated they lacked training in this area (see Chapter 7), it is clear that this represents a worrying omission, and one that has been highlighted in previous research findings. Berridge and Brodie (1998), in their detailed study of 12 children's homes, similarly found that behavioural control was a major preoccupation of staff. Interestingly, this was the area in which they had received *most* training and it was not so much that staff lacked a general awareness of how they should act but that this was not being operationalised. A main explanation for this was that they lacked confidence in (mostly local authority) managers should an allegation be made. Consequently, staff sometimes adopted passive attitudes towards young people's behaviour and, for example, did not prevent them from leaving the building late at night.

Only one (private) residential home lacked any formally agreed policy or practice guidelines governing children's behaviour. Although the new manager remarked that they were presently formulating these, little evidence of this process could be found, even two months after the main fieldwork had been undertaken.

Overall, it seems that workers felt it was important to have clear and concise declarations of unacceptable forms of behaviour, as well as governing principles of care surrounding mutual respect, protection and safety. For example, most policies stated that any form of physical violence, 'bullying' and offensive language would not be tolerated and that young people had the right to feel safe at all times. These 'guiding principles' were seen by workers, and especially senior staff, as providing important benchmarks for what was acceptable behaviour, even though many workers recognised that in practice they would be unable to enforce them all the time.

Young people's assessments of policies and procedures

Only a quarter of the young people interviewed discussed residential policies. Young people's awareness of formal policies regarding young people's behaviour in the residential setting related strongly with those homes exhibiting high levels of violence. Knowledge of behaviour policies which revolved mainly around the use of sanctions, police involvement and the more general complaints procedure seemed to be generated through practice, that is, through direct experience of one or more of these procedures.

While very few young people made mention of the *moving-in packs*, they were aware of the more informal rules and regulations regarding, for example, curfews and smoking, and for some young people such rules were generally positively (albeit reluctantly sometimes) regarded:

> Jessie: ... I've got a lot of freedom here as well and I've never had boundaries which I've got here. I was not used to that, so I rebelled against everything they say to me. I've got used to it now but at first I couldn't handle the rules coming in on time and not being able to do this and that, I've never had that before.
> Interviewer: Do you prefer having boundaries?
> Jessie: I always wanted boundaries, like I've been in care for 10 years and I always wanted to be in a children's home.
> (Jessie, aged 16)

Most young people were also aware that physical peer violence would not be tolerated and would necessitate some form or staff intervention. However, as the following extract illustrates, they were also acutely aware that the implementation of some behavioural policies lapsed in practice and that staff members were inconsistent:

> Interviewer: Is that a policy here, that staff have to break up every fight that happens?
> Melissa: They are supposed to, restrain us, but it depends really. If you've been warned like to stop annoying the person, like well you say if that person turns round and hits you, it's your own fault they are not going to do anything. And if that person still carries on and winding people up then that's it, he gets into a fight, staff won't do anything.

Interviewer:	And all staff members are the same, or do some staff intervene more than others?
Melissa:	Some staff will. It depends on what kind of day it's been really. If you've been really hectic all day then a fight starts out sometime I think I can't be bothered, and I'll leave it and other days they will intervene but they need to know what is going on first before they do that. They might if there is other people round watching them and might ask them what's happened, and then if they feel its necessary to break it up then they will do.

(Melissa, aged 16)

As stated earlier, in homes in which they applied, formalised reward and punishment systems were well known to residents. This was particularly the case in the two all-male children's homes.

However, most young people were quite aware that sanctions and restraints were successful only if they were consistently delivered and as the following extract illustrates, if they were taken seriously by young people. The young person here is discussing the home's policy to remove and replace a young person for violent behaviour:

Interviewer:	What sort of things would the staff do (to prevent violent behaviour)?
Lisa:	(they can say) 'I can get you kicked out if you don't quit it'... and that's going to stick in your head isn't it and going to make you think... 'well if I like it here I don't want to get kicked out I'm going to quit'... but if I hate that person I'm going to carry on, who cares if I get kicked out.
Interviewer:	So it depends if the young people want to be here or not?
Lisa:	yeah... I think that's how it works in a way... but as I say it's different for different people.

(Lisa, aged 16)

Similarly, as suggested in earlier chapters, young people were also aware that while the reactive interventions could put a stop to a physical fight happening in front of them, they were often futile and did nothing to prevent the more hidden, and often systematic forms of bullying/violence.

Interviewer:	And have you told staff they do this (young people banging on his door and coming into his room at night)?
Dan:	Yes.
Interviewer:	And what have they said to you?
Dan:	They just said when they do it again just come down and tell us.

Interviewer:	And do you go down and tell them?
Dan:	Yes, but it doesn't stop it happening.
Interviewer:	And what are the consequences for Ramon and Richard doing this to you? Do they get told off? (shakes his head) Do they have privileges stopped or? (shakes his head) Nothing?
Dan:	No.

(Dan, aged 15)

Interviewer:	If you did tell them what do you think staff could do about it?
Tony:	Nothing.
Interviewer:	There's nothing you think they could do?
Tony:	Well all they can do is put the kids on one-to-one (supervision) and when the kids come off one-to-one they just start it again.

(Tony, aged 14)

Interviewer:	And were you able to tell staff?
Jonathon:	I told staff in the end, and then the kid goes aah you've told staff ain't you, about the bullying, you're dead now. That was why I got really scared so I talked to staff about that. So staff have gone and told him if he ever touches me again, I can get him nicked straightaway.
Interviewer:	So did it stop them?
Jonathon:	Well, it didn't stop until he got nicked twice.
Interviewer:	When you say nicked, what do you mean?
Jonathon:	Arrested.
Interviewer:	Okay.
Jonathon:	Like he hit me, I got him arrested, then he learnt his lesson.
Interviewer:	So it didn't happen once he got arrested?
Jonathon:	No.
Interviewer:	And are you happy with how staff handled that situation?
Jonathon:	No. He'd done it all over again, bullied me, punched me, kicked me, actually wounded me by pushing me down the hill.

(Jonathon, aged 13)

At other times young people were simply let down by residential policies and procedures (or often lack of):

Interviewer:	I know you all got together and wrote a letter to staff about it all, before that had you complained to staff about it?
Ewan:	Yer a couple of times.

Interviewer:	And what happened there?
Ewan:	They just said they'd try and arrange a meeting with my social worker.
Interviewer:	And did that help?
Ewan:	No they didn't do it.
Interviewer:	Do you feel they did enough to protect you?
Ewan:	No... not really.

(Ewan, aged 13)

Children's rights

Some workers (11) were very clear about the positive role that a children's rights perspective could play in relation to protecting children from peer violence. Senior workers often referred to the Children Act 1989 as encapsulating the need to implement strategies to strengthen children's rights. It is important to recognise that although the Children Act is much more broad-ranging than this, workers mentioned its application only in relation to children's rights' issues. Often these workers stressed the need to involve and consult with young people concerning how best to safeguard them from harm but also recognised that, in some instances, children's wishes would be inconsistent with their own protection, as illustrated by the extract below (although the worker misinterprets the legislation).

> Like with the Children Act, I really think we need to listen to children... and we need to take on board what they're saying to us... but with that we also need to make sure that they're aware of responsibilities that comes with that... at the end of the day we are the adults... and if the choices that they're making are actually wrong... we're gonna have to make choices for them. (Residential Social Worker, male)

However, only one worker explicitly felt that children and young people should have a formal procedure (recognised by external management) to ensure they had a greater say in the policies and practices governing residential provision. Unfortunately, not all residential workers held positive views concerning the implementation of children's rights. In fact, we found a great deal of misinterpretation about what children's rights meant in practice. Indeed, myths about child domination and omnipotence had grown around the area of children's rights (Utting 1997).

> They (young people) often feel that I can please myself and we get 'you can't stop me'... and we can't do anything and in a way they're right because the legislation does that and they're all jammed up on it. (Residential Social Worker, female)

...the thing has gone full circle and you don't have complete control, the kids have complete control, the kids have more power than you have. (Residential Social Worker, male)

The Children Act 1989 does not state that children's wishes should predominate and acknowledges that young people's perspectives and the safeguarding of their welfare do not always correspond. The Support Force for Children's Residential Care (1995) emphasised in their final report that:

> A positive ethos towards rights and empowerment carries with it the need to develop both self-control and external controls for individuals and the group. Working together managers, staff and children need to strive for an ethos, structure and daily living environment that provides positive opportunities whilst at the same time creates boundaries around what is acceptable. (p. 48)

However, we must question if it is realistic to expect residential workers, who themselves often felt excluded from the consultation process, nevertheless to empower young people in such a way. Ultimately, both groups need to be included in policy and practice development processes to ensure that their views and wishes are taken seriously if a positive environment surrounding children's rights is to be achieved (Barter 1997).

Young people's meetings

In theory, one forum in which young people had the opportunity to raise issues and topics that were significant to them was in the context of the young people's meetings. All the homes except one claimed to operate (or in the case of three homes were in the process of setting-up) young people's meetings. These seemed to be designed and used in very different ways, to different ends by individual homes, individual staff and by the young people themselves. For example, young people's meetings occurred every night in one home, once a week in another, two homes stated that in principle they occurred once a month, while another admitted to taking place only 'when we can find the time'. Furthermore, the ambivalence surrounding staff's commitment to hear children's voices and opinions with concerns over young people 'having complete control', as expressed in their accounts relating to the Children Act and children's rights, could be seen at work in their approach to the young people's meetings. Indeed, very few of the homes had clear or consistent rationales for the organisation of the young people's meetings. The following extract illustrates how many of them begin as an opportunity for young people to share their thoughts and opinions, but often shift from young people's problems to staff concerns:

> Yeah, young people, they themselves would have a, where it's like, it's their meeting, they talk and we listen, kind of thing. Where they talk and

like we listen and a note's been made of it and then we obviously discuss with them certain issues which they, which we feel that they need to be aware of. And it could be from playing their tape recorders loud at night, to not settling to bed, causing riots, lending and borrowing things, for example, it's come up a number of times. (Residential Social Worker, female)

In the main, the agenda for the young people's meetings was controlled in almost all cases by the staff. Staff suggested that the meetings were designed for young people to raise issues such as bullying:

> If a young person in the house is experiencing any difficulty, they take it to the meeting. (Deputy Manager, female)

> We'd use the forum of the kids' meeting, every evening, to discuss bullying if that was on the agenda or whatever they want. (Residential Social Worker, male)

In practice, the young people themselves reported having little control over the agenda of meetings. In some cases they were perceived as a source of discipline and punishment. This was particularly the case in homes in which there were high levels of violence (which ironically had regular 'young people's meetings').

> Interviewer: Do you get the chance to say things like this in the meeting that it's not fair that people are getting rewarded if they behave badly?
> Stuart: Well the meeting isn't really for us, it's for the staff to have a dig at us. First of all it goes round asking everyone for points and comments what's on the cards, then it goes straight to the staff and they pick up on everything, you've been bad, you've been inappropriate blah, blah, blah, and if I went around saying 'oh you didn't open the door quick enough, you didn't answer the phone quick enough' they would give me a red card, but its OK for them to do it.
> Interviewer: So it's all niggles and stuff like that?
> Stuart: Yeah and it's all one-sided, it's all just... When things go their way OK, when it's back in their face they don't like it at all.
>
> (Stuart, aged 15)

> Well like the young people's meeting for me is like a punishment 'cause we sit down at the dinner table and listen to this crap and talk rubbish. (Lisa, aged 12)

> Ross: But I think staff here are against, not against the kids but, I mean but won't fight for, not like literally but if there's

	like I've got a meeting, the staff will act as a someone who is trying to put me down not bring me up, you know.
Interviewer:	Not there to support you, in a way that you want?
Ross:	Yes, they're against me as in you know 'well maybe if you hadn't have done this then...' but they are not trying to support you.

(Ross, aged 14)

Even when there was a clear and consistent commitment to organise young people's meetings solely as a forum for young people to raise issues of concern to them, peer conflict was a common outcome:

> We've stepped in a few times at meetings before it got to that (verbal conflict between young people) but never had any violence. They've (the young people) asked for them, they chair it, they minute it. It started by bringing issues up. Yeah, we don't want it being a bullying session where we're invited in. (Residential Social Worker, female)

Interviewer:	Has that happened?
Staff:	It has happened where we've stepped in as staff. We don't usually step into their meeting, we're just at the background. It's theirs, but we're there in case 'owt goes on. Er, and occasions, though, where it was three against one (we say) 'now hang on, no, this isn't how it's done, it's not meant for this. You've all got your say now let's have it corrected.'

(Senior Residential Social Worker, male)

Alternatively, they would not be taken seriously by young people themselves:

> We've started to try and have, again, after the staff meetings we then have a forum for the, young adults to give their points of view across and to write down, you know, any bits and pieces that they want to bring up to do with the house or the staff or whatever it may well be. But unfortunately there might be one or two who take it seriously, by and large, the majority of them, like young lads in general just, someone says something or some word is said and then all of a sudden it's bursts of laughter. (Residential Social Worker, male)

And even when young people felt able to raise issues such as 'bullying', there would often be no policy or procedure to handle such disclosures, and thus they felt it was in one boy's words, 'a waste of time', which relates back to previous issues regarding non-disclosure and lack of effective intervention.

In sum, the overriding theme regarding why young people's meetings were either not taken seriously, or why they turned into meetings conducted and controlled by staff concerns, pivoted around wider issues regarding the unequal power relationships between young people as 'children' and staff as 'adults' as articulated by Julie below:

Julie: It's really our meeting, it's not them trying to talk.
Interviewer: Right. So do you think that you should do more talking, that you should have more control over the meeting maybe?
Julie: Yeah, yeah.
Interviewer: Yeah. What you've said to me today, what you'd like to see happen, have you ever brought that up in a, in a young people's meeting?
Julie: Yeah, but they, they will say, 'Oh, it's, it's, we're here and we … have to do this' and you don't say very much and all this.
Interviewer: So you, so have you tried to talk about it?
Julie: Once.
Interviewer: Once, but, and what was their response?
Julie: We like, they say, 'It's your choice of meeting, anything you wanna bring up', then if we don't, they bring up something that we do wrong or what we do right. It's mostly what we do wrong and do right, it's not how we feel, it's not how they, they … it's just you done this right, you done that wrong.
Interviewer: Right, and have you told them that you want to talk more about how you feel in a meeting?
Julie: No, not really 'cause they won't listen.

(Julie, aged 13)

Having looked at the institutional policy and practice guidelines we now focus on the organisational factors that participants identified as representing major hurdles to reducing the presence of violence within homes. Not only were workers much more likely to raise organisational issues than were young people, but proportionally more senior workers and especially managers introduced these factors. This is unsurprising given Sinclair and Gibbs' (1998) assertion that heads of homes provide the link between the structural (organisational) characteristics of the home, on the one hand, and its day to day practices on the other.

Referrals

The most frequently stated organisational factor identified by workers related to referrals (38). When this category was looked at in more depth four main issues arose: lack of information at referral (9 homes), control over referrals (7 homes), lack of admission procedures (7 homes) and unplanned emergency placements (6 homes). Some homes (4) were represented in all of the above categories. Only one (local authority) home did not experience any of the above difficulties, significantly this home exhibited the lowest level of violence within the sample.

Lack of information at referral

Workers from nine homes stated that a common problem concerned the lack of adequate background information provided by social workers at the time of referral. Numerous examples were provided where, once young people had moved in, 'missed' details were received revealing their previous known involvement in violence (mostly physical), bullying or abuse, including the perpetration of sexually harmful behaviour. In other instances, it was not until the behaviour of the young person caused 'warning bells' for staff did their previous involvement in such activities become known. This is consistent with previous research findings and constitutes a significant area of concern (Farmer and Pollock 1998). Some workers felt that social workers purposely withheld details of this nature to ensure a successful referral.

> It's a huge problem here, not getting the right information being passed on to us. For example, we recently had a girl admitted and if we'd known her full history at the time I wouldn't have taken here, but we didn't find out till it was too late. (Manager, female)

> Referrals are a bit hit-and-miss here, we get as much information on each kid as much as possible, but we've had important facts missed and sometimes I believe that it's done on purpose just to get them in. (Senior Residential Social Worker, male)

Paradoxically, workers in one home for young people providing detailed assessments, complained that occasionally a young person's problems were 'talked up' by their social worker to secure a successful referral, when in fact their behavioural problems did not warrant such intensive intervention.

> To give you a concrete example, we had a kid here who was described as being violent and sort of throwing property around the place. When I rang up the previous home that he'd come from, he'd chucked a plate across the room and it had smashed, and that was described as very violent behaviour, and that was the only incident he had ever been involved in. (Manager, female)

This lack of information-sharing places children and young people at risk as it prohibits targetting of staff surveillance and supervision, reduces the effectiveness of intervention and leaves the needs of very challenging young people unrecognised and unmet. For example, whilst undertaking fieldwork in one home, a girl arrived who was related to another resident. It later transpired that concerns had been raised that this relative may have previously sexually abused her. The head of home said that she would not have agreed to this placement if she had known the full history at the time of referral.

Control over referrals

Overall senior staff in 6 of the 14 homes stated that they were generally unable to control referrals on the basis of a young person's previous history of violence. Although senior staff in two other homes were consulted for their assessments regarding the appropriateness of referrals, their evaluations were sometimes overridden by external managers who 'instructed' them to admit a young person against their judgement. The most frequently stated concern surrounded the referral of a young person with a known history of physical or sexual violence, whose requirements were felt to be too great for the home and where the potential risk to the safety of the wider resident group was significant. Staff in these homes felt that the needs of the current peer group were not taken into consideration when an admission was made. Workers also stated that, at times, the challenging needs of the present peer group meant that any additional referrals would, in their opinion, make the situation unmanageable; again these evaluations were sometimes disregarded. Some workers felt that the referral system was more to do with the economics of 'heads on beds' than what was in the best interests of the children. In these homes, inappropriate referrals were linked by staff to higher levels of violence.

> The gate-keeping here by senior management is appalling, that's not including the head of home ... For example, like with referrals, we'll say a particular young person is unsuitable and they overrule our assessment, even though we try and dig our feet in ... which means that young people get taken from high-risk situations and placed here into another high-risk situation. We haven't got the forum to challenge it so we can't do anything about it. (Senior Residential Social Worker, male)

> It's heads-for-beds, they don't match our skills to young people's needs. We're supposed to be long-term, but if they want a young person in that night, even if it's against our criteria we have to accept them. (Senior Residential Social Worker, female)

> You'll probably hear this phrase again and again, 'bums on beds', I don't have any doubt in my mind that we just take any, no matter if they fit in with what we are supposed to do ... we've had kids here recently who have been very messed-up, dangerous for us and for the other kids and that's not right. (Residential Social Worker, male)

It's just all about money, even here, we keep kids too long... it ends up just crisis management, and we take kids if one comes along, regardless if they are inappropriate or won't fit in with the group. (Residential Social Worker, female)

Senior staff in six homes stated they were able to influence referrals, including if there were concerns about violence. Four of these homes would accept a child or young person with challenging or violent behaviour if an acceptable care plan to address these issues was in place. This meant, for example, that the young person must be receiving professional counselling for their behaviour, that additional resources would be made available (generally to employ an extra worker to undertake individual supervision) or that an alternative placement would be found within a specified duration which could meet their needs. These senior staff stated that, ultimately, it was the head of the home's decision whether to accept or reject a referral and that, by and large, external management did not interfere. One local authority and one private home at the time of fieldwork would not accept any children or young people with violent behaviour, due to the disruption this would cause to their long-term settled resident group. Another home's referral criteria stipulated that all young people must be in full-time education, something with which many young people with violent behaviour would find difficult to comply. Sinclair and Gibbs (1998) identified that the autonomy of head of homes in decision making processes was a key factor in their evaluation of 'good homes'.

Lack of planned admission procedures

Just under three-quarters of homes appeared in principle to have a planned schedule for admissions. In general, these processes covered the gradual introduction of the new person to the home, and providing time for the established peer group to become used to the presence of another young person. It was felt that this reduced anxiety for both a newcomer and the established group, thus lessening the risk of any antagonism which may arise. It was stated that this planned process would take approximately 2–3 weeks and was, therefore, restricted to longer term placements. Staff in seven of these homes commented that, although these procedures were present in principle, in practice they were rarely adhered to. Consequently these workers felt that children and young people were rarely provided with any substantial preparation for the placement or ability to determine for themselves if this was appropriate for them.

> If our admission procedure was followed at the beginning there would be less of this, as we would be able to see if they fit into the group. Our policy for admissions takes three weeks from tea to weekend stays, but it never happens, it's just a paper exercise. (Residential Social Worker, male)

> I would prefer for us to stick to our planned admission procedure, which takes between three and four weeks, but it's all crisis management so it's not really taken into consideration, which is shocking as it affects the whole group and can lead to huge problems that may otherwise have been avoided. (Manager, female)

In homes where the preparation process involving day visits, overnight and weekend stays was followed, integration of a new resident was perceived by staff as occurring more smoothly. They felt that they were able to observe how the new arrival interacted with the other young people within the placement and develop some idea of how they would fit into the established group. In a small number of cases, a young person had the placement offer withdrawn on the basis of the negative impact they had on the residential setting within this preparation period. However, and as many staff acknowledged, young people often presented their best behaviour and their 'true' character would generally emerge much later once the 'honeymoon' period was over. Indeed, as we have already seen in Chapters 3 and 4, a new admission can challenge the composition of the peer group hierarchy, which may result in increased levels of violence. Despite this, phased introduction was viewed as a useful procedure and the lack of adherence to it was viewed as problematic. One of the main causes of this was emergency admissions to homes that were supposed to be for longer term placements only.

Emergency admissions

Staff in six homes remarked that, although their establishments were designated as long-term provision, they were nevertheless frequently used for emergency admissions, a situation which they felt often led to problems surrounding instability within the peer group. Thus, alongside the above organisational issues, the problem of having short-term placements for young people, whose needs were unknown, alongside an established peer group often caused disruption, anxiety and led to 'acting out' behaviour within the wider group. Although many of these issues were often resolved relatively quickly, this was not always the case. Interviewees provided numerous examples where emergency admissions had so disrupted the home's environment that the gradual progress made with young people in their care had been jeopardised in a matter of days.

> Just one young person can affect the whole group very negatively. All the good dynamics that have been built up over a long time crumble in a matter of days, the whole group can become unsettled, the young people panic and do stuff out of character, try and act tough so they get left alone. It can lead to real problems and all the progress they have made goes down the drain... it's very disheartening when you know it could have been avoided in the first place. (Manager, female)

Size and structure of the building

Thirty-one workers in eight homes stated that the physical size or layout of the building affected the degree of violence present. The most commonly stated problems were that either the building was too large, or that the structure of the home prohibited effective supervision. To compensate for this, some of the homes restricted young people's movements to certain areas (some of these issues are discussed further in Chapter 7). In one home, for example, many of the fire doors that were meant to be kept permanently closed were left open so that staff could more easily supervise all areas of the building. This clearly raises other safety concerns. Two homes had installed CCTV cameras. In another establishment, mirrors were strategically placed to enable staff to observe communal areas from their office. At another home the bedrooms were completely separated from the main part of the building; consequently, one worker spent most of her shift sitting on the stairs to ensure nothing untoward was occurring. On the other hand, workers in two other large homes felt that the size was an advantage, allowing young people a high degree of privacy as well as enabling a range of activities to take place simultaneously without young people competing for space. In only one case did workers feel that the building was too small. This meant that young people often became frustrated with the lack of space and privacy and caused major problems when residents needed to be kept apart. However, all the homes we visited had gardens and these were universally seen as an important space for young people to 'let steam off'.

Overall, the most important aspect of the buildings for young people themselves was said to be the general state of the décor and the amenities provided. Although most of the homes were well-decorated and had a good range of facilities, 3 of the 14 homes were singled out for criticism. Young people in these homes highlighted the dilapidated state of the building, which they found both depressing and stigmatising, especially when friends and family visited. For example, one of these settings was in a state of general disrepair, there was only one sofa (which, as young people pointed out to us, was upholstered in former British Rail material!), the TV was old and frequently did not work, there was no video or computer and the garden resembled derelict scrub land. As the young people in this home pointed out to staff at a meeting which we attended, the lack of amenities meant they were frequently bored and frustrated, which manifested itself in increased levels of disruptive behaviour. Some young people elsewhere felt that their building was too big and that it subsequently felt unsafe, especially at night-time when staff were absent. Only two homes had shared bedrooms. This was viewed very negatively by adolescents (and there was great competition between young people to acquire one of the single rooms), whereas younger children enjoyed the companionship it provided. However, sharing does involve obvious risks – consequently the residential home for adolescents had plans to discontinue this practice in the near future.

Function of the children's home

In their explanations of differing levels of violence, 23 workers raised, in a number of ways, the issue of the home's function. When asked what was the specific function of their residential home, many participants either offered the age-range they accommodated and/or the length of stay. Apart from these two factors, most homes did not appear to have any more of a definite remit, reflecting previous research findings (see Berridge and Brodie 1998). Exceptions included two units that catered specifically for young offenders or provided young people with an assessment of their long-term needs, and two homes that were used to prepare children for fostering.

Overall, seven homes stated that their general functions were frequently disregarded, leading to difficult mixes of young people by age or length of stay. Thus, although eight homes were thought to be offering long-term provision, many experienced frequent short-term placements. Short- to medium-term homes were found to accommodate young people for much longer than the prescribed time-period, in one case for over three years longer than originally planned. Workers in these circumstances argued that these breaches in the homes' specifications increased the likelihood of violence.

> We're supposed to be long-term here but we're constantly used for emergency and short-term placements... For the kids who see this as their home, this is very difficult, especially as the settled dynamics change when a new admission comes, especially if we can't meet their needs... the levels of violence and abuse go right up then. (Manager, male)

> Some kids have been here for three or four years, supposedly the length of stay is only up to one year. Inevitably, the kids get pissed off with the lack of movement and we struggle to accommodate their needs on such a long-term basis, so they become frustrated and this can lead to acting out behaviour and confrontation. (Residential Social Worker, female)

Ten young people raised the issue of the function of homes in discussions with us about violence. These reflected workers' ideas about the placement of 'challenging' young people and age restrictions. Young people thought it was inappropriate to place especially challenging young people in 'ordinary' homes due to the adverse effect this had on their living environment. Most often, this referred to young people who exhibited highly violent or criminal behaviour or those who had mental health problems. Two young people in a long-term home spoke about the high level of stability they enjoyed and praised the role their head of home had taken in refusing the admission of young people who might disrupt this. In contrast, young people in another establishment specialising in accommodating very disruptive young people whose previous behaviour had led to multiple placement breakdowns, revelled in the 'prestige' this reputation brought, as is illustrated by the young person below.

It's a pretty good home this, 'cause when you come in this home, you have to be pretty mature to come in this home 'cause it's an hard home to be in, you know 'cause it's got a reputation this home has for like... you know if like people are annoying, they'll threaten to send them here. (Bronwyn, aged 14)

Staffing levels

Observation and supervision were seen as important components in professional protection strategies, so it is unsurprising that staffing levels were highlighted in relation to this. Overall, workers in four of the 14 homes seemed satisfied with the ratio of staff to young people. Generally in these homes, 1 staff full-time member was on duty for every 2/3 young people. Furthermore, staff in five homes insisted that they had adequate levels of staff. Yet, in three of these homes, this was mainly because they had not been operating at full capacity for some period. These workers warned us that this situation may change at any time which would, in their opinion, cause problems with staffing ratios. In four homes, staff felt that staffing levels represented a significant problem that needed to be addressed. For example, in one home, two staff members were expected to supervise over ten young people in a large building, as well as undertake administrative work at the same time. This often left a single worker on the 'shopfloor' whilst their colleague concentrated on office-based tasks. In contrast, both Berridge and Brodie (1998) and Sinclair and Gibbs (1998) concluded that staffing levels in residential care were not a particular problem at the time of their studies. Importantly, they both also concluded that staffing ratios in themselves were not a main determinant of the quality of care.

On a somewhat different aspect of staffing, one disconcerting practice had been implemented in one of the homes in our sample. Staff shifts were from 3.30 p.m. to 9 a.m. In between these hours, no staff were present in the building as all the young people attended the establishment's own school. Not only does this raise issues for us concerning the reduced opportunities staff have for both formal and informal information-sharing and team building, as well as other professional and administrative duties, but also for the welfare of the young people. For example, while we were undertaking fieldwork at the home a 'flu outbreak occurred, with some of the young people becoming unwell and being prescribed antibiotics. But all had to attend school, with some spending the day in the sickroom, rather then being tucked-up in their own beds. This seemed unacceptable not only to us but also to the young people concerned.

Young people highlighted two staffing issues. First, some complained that due to low staffing levels, workers were rarely available to talk with, except at limited prearranged times. Second, young people stated that, because of the depleted staff levels at night, this period was often the most unsafe for (generally pre-planned) violent episodes.

Having explored the main organisational factors that workers, and to a lesser degree young people, associated with increased levels of violence, the final section of this chapter related these to the homes' position on the violence continuum, introduced in Chapter 2.

Relating organisational and structural factors to the violence continnum

To recapitulate, the continuum of violence was developed to provide a theoretical mechanism by which we could capture the overall impact of violence within the 14 residential settings. We drew on Kelly's (1987) definition of violence as a continuum of physical, emotional, verbal and sexual abuses of power at individual and group levels. A continuum can thus incorporate a range of violent behaviours from isolated flashes of physical violence to systematic, prolonged verbal attacks. Thus, young people's and staff's evaluations of the impact of violence within each home have been combined and reordered to aid comparison (see Figure 6.1). As previously stated, we are not presenting this model as an explanatory construct, but rather as an exploratory framework. Bearing this in mind, the figures below present each of the organisational factors identified by participants alongside the individual home's position on the continuum. Following this, some of the structural factors associated with each home are presented to provide context for the organisational processes.

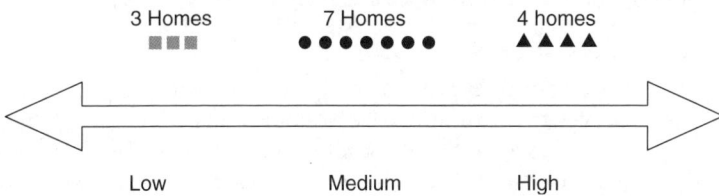

Figure 6.1 Diagrammatic representation of the violence continuum

Notes
Low-level violence only   ■■■
Intermittent high-level violence ●●●●●●●
Persistent high-level violence   ▲▲▲▲

Organisational factors

Some interesting findings emerge from this impressionist overview of the data (Table 6.1). First, it appears that the residential homes with the greatest level of violence (triangular) are also those with the most negative organisational

Table 6.1 Organisational factors and the violence continuum

Organisational factors	Problematic	Non-problematic	N/A
Lack of information	▲▲▲●●●●● ■	▲●● ■ ■	
Control over 'violent' referrals	▲▲▲●●●●●	▲●● ■ ■ ■	
Lack of admission procedures	▲●●●●● ■ ■	▲●●● ■	▲▲
Emergency admissions over criteria	▲●●●●●	▲● ■ ■ ■	▲▲●
Site	▲▲▲● ■ ■ ■	▲●●●●●●	
Function	▲▲▲●●● ■	▲●●●● ■ ■	
Staffing levels	▲▲▲●	▲●●●●●● ■ ■ ■	

Note: See notes section, Figure 6.1.

factors. In contrast, homes located towards the lower end of the continuum (square) seem to present fewer of these problem factors. Homes within the middle range (circle) are more evenly distributed across the two categories. Overall, the above dispersal seems to suggest that homes can bear some negative organisational factors without this impacting on the overall experience of violence. For example, although all low-level violent residential homes had inappropriate premises, this factor may have been compensated for by the relatively high staffing ratios also found within these homes. However, the accumulative impact of negative organisational factors is apparent. Consequently, it may indeed be futile, as Brown *et al.* (1998) argue, to try to change violent 'cultures' within residential homes without first removing organisational barriers to improvement.

Structural factors

Two possible associations appear to emerge when we impose structural factors onto the violence continuum: size of home and gender mix (Table 6.2). Both of these findings are reflected in Sinclair and Gibbs' (1998) large-scale, quantitative and qualitative study of 223 children in 48 homes. Homes with more than six residents do seem from our indices to increase the likelihood that violence may occur. Similarly, Sinclair and Gibbs also found that in relation to their positive intermediate outcome measures (which included among other things bullying and physical violence), residential homes with six or fewer places offered higher standards of care. Our findings also indicate a tentative association between single-gender resident groups and increased violence and verbal attacks. This pattern increases if we take into account the fact that one high violence home, although located in the mixed-gender category, had in practice (but not in remit) been single-sex (female) for most of the previous 12 months. If we move this into the single-gender category, three out the four high violence (triangular) homes would be situated there.

Table 6.2 Structural factors and the violence continuum

Structural factors		
Age	Adolescents ▲▲▲▲●●●●● ■■■	Younger children ●●
Gender	Mixed ▲▲●●●●●●●■■	Single-sex (male) ▲▲●■
Size of home	Under 6 placements ●●●■■	6 placements and over ▲▲▲▲●●●●■

Note: See notes section, Figure 6.1.

Table 6.3 Sector and the violence continuum

	Local authority	Private	Voluntary
Sector	▲●●●●●●■■	▲▲■	▲●

Note: See notes section, Figure 6.1.

Table 6.4 Length of stay and the violence continuum

	Short	Short/medium	Medium/long	Variable
Stay	▲	▲●●	▲●●●●●■■	▲■

Note: See notes section, Figure 6.1.

Regarding age-range, although all four high violence (triangular) homes were situated in the adolescent category, we had only two homes for younger children in our sample and should therefore be cautious in seeking any conclusions from this. In fact Sinclair and Gibbs (1998) found that violence towards other children was far more common among younger residents (under 12 years of age) than those aged 16 or over (90 per cent as opposed to 27 per cent respectively). In explanation, the authors surmised that as residential care is rarely used for the under 12s, it is likely that their behaviour made it impossible to be contained elsewhere. Indeed, on a later ratings scale, it was found that younger children were much more 'disturbed' than their older peers.

Our sample distribution prevents us from drawing conclusions regarding either sector or length of stay (Tables 6.3 and 6.4). To provide some context, Sinclair and Gibbs (1998) compared 2 samples of children's homes, provided by the public (48) and private (15) sectors. As they state, it is not known whether in the private sector the discipline of the market has resulted in higher standards, or that the desire for profit had driven down the quality of care. Overall, young people in public homes in their study reported a much higher degree of 'misery' than their counterparts in private establishments. This difference was mostly accounted for by increased levels of 'bullying' and sexually harmful behaviour. In addition, workers in the private homes were more satisfied with their jobs, had clearer expectations of their role and had fewer concerns over keeping order. In our small qualitative sample, only one of our three private sector homes reflects this wider picture.

Summary points

- Most homes in our study had produced policies and procedures setting-out their expectations of residents' conduct, including violence. These were included in *moving-in packs* for new residents.
- Staff were concerned and confused about their ability to physically restrain young people when required.
- Some staff felt that violent behaviour could be attributed to the lack of information provided when new residents were referred; their home's inability to challenge inappropriate referrals; poorly planned admissions and emergency referrals.
- The large size and layout of some buildings made young people's behaviours more difficult to supervise and control.
- Young people were concerned that, in some homes, the low staffing levels made it difficult for them to find opportunities to talk with staff. Also, the lack of staff working through the night meant that this was the most unsafe period.
- Though any conclusions are only tentative, there was some suggestion that homes experiencing most problems with violence contained the greatest concentration of negative organisational factors. In addition, larger homes in our sample (more than six residents) and single-gender homes also seemed to experience more violence and verbal attacks.

7
Evaluating Working Practices

> They are supposed to restrain us but it depends really...depending who's on (duty) and who's watching.
>
> (Colin, aged 15)

We now turn to consider young people's and staff's experiences and evaluations of responses to violence. Accounts of the level of intervention associated with each of the main forms of violence will be explored, including consistency within teams, problems of identification and mechanisms for information-sharing. Building on this, the different forms of intervention employed within homes, both informal and formal, will be discussed. Perceptions surrounding the appropriateness of these measures, evaluations of their success and young people's opinions about staff actions will all be examined. The final section of this chapter considers working methods for anticipating and reducing peer violence within residential settings. However, before focusing on intervention, we initially explore young people's own help-seeking strategies, first in relation to peers and then to staff.

Seeking support and issues of disclosure

'It's good to talk'/'Can't talk won't talk': the genderisation of seeking emotional support

The majority of young people reported using their peers as a source of support. While most felt that they could not disclose all their experiences to staff, almost all residents could talk to another young person within their current placement reflecting a positive aspect of peer relations within residential care that previous research has highlighted (Emond 2002). Indeed, peers were the first port of call in all incidents later disclosed to staff. But the type of support sought and perceptions towards seeking support differed greatly between the genders. For example boys were predominantly disclosing their experiences to their male peers and seeking support only in terms of intervention. And as the following extracts illustrate, the main type of intervention took the form of physical contact violence framed within ideas of retaliation, protection and revenge:

Stewart: If he (fellow resident) does it to me (physically assaults him) sort of thing...but I know for a fact he wouldn't do it to me because I know him...
Interviewer: What would you do if he did hit you?
Stewart: I would pick up the phone and I tell you what, in five minutes he'd be dead...and he if he hit Frank (friend) I would jump on him.

(Stewart, aged 15)

On closer analysis of the boys' accounts regarding seeking support, many consciously avoided discussing with their peers how they felt using a discourse of 'can't talk, won't talk' often framed within a narrative of personal responsibility, where they felt they had to take it upon themselves to deal with their experiences of violence:

At the end of the day I'm responsible for...that is something I have had to learn living in care and that is you have to be able to stick-up for yourself and what you think...otherwise people just take the mick. (Martin, aged 14)

I sorted it out myself...'cause I'm not little like Neil...nobody is going to pick on me like that. (Ross, aged 15)

I have a good relationship with staff, but I just can't talk to them about why I do things or how I feel. I've never been able to do that. (Donatus, aged 14)

However, there were some boys in mixed homes who had developed close (platonic) relationships with older girls within the home and whom they were able to confide in and sometimes share their insecurities:

Connor: I've known Jessie for a long time, since I went out with Vicky and then I moved in and got to know her even more, so...
Interviewer: So is she like you're main kind of emotional support (nods) if you needed to chat to someone, if you had problems?
Connor: I speak to Jessie.

(Connor, aged 14)

Girls were much more likely to use their female peers as a source of emotional support. While they too drew upon their friends to retaliate, protect or seek revenge on perceived 'bullies' or 'irritants' (see Chapter 3), they also took solace in sharing their experiences with each other as the following quotes illustrate:

Alicia: I do feel happy, but most of the time I go talking to my friends (female), because they understand and they've most probably been through it.
Interviewer: So would you rather talk to someone who's been through the same experience as you?
Alicia: Yeah yeah.

(Alicia, aged 14)

Thus, for girls, disclosing and sharing experiences with their peers was an acceptable response and form of interaction and often took the form of *emotional* support. For the majority of boys, seeking *functional* support, often in the form of physical violence (framed within a clear narrative of revenge, protection and retaliation) was the only acceptable response, because of the perceived association of emotion with femininity and emotional release with emasculinisation (Frydenberg 1997). Thus, a consequence of boys' non-disclosure also meant that many serious incidents of physical violence and intimidation went undetected.

In contrast to young people's use of peers, staff were rarely used as a source of emotional support following violence. While there were gender differences regarding young people's reluctance to use staff in this way, there were a number of explanations offered by both boys and girls. Some of the reasons included:

Lack of trust (the feeling that staff as adults wouldn't believe them, particularly in cases of male–female sexual harassment)

> I would never tell a member of staff... because I don't trust adults. When I was living back where I used to live, the reason I was always out was because I don't like adults. I try to spend as little time as possible with them. (Melissa, aged 15)

> They just think it's the girls make accusations... I don't think they took us at all seriously. (Megan, aged 16)

Futility (the feeling that staff would not be able to solve the problem)

Interviewer: If you did tell staff what do you think they could do about it?
Cole: Nothing.
Interviewer: There's nothing you think they could do?
Cole: Well all they could do is put kids on one-to-one (supervision) and when the kids come off one-to-one they just start again.

(Tony, aged 14)

Make matters worse (the feeling that staff involvement may exacerbate the situation)

> Simon: Every kid in this unit has been bullied.
> Interviewer: And did you tell a member of staff?
> Simon: Not really.
> Interviewer: So do you think the staff then didn't know what was happening?
> Simon: Well, no they don't know because no-one was telling them, it just makes it worse.
> Interviewer: Do you think? (nods) Is that why you didn't tell?
> Simon: Yeah.
>
> (Simon, aged 15)

Lack of empathy (feeling that staff cannot 'understand' or 'relate' to young people's experience/lives because they have no direct 'personal' experience)

> (discussing another boy's challenging behaviour)
> The staff are like trying to get him help and things like that but most of them just don't understand. (Lauryn, aged 14)

> Interviewer: Are there reasons why you don't tell staff (about fighting in the night)?
> Dan: They patronise us.
>
> (Dan, aged 15)

> I just can't talk to none of these members of staff. (Richard, aged 14)

Loss of privileges (fear that informing staff could entail loss of privileges for both young person involved and peers)

> Interviewer: Would you rather staff did or didn't know about the fighting?
> Jonathan: Didn't.
> Interviewer: Why's that?
> Jonathan: Because we'd all get in trouble and we wouldn't be able to go out on trips and have our money and everything.
>
> (Jonathan, aged 14)

Culture of non-disclosure (often fear of being thought a 'grass')

> Interviewer: Do you think staff know (about the frequent fighting at night)?

Stewart: Some of it they find out about, but not much 'cause they'd get it worse if they went to staff and grassed.

(Stewart, aged 15)

Interviewer: What do you think might happen if you told staff?
Ewan: Makes you a grass doesn't it?

(Ewan, aged 13)

Indeed many of the above accounts suggest that the cultural and social divide between adults/professionals and children/clients is a powerful barrier to communication between staff and young people. Again there were gender differences regarding why staff were not deployed as a form of emotional support and the ways in which – and situations that – staff were indeed called upon to support young people.

Identical reasons were reported for boys not to involve staff as a source of emotional support (although there were one or two boys who disclosed their feelings to key workers or social workers). Informal codes of 'grassing' particularly among older boys were strong and often woven into wider peer group dynamics (especially the more hierarchical settings). When staff were approached by boys, it was often to request their intervention in the form of restraint, formal warnings, sanctions (e.g. loss of privileges) and sometimes police involvement. Indeed staff were often only sought in cases of high-level physical violence.

Girls' reasons not to involve staff as a source of emotional support included were very different and linked to particular types of violence. First, some girls (and one or two boys) reported being 'too scared' to involve staff:

Too scared

We were just too scared to say anything... he didn't have no limits man, he'd quite happily slice someone's eyes out... he was just sick. (Megan, aged 16)

Although more girls reported being too scared to inform staff, it may have been more difficult for boys to admit to their fear of involving staff, because of the difficulty of positioning themselves as vulnerable and 'weak'. Other girls avoided involving staff because they feared repercussions and as the following quote illustrates, 'didn't want to get into trouble':

Avoid trouble

Interviewer: So, did she want to tell staff that they were doing this to her? (racist name-calling)

Melissa: She didn't really want to get into trouble by staff, that is why she always came to me to speak to me.

(Melissa, aged 16)

The need to maintain an emotional distance from staff in an attempt to maintain some privacy was especially important to many girls, as one succinctly points out:

Privacy

Some things I just keep private... it's none of their (staff's) business. (Christine, aged 14)

Indeed, the need for privacy was strongly linked with the high levels of non-disclosure and reporting of physical sexual violence and sexual harassment – the implications of which are discussed later in this chapter. Conversely, however, girls were more likely to involve staff in both low-level and high-level physical forms of violence and were twice as likely to involve staff in verbal conflicts and disputes. In homes that actively fostered positive relationships between staff and young people, however, there were fewer gender differences and young people readily used staff as emotional support and were happy for them to intervene, perceiving such intervention as successful. Such a culture, however, applied only to two homes, one for younger children, the other for a mixed-age range.

Gail: If anyone's getting a bit angry, they just go to staff and talk to the staff... or they can get to talk to one of the kids who live here.
Interviewer: And that sort of makes, can make people feel better then?
Gail: Yeah yeah.

(Gail, aged 14)

We do go to staff, we do. We do have quite a good relationship with staff that are here, so if there is a really big problem and we felt we couldn't talk to any of the other young people, we'll all go to a member of staff. (Kelly, aged 13)

In addition, the residential home complaints procedures were generally not viewed as relevant by young people who felt disinclined to use such formalised processes. Some young people had used the complaints procedures for more formal aspects of their residential experiences, especially issues surrounding the appropriateness of placements and their social workers. They were less willing to use such formal systems for personal problems; overall, only eight young people had used the complaints procedure, and nearly all these related to incidents of high impact physical violence.

Just under half of homes (6) did use some form of children's advocacy service, which was to a greater or lesser extent independent from the management of the home. In the majority of homes this had still not been implemented although every child who is looked after should have access to this service. However, young people did not routinely use this as a way of addressing their personal concerns, in fact no young people we spoke to had used this service regarding personal issues. Advocates were sometimes used to assist young people with broader organisational aspects of their residential experiences.

The reluctance of many young people to disclose to staff their personal experiences of violence is an obvious barrier to safeguarding young people's welfare (see also Lindsay 1991, Aiers and Kettle 1998, Wallis and Frost 1998). This is particularly the case with covert violence. Furthermore, other issues including staff consistency, differential expectations of behaviour and child/professional relationships, all significantly impact on young people's residential experiences in this area, as we shall see in the following section.

Evaluations of staff interventions

Physical violence

Forty-five young people (from 10 homes) spoke to us about intervention and physical violence; 19 young people referred only to low-level violence and 26 to both low- and high-level. The most striking finding concerning intervention was the consistency in both staff's and young people's accounts of overt physical violence within homes. In all homes where physical violence was present, both groups categorically stated that all forms of 'public' physical violence between young people would trigger some form of intervention by staff, up to and including the use of physical restraint if conciliatory methods had been unsuccessful. Reassuringly, all young people stated that in their experience most forms of physical violence, if observed by staff, would be swiftly stopped.

Yet this does not, mean that all staff and young people thought this was always the correct response to physical violence in all contexts (see vignette analysis in Chapter 5). A minority of staff (14) stated that, on occasions, retaliation to continual provocation involving low-level physical violence was a justified reaction, which did not, in their evaluations, always necessarily require staff intervention. However, even these staff stated that they would always intervene in line with practice guidelines.

> We have to stop everything, which means that the kids never get an opportunity to develop self-control, as we're always providing the boundaries very early on so they don't learn it for themselves just in case they get hurt... but guidelines have to be followed. (Residential Social Worker, male)

Hence, although staff exhibited differences in opinion about what, if anything, constituted a 'fair' or 'justified' use of force, they nevertheless stated that these personal evaluations did not interfere with the consistency of their professional response to overt physical violence. Indeed, only two workers could recall instances where staff had purposely failed to intervene in a physical fight between young people.

Young people provided a slightly different picture to the one offered by staff regarding consistency in working practices. Over one-third of young people (26) provided us with first hand accounts of physical violence in nine homes where staff had either failed to intervene or had delayed their response. Half of these accounts were from the perpetrators of the physical violence and over one-third from bystanders who supported the attacker. Only a minority of victims spoke to us about staff non-intervention, possible reasons for this are suggested later in this section. In most of these instances the physical violence was low impact, although 14 young people spoke about high impact physical violence (in regard to the severity of the attack). In none of the examples provided were weapons involved and most cases relayed to us concerned individual rather than group violence.

> I mean if staff get annoyed and that, and kids have been threatening them and screaming in their faces and winding us up, then sometimes they can be a bit slow to stop the fight you know. They'd walk over to it as they are fighting and not run to split it up. (Tim, aged 12)
>
> They are supposed to restrain us, but it depends really. If you've been warned like to stop annoying that person, and then that person turns round and hits you, some won't do anything. It depends what kind of day it's been really, if it's been really hectic they might just leave it... depending who's on and who's watching. (Colin, aged 15)
>
> Wendy was picking on the younger ones and eventually they beat her up, and the worker that was on said that it was her own fault because she started picking on the little ones and so she didn't stop it. (Bianca, aged 13)

When we looked at the contexts in which accounts of 'non-' or 'delayed' intervention occurred we found that the majority of cases surrounded very specific circumstances. In addition, all the young people identified only a minority of staff in each home who would intervene in this selective manner.

Professional non-intervention was generally contextualised within young people's accounts of 'deserving victims', perhaps more accurately described in this instance as *provocative-victims*. The majority of these violent attacks occurred in the context of retorts to deliberate and repeated provocation by the 'victim', often over a prolonged period. When we compared accounts within individual homes we found a high degree of consensus concerning which residents, both past and present, were perceived as being provocative-victims. Accompanying this was a general recognition amongst the wider peer group of the frustration and misery that the behaviour of these young people could cause, although this was often countered with the statement that it did not affect them to the same degree.

> Everything was nice here before she came, now it's all sad 'cause she just makes everything worse, 'cause she just winds us all up and ruins all our games...I hate her and I hate living here now. (Shyama, aged 9)
>
> We all got annoyed with her behaviour...a few of us did actually physically hurt her...but staff couldn't do anything, 'cause they had warned her that if we did hit her they're going to turn their backs 'cause she drove us to it. It would be wrong normally, but because of what she's been doing...they didn't get in trouble for it. (Melissa, aged 16)

In nearly all these homes, young people stated that staff had attempted to minimise the provoking behaviour; unfortunately in most cases this intervention had been unsuccessful, probably reflecting the very complex problems and needs of the young people concerned. In a number of cases, the increased staff attention that provocative-victims received meant that the wider group, and particularly younger children, often became resentful, which consequently exacerbated the situation. The most common advice from staff was for young people to ignore the provoking behaviour as it was only attention-seeking. However, many felt this showed how staff did not understand or take seriously the pressure of living in an environment where someone is constantly confrontational.

> ...he just stared calling me 'dirty little slag' and the staff have gone 'just ignore him', but how you ignore someone who is in your ear going 'you dirty little slag' and everything? You can't. (Megan, aged 16)
>
> She was bullying us 'cause she was winding us up on purpose to make us hit her so she could run off to staff and get us in trouble...she was coming up in my face and saying things about mother, so I hit her. We're told to ignore her, but how can you?...It's not fair on the rest of us having to put up with it. (Bianca, aged 13)

Some young people stated that individual staff had forewarned the provocative-victim that if they persisted in their aggravating behaviour, they would cease to intervene in any subsequent reprisals. In the majority of these cases the sanctions that would have routinely accompanied the use of physical violence were reduced.

Consequently, in these specific contexts, the non-intervention, or more accurately the delayed intervention, of some staff was generally viewed by the majority of the young people concerned as reasonable, as long as the violence in *their* estimation was 'acceptable' (which may not necessarily relate to the research categorisations). This may reflect the fact that many of these accounts were from the perpetrators of the physical violence, although one-third of accounts came from witnesses who shared this view. Overall, young people felt that the actions of these staff reflected their ability to view the situation from their perspective and to recognise the unreasonable demands that such antagonistic behaviour placed on their self-control.

We spoke to a number of young people identified by others as provocative-victims. Often, these young people described themselves as victims of bullying and of being excluded from the peer group for unknown reasons. None of these young people stated that they felt they held any responsibility for the actions of the other young people towards them, although we knew from staff that they had been spoken to about their provoking behaviour on numerous occasions. Only a few of these young people spoke to us about staff's non-intervention. Generally these young people craved staff attention and approval and it may perhaps have been too uncomfortable for them to admit that, on some occasions, these same staff intentionally failed to protect them.

> Interviewer: Why do you think staff didn't try and stop them hitting you right away?
> Brennan: I'm not sure... They (staff) do try... the other kids push me around... they think they're staff but they're not... I tell staff and they sort it out... I think they (staff member on duty) probably didn't see properly or something 'cause I can't really see why they'd let them hit me.
> (Brennan, aged 12)

It appears from young people's accounts that non-interventionist practices most commonly occurred when a clear consensus emerged which identified a young person as a persistent provocateur. This enabled a climate of victim culpability to be established within the home (at least between the majority of young people and some individual staff). However, most young people stated that, outside this specific context, non-intervention in physical violence did not generally occur and was looked on unfavourably.

Some young people (8 – mainly victims or witnesses) identified that a minority of staff had been disinclined to respond to a physical incident, even when there was no prior provocation ascribed to the victim. This was generally viewed as unacceptable and being staff-related rather than reflecting young people's circumstances.

> I had a fight here once and I didn't feel safe after that 'cause staff didn't even come up, three staff members were just sitting downstairs and they could hear thumping and the screaming and swearing and it was only

'cause a young person heard it and got staff. They couldn't be bothered to go and see what was going on. (Claire, aged 14)

The perceived success of interventions into physical violence related largely to the subject position (perpetrator or victim) of the young people themselves. As most acts of physical violence were viewed as justified by the young assailants, any intervention was generally viewed as an unwarranted intrusion. A minority of perpetrators, however, stated that on specific occasions they were pleased the intervention had occurred, fearing they would otherwise have been unable to control the level of physical violence, described in terms of 'losing it'. These young people felt uncomfortable with their loss of control and the possible consequences this may have had in respect to criminal charges and being moved from the home.

Interviewer: So were you glad that staff intervened in that situation?
Melissa: Yes, 'cause I knew that I could have hurt him really badly and I could have gotten myself into a lot of trouble, put in secure 'cause I had gone to him with a knife but staff noticed what was going on and stopped it.
(Melissa, aged 16)

In contrast, victims generally confirmed that they welcomed the intervention at the time of the incident, at least in respect to low-level violence. However young people's assessments of interventions into high-level violence present a very different picture. Although the majority of young people were happy with the immediate intervention, mainly due to saving them from possible physical injury, this positive evaluation diminished over time. Consequently, 21 young people indicated that staff interventions had been unsuccessful due to the inability of the response to stop the violence recurring. This may reflect the fact that, as we have seen, most high-level physical violence took place within wider power dynamics rather than isolated arguments. In fact, intervention into all forms of violence was generally viewed by young people as being most successful in relation to the resolution of individual disputes.

We also asked young people about staff's ability to de-escalate a potentially violent situation. Most young people described more positive outcomes of de-escalation and, indeed, intervention generally when they had developed a good relationship with the staff member involved. This indicates the need to situate intervention in the wider working practices of relationship-building between staff and young people. Staff who received the most positive feedback were those who used (non-humiliating) humour, were seen as being able to empathise with young people, listened to their views and took their grievance seriously. They were also seen as being impartial and interested in the young person's wider social world. Staff who received less positive assessments were those who did not take young people's views seriously, or where young people lacked trust in their consistency and ability to respond in an impartial manner or were viewed as just 'doing a job'. This was evident in relation to young people's assessments of all forms of violence, not just physical.

> Like, if Alex (worker) intervenes then that's OK 'cause he's pretty OK for a worker. You can have a laugh with him... he'll listen to what you've got to say and won't take sides... but some here don't give a shit and just blame us for everything, even when it's not our fault, don't listen to a word we have to say. (Ewan, aged 13)
>
> How you respond depends who's on duty, 'cause if it's a staff member you like then you're more likely to listen to their point of view and think about what they've said, but if it's a member of staff who doesn't take you seriously or listen to our side of things, why should we listen to them... some are here 'cause they care, others 'cause they're paid and it shows. (Alicia, aged 14)

Staff's strategies generally reflected young people's earlier evaluations. Many stated that staff used contrasting methods to try to defuse a violent situation from developing. Staff acknowledged that often individual factors played a major role in how effective their efforts at defusion would be, specifically how well liked or respected the worker was by the young people concerned. When we asked staff how they recognised that a situation was developing, responses generally surrounded the intuitive ability of staff to sense that something was amiss due to the atmosphere in the children's home.

> You just get to know something is up... you can feel the vibe that's going around. (Residential Social Worker, male)
>
> Generally you can sense something is not right, an atmosphere, a feeling you just get. It's difficult to explain, I think it just comes with experience and a bit of common sense. (Manager, male)

Play-fighting

The only situation where young people were allowed to engage in some form of physical violence was with play-fighting, although this was rarely officially sanctioned. In nearly all the homes (12) play-fighting between young people was not allowed. This was generally due to the play aspect quickly escalating to real violence, where one or more of the participants might be physically harmed. Staff nevertheless generally perceived play-fighting as a normal aspect of (generally male) childhood behaviour and, thus was considered acceptable in specific contexts. But the majority of these staff felt that this aspect of normal peer relations could not be safely transferred to the residential setting. Staff considered that the young people with whom they worked lacked the self-control needed to ensure they stayed within the rules. In addition, some staff felt that what may be genuinely perceived as play-fighting by some may not be viewed in the same way by other young people. Play-fighting may be used as a camouflage for the actual power inequalities.

> We certainly don't encourage play-fighting because, inevitably, someone does get hurt... we nip it in the bud and that might seem a bit strict, but often you find that one of the kids is quite relieved 'cause it's usually the stronger one who starts it. (Residential Social Worker, male)
> Play-fighting is strictly prohibited, 'cause in a blink of an eye it gets out of control, they just don't know when to stop. (Manager, female)

A minority of staff (9) felt that play-fighting allowed children a safe form of physical expression and that adhering to the associated 'rules' enabled young people to develop their self-control. Some staff felt that with careful supervision children should be allowed to engage in play-fighting as part of normal development.

> It's healthy, they're just like little puppies. There's not any kind of aggression in their play-fighting, there is a purpose behind it, although they don't realise that. It's like a form of bonding and rule-learning, but mostly other staff do not see it as acceptable. (Residential Social Worker, female)

As these staff worked in homes where play-fighting was not formally allowed, this led to some inconsistency between staff and possible confusion for the young people in their care, as the above participant later observed.

> I suppose the lack of consistency must be confusing for them. I'd not really thought of it in that way before. (Residential Social Worker, female)

Play-fighting was allowed in two homes but within very strict guidelines. For example, one of the homes for younger children allowed play-fighting in certain contexts and always with staff supervision. In these play situations staff constantly reminded children of the rules and policed them strictly. For example, 'wrestling' contact was allowed in moderation but punching, slapping, hitting or kicking was prohibited, with the game being stopped immediately if any of the above actions were used.

Although play-fighting was generally not allowed between young people, in some homes it did occur between staff and young people, most specifically between males. In this context, staff would jokingly 'fight or wrestle' with boys in an atmosphere of joint camaraderie. This was often seen as a way of cementing male relationships and having 'a laugh', an important element in residential work with children and young people. In the course of our fieldwork, we observed a number of such situations where young people initiated play-fights and seemed to enjoy the opportunity to have 'safe' male physical contact with adults, which they may otherwise be unable to experience.

But in one home play-fighting seemed to be used routinely, even when it may not have been the most appropriate form of interaction. In one instance, two young men had just been reprimanded for fighting, when the same staff member started a play-fight with another young person. In the same home, an inexperienced staff member joined in with the general ethos of play-fighting, perhaps slightly unwillingly. The situation soon got out of control and another staff member had to intervene to restore order, and save his colleague from asphyxiation! The possibility that play-fighting may also be used inappropriately by staff as a mechanism to initiate physical contact with young people for their own satisfaction is also a risk that must be considered. In addition, we sometimes questioned the use of play-fighting in situations where violence was present in the peer group, or where such behaviour may serve to reinforce the 'hard masculinities' present in some homes.

Non-contact violence

Young people's assessment of the success of interventions into forms of non-contact violence were less straightforward, and overall less favourable. Discussions were generally phrased in terms of bullying. Young people felt that this was often the most difficult aspect of residential life and one which was the most difficult to control due to its hidden nature. Most young people stated that, as a general rule, staff did not allow bullying to occur, although how successful they were at ensuring this was sporadic. Overall, 26 victims of bullying provided assessments concerning intervention. Of these 17 felt the strategies used by staff had been unsuccessful as the intervention had failed to stop the bullying.

> I didn't want to tell staff 'cause it's like I should be able to deal with this but then when you do it doesn't help so what's the point? He just stopped being so obvious about getting me, like he'd wait till I was alone or make it seem like an accident that I got pushed. Then he was taken off 'cause he'd done something outside and I can't tell you how happy I was, like having a party or something, 'cause I knew he'd not be coming back. (Ross, aged 13)

The above extract illustrates the difficulty of intervening in bullying cultures when victims are reluctant to report their experiences and 'bullies' often simply adopt more masked tactics. The reasons why children may be reluctant to identify themselves as victims of bullying are varied. Their perceived inability to exert control over the situation and the lack of power this implies may be crucial components in this process. Another possible reason may be more pragmatic – fear of reprisals. Unfortunately, in some cases discussed with us, the intervention itself was viewed by young people as contributing to the problem.

> I told staff in the end and then the kid goes, 'ah you've told staff you're dead now', and that's when I really got scared and he done it all over again, bullied me, but just did it more hidden, still punched me, kicked me...In the end he actually wounded me, broke my wrist, I couldn't move 'cause it was such pain and then he got arrested and left. (Ewan, aged 13)

The intervention strategies aimed at changing bullying behaviour were often viewed by young people as being largely ineffectual. Most stated that 'bullies don't listen' and many held very pessimistic views on the potential for change. Some individuals did, however, talk to us about their previous bullying behaviours and how staff helped them to see that what they were doing was unacceptable.

> Until staff sat me down and really talked about what I was doing and how it made Peter feel, I didn't really think I was doing much...but the way they put it made me think it was unfair of me and that I was sort of picking on him. So I stopped then. (Adrian, aged 16)

None of the young people who had been persistently bullied stated that the bullying had stopped without staff intervention – and the only intervention that worked, according to most victims, was the permanent removal of the perpetrator. Some positive outcomes of intervention where both the victim and the bully had remained in the same establishment were provided but these were rare. Generally, these positive outcomes concerned bullying which had occurred for only a limited time and where the pattern was not ingrained. They were also more likely to occur in homes which had developed good relationships between young people and staff and where all forms of violence, including bullying, were uncommon. However, in the majority of cases young people stated that the bullying stopped completely only when the perpetrator had left the setting.

Young people showed very little concern towards the needs of the young people inflicting the pain, or interest in why they may be acting in this way. Many felt the only way they would change would be to experience bullying themselves. Others felt they should be isolated from other young people, holding out little hope that they would be able to change their behaviour. Unsurprisingly, all young people prioritised their own needs and the needs of the wider group over those of the individual bully; whereas young people often felt that workers prioritised the needs of the minority over those of the group.

Some level of staff inconsistency was reported by young participants in both identifying and responding to this form of intimidation. In five homes, some young people (14) stated that *individual* staff were 'known' to let bullying occur unchallenged. In another home all young people told us that the majority of the staff team (except one worker) had ignored or minimised the presence of severe physical and non-contact bullying over a prolonged period.

Unlike physical violence, this non-intervention was predominantly viewed as unacceptable. Bullying was seen as a misuse of power and, therefore, staff non-intervention could not be morally justified as with provocative-victims, but was seen to be solely staff-related. When asked why they felt staff may be acting in this manner, the main reasons proposed were 'laziness', being unconcerned with young people's welfare or that these employees thought young people should learn to deal with the behaviour themselves.

Staff's own evaluations both reflected and contrasted with young people's assessments. Non-contact physical violence was unanimously considered by staff as being the most difficult form of violence to identify and confront, due to its hidden nature rooted in wider power dynamics. Staff described its covert nature as 'undertone', 'undercurrent' and 'backdoor' violence. Workers frequently remarked that they had to be extremely observant of young people's interactions in order to recognise the very subtle signs of non-contact violence. What may seem perfectly normal behaviour in itself, when viewed from a wider perspective may indicate a misuse of power. Thus, some staff felt that in residential work, rather like research, it was essential never to take things at face value.

> You have to look very closely, it can be very subtle... just a flick of the head, doesn't need to be verbal even, kids just sort of know... You have to be very observant in this job and recognise that things that appear normal or straightforward may not be. (Senior Residential Social Worker, male)
>
> Log everything, then you can see over time what's actually going on, as having things written down can illuminate signs you may miss or dismiss as irrelevant or normal, but viewed as a whole show subtle patterns of domination between kids. (Residential Social Worker, female)

Although most staff felt there was consistency of intervention with overt physical violence, they were less confident about non-contact forms. A number of staff argued that it was virtually impossible constantly to monitor and evaluate every minor action within this wider perspective when immersed in the detailed dynamics of residential life. Subtle signs that may indicate all is not quite as it seems could be missed.

> I think we can't always stand back and have a wider view. At the end of the day, a lot of the stuff we do is crisis management, we're all in too in-depth to even notice the stuff that's going on. (Residential Social Worker, female)

The identification of non-contact violence requires a greater role for staff in detecting signs through 'active' observation: continual assessment and interpretation of behaviour, including very subtle changes in young people.

> Kids don't usually come out and say they are being bullied... you have to do the legwork. They won't say it directly, you have to look out for the signs, mood swings, acting out of character. One of the main problems is you end up trying to deal with the bully when the victim isn't complaining, and that can be difficult. (Manager, male)

Consequently, there can be inconsistency in both identification and intervention. In over one-third of children's homes, where the surreptitious nature of non-contact violence was recognised, staff could still recall at least one occurrence when this form of violence had been present without their knowledge for a significant length of time (ranging from two to four weeks).

Taking into consideration the difficulty of recognising signs, staff in five homes reported that some of their colleagues regularly downplayed or 'missed' significant indicators of non-contact violence. Consequently, they neglected to intervene in situations that, in the participant's opinion, warranted some form of staff response. Three out of these five homes had been identified by young people in their evaluations of inconsistency. In one (local authority) residential home the manager had to plan the staff rota around a number of non-interventionist staff to ensure they were accompanied by their more observant and proactive colleagues to safeguard the children and young people in their care.

> There are times when you look at the rota and you think 'that's a strong shift' and then you look at the other shifts and think 'that's quite weak', there's going to be trouble on that day, and I think the kids are perceptive enough to do the same. (Manager, female)

> Sometimes I know that staff have not intervened when I would, kids know they can say and do things in front of certain staff and not others. (Senior Residential Social Worker, male)

Several reasons were presented by staff in their explanations of this inconsistency, including: staff feeling intimidated themselves by the young person concerned and, therefore, being unwilling to intervene; the young person being popular with staff (which may have been purposely manipulated by the young person), who are therefore less likely to perceive them negatively; staff wanting an easy shift with no conflict; staff minimising the impact of such violence; and viewing bullying as something young people should sort out themselves. Staff also felt that some inexperienced staff, if not well supported by their senior colleagues, may ignore signs due to being unsure how to intervene.

Furthermore, a number of these participants thought that some staff did not support them in their attempts to intervene in covert forms of non-contact violence and intimidation. In some cases staff felt that colleagues had undermined their involvement.

> Like now, I believe that an older girl here is bullying a younger one, maybe very subtle but it's definitely going on, but it's not addressed as the older one is very confrontational. So workers prefer not to run in with her... up to the point of not backing me up when I've tried to challenge some of her behaviour, some here have even belittled my attempts in front of the young people. (Residential Social Worker, female)

Disconcertingly, in one (local authority) home issues of intimidation within the staff team were identified as undermining the team's ability to respond to similar issues within the resident group. In two other homes, inconsistency in response to non-contact violence was identified as being a problem in the past but had been worked on within the team recently and a higher level of consistency achieved.

Problems are further compounded by young people's own positioning and repositioning of themselves in respect to violence generally. This is especially relevant concerning 'bullying' which, as we stated earlier, was how many staff defined non-contact violence. As a result we need to consider how bullying is perceived within children's homes and the implications of this conceptualisation for intervention. As non-contact and physical violence associated with bullying are often covert, the denial of the victim status often hampered professional attempts at intervention. Staff in many homes asserted that young people were often very reluctant to inform them of bullying. Staff felt that this was due to the fear of making the situation worse, through reprisals for 'informing' and young people's recognition that staff could not protect them at all times. There also seemed to exist a code of not 'grassing' in some homes, especially all-male establishments (or at least male dominated), and where persistent young offenders were placed.

> All the time I've been here no boy has ever complained to me about bullying, but I know for damn sure some have been bullied but they won't grass. (Residential Social Worker, male)

> I know kids here have been bullied and have been too scared to tell us. It's very common for kids not to be able to talk to staff, they have to be confident in staff to deal with it without dropping them in it. (Manager, female)

> Interviewer: So do you think lots (of young people) here don't tell (staff about bullying) 'cause they'll get called a grass?
> Ewan: It's not just 'cause you'd get called a grass, but 'cause you'd get beaten up for it. If you tell staff then they really kick your head in.
> (Ewan, aged 13)

Similarly, instigators of bullying were generally reluctant to own up to bullying (see Chapter 5), although a minority of young people seemed to revel in their bullying label.

> Often young people get very upset at being called a bully and will not accept that their behaviour constitutes bullying or any form of intimidation on their part. (Residential Social Worker, male)

> When it comes to bullying, I'm sorry but there's nothing they can do. I'm a complete bastard, I like going round picking on people especially if I don't like them... I've been talked to about it (by staff) but I never listen so I don't know what they're chatting about. (Reece, aged 16)

Without a 'victim', denial by the instigator and reliance on only very subtle indicators, many homes were struggling with how to identify and respond to these very sophisticated misuses of power. In response, many children's homes had adopted a *no-victim stance* where a young person does not have to make a complaint, or even acknowledge they are being bullied, for staff to intervene when possible signs of bullying were observed. This is designed to relocate the 'blame' away from the victim and place it in the hands of staff.

Interestingly, two homes had developed a 'bullying book' in addition to their general record-keeping, where all incidents of bullying were documented. This was used by staff to challenge young people's denial of their bullying with accumulative evidence, to highlight the significance of their actions and, additionally, to emphasise to the young people concerned staff's vigilance in spotting signs of bullying and their commitment to action. Workers in these homes were convinced that these records enabled a much wider perspective on bullying to develop within the staff team and allowed patterns to be recognised concerning young people's behaviours. In addition, they could also highlight possible inconsistencies in intervention within the team, which could then be rectified.

Verbal attacks

Verbal assaults were the most common form of violent experience by nearly all our young participants at some time. Close analysis of the data indicated that 'name-calling' and swearing were common aspects of young people's social cultures within the majority of the homes in our sample. Overall there seemed to be much variation in staff response, both within and across homes. Within homes, young people and workers agreed that staff groups acted inconsistently and that this also depended on the social climate in the home at the time.

Comparing homes, we found generally that those homes situated towards the lower end of the violence continuum responded more strongly to verbal attacks than homes which experienced greater physical and non-contact forms of violence. Verbal attacks in high violence homes were more likely to be viewed by staff as part of young people's routine social interactions. These staff stated that although they disliked the language, there was little which could be done about it.

> You can't stop it (verbal attacks). If you did, you'd be doing very little else all day. (Residential Social Worker, male)
>
> Don't really mean much, they're just all so used to it... if they carry on too much we do tell them to stop. (Deputy Manager, male)

Some staff felt that the constant reprimands that would be required would be counter-productive, as this would hamper wider positive relationships with the young people.

> If you keep on at them about the language it just ends up winding them up more, so it's really quite counter-productive. (Residential Social Worker, male)
>
> You can't sanction every minute, which is what we'd be doing. If they're using bad language they're not hurting a kid. They all use it, it's the norm actually. We do say but we'd be doing it every minute of the day – you can't be at the kids all the time 'cause that irritates them. (Manager, female)

However, research has been undertaken into a residential unit that successfully challenged swearing and sexualised language among young men (Kendrick and Mair 2002).

We found much more consistency in relation to racist insults, which would generally receive a swift response from staff (and young people themselves). In addition, verbal attacks were more likely to receive a formal response if personal information was used or wider power issues were suspected. Generally, it was the physical retort that received the most attention from staff rather than the verbal attack that preceded it. In four homes, all towards the lower end of the violence continuum, verbal abuse was not allowed and any such behaviour would be met with a swift revoke.

We don't use bad language here. All the kids are very aware of that... we don't let anyone abuse or insult another person... This is their home so why should they have to put up with that... if you allow that to occur then one thing can lead to another. (Manager, female)

Sexual violence

Staff often did not mention spontaneously sexual violence in their discussions with us. Bullying and physical violence dominated their concerns. Indeed, some were reluctant to discuss their experiences in this area.

Overall, 20 incidents of what staff defined as 'serious' sexual violence had occurred over the past year in the 14 homes. In all these cases either pervasive sexually abusing behaviour or single incidents involving aggressive or coercive elements were present. Concern seemed most apparent where the sexually harmful behaviour had occurred between males, where the victim was significantly younger then their assailant or if the behaviour was persistent. Least likely to receive professional attention was sexual violence from females, or situations involving male sexual violence against a same age female peer, where no other overt physical violence appeared to have taken place.

Compared to other forms of violence we found major discrepancies concerning how even serious incidents of sexual violence were approached both within and across homes, and an even greater lack of clarity in relation to sexualised behaviour generally. This was an area which staff were obviously uncomfortable discussing, where many felt unsure of their abilities and complained that they had received insufficient training. Consequently, and understandably they lacked confidence in their professional judgements. It seemed that issues concerning sexuality were generally given little priority in many homes, except in relation to deterring sexual relationships between residents. Some homes had developed more positive initiatives, which we discuss later. Unfortunately, these are the exception rather than the rule.

Parkin (1989) suggests that the origins of such confusion lie in uncertainties about what are public and what are private concerns. Public care sits within the intermediate zone between these two spheres. The policies and procedures belonging to the public world do not translate easily into the private world of sexuality.

However, we found that, even where serious acts of sexual violence had occurred, this did not necessarily result in a full child protection investigation or conference, although the need for this is stated clearly in official guidance (Department of Health *et al.* 1999). Although staff told us about 20 incidents, only 8 resulted in a conference taking place. We return to this important area in the next chapter. These findings are consistent with Farmer and Pollocks' (1998) study on sexually abusing and abused children in substitute care and, therefore, seem to portray the general position of residential practice in this area. These authors conclude:

> The overriding message from this evidence is that imparting information about sexual matters is given little priority in residential care and that this is sustained by a lack of confidence in this area among workers about what is allowed and expected and about their own abilities to take on this role...The position of local authorities is not an easy one but if young people are to have the benefit of information which will enable them to make a choice about their sexuality...the present passive approach will need to be rethought. (p. 127)

Disconcertingly, we found examples of young people who had informed staff about an incident involving sexual violence but who were not believed, or their experiences not taken seriously. This seemed to occur most often when the victim was viewed as sexually promiscuous, if they had made a previous inconclusive allegation, or where staff believed a consenting sexual relationship had been present between the people involved. Some staff added that, although they had taken an allegation seriously, external agencies had not, illustrated below when a 14-year-old boy reported unwanted sexual touching by a female resident.

> When the police arrived they almost laughed about it – he (the young man) was very angry and they were like 'Oh you lucky thing'. (Senior Residential Social Worker, male)

We have already seen how reluctant young people were to discuss with staff their experiences of sexual violence. Indeed, in all the above cases staff had not been the first avenue of support to which young people turned. Given staff's reluctance to engage with young people on issues of sexuality generally (including exploitative or inappropriate sexual behaviours), there seems little possibility of progress occurring in this area unless staff's lack of knowledge, confidence and expertise are recognised and addressed in training and management. Dealing with teenage sexual behaviour is difficult enough, let alone when it also involves looking after other people's children.

Having considered the level and consistency of intervention in children's homes, in the next section we explore the methods of intervention employed, the different forms these took and how some homes were implementing proactive working strategies to combat violence in their homes.

Summary points

- Most young people initially turned to peers as a source of support rather than staff. Girls used their friends for emotional support but boys were less likely to discuss their experiences and feelings, instead concentrating on their response.

- Young people and workers agreed that most overt physical violence would be promptly stopped by staff. However, it did not necessarily prevent violence from recurring.
- Staff who were most successful in de-escalating a potentially violent situation were those whom young people felt effectively used humour, could empathise with young people, listened to their views, took their grievances seriously, were considered impartial and took an interest in young people's lives and culture.
- Young people felt that staff were generally unsuccessful in dealing with bullying. Responses were inconsistent.
- Verbal attacks were the most common form of violence experienced by young people. Homes responded to this very differently. Racist insults, in contrast, received a swift response from staff and young people alike.
- Responding to sexual violence was a problem for staff and there were major discrepancies. Staff lacked confidence and skills in this area. Even serious acts of sexual violence did not always receive a full child protection response.

8
Responding to Violence – Methods of Intervention

> Sometimes we get put on LOPS, that's loss of privileges, even though we don't deserve it, but mostly I think that staff are pretty fair, some rules are for their convenience like, but I reckon that most are fair 'cause they're to keep us safe.
>
> (Fiona, aged 13)

> Basically all you can do is tell them to leave it out, separate them 'cause it goes in one ear and out the other. It (supervision) has little effect on bullying, as much as we try through being very vigilant, we try and protect by presence, but that's not going to stop them when they're able to get another child on their own.
>
> (Residential Social Worker, male)

Building on from the previous chapter we now turn our attention to look in more depth at the range of methods used by staff to respond to peer violence. Initially we concentrate on exploring the range of interventions found within homes including; sanctions, physical restraint, meetings and formal child protection procedures. Following this we look at proactive working methods aimed at reducing the presence of violence and finally consider staff's wider perspectives on how peer violence within residential settings could be prevented.

Sanction-based interventions

Nearly all homes operated a system for controlling young people's behaviour based on negative sanctions. However, many staff in the majority of homes stated that they were fairly limited in what they could actually do.

> There's very little we can do in reality, send them to bed a few minutes early or stop them going out one evening, but really our hands are tied due to the guidelines and the kids know that, so they can weigh it up to see if it's worth it. (Residential Social Worker, male)

The most commonly used negative sanctions, universally referred to as 'loss of privileges' included: 'early beds' (generally going to bed 10–20 minutes earlier than the young person's allotted time); loss of evening or weekend activity; pocket money held over for another day; not allowed to watch the evening's video; not allowed TV in room; loss of *extra* money (additional to allocated pocket money allowance); not allowed extension of normal bedtime at weekend; restricted to the building unless on planned activity; loss of single bedroom or preferred bedroom. The effectiveness of these sanctions was difficult to determine. Overall it seemed that staff felt sanctions were most effective with younger children and those who were less involved in negative (generally meaning offending) peer cultures.

> Sanctions don't really work, as in punishment – taking something away rather than giving them it...children get used to sanctions and there's not a lot you can do anyway. (Residential Social Worker, female)
>
> Our system here works best with the younger kids, but is less effective with the older, deviant lot. Someone who's out selling drugs all night doesn't care if he can't watch TV in his room for an extra hour or not. (Residential Social Worker, male)

Through both our discussions with young people and observations in the homes, the central role that sanctions played within many of the residential settings was clearly evident. Homes that had formalised reward and punishment systems were well known to residents, this was particularly the case in two of the all-male children's homes:

Martin:	There are certain sanctions they can give you, I wouldn't call it blackmail, but if they say if you do this you are not going to get the telly tonight or a cigarette and your gonna-think...oh.
Interviewer:	So if a fight broke out what would the sanction be for that?
Martin:	Probably a red card, which is off systems. Say I mean instead of like, let's say you get a weekly wage with our points system, you get points. You can get about 340 in a day, a red card, take you off systems for an hour.
Interviewer:	So you can't pick up any points in an hour?
Martin:	Yeah or spend points, say you can't have any cigarettes, can't get the telly, things like that, so you have to be good to get off it and they write our targets so if they are fighting they write on it 'don't fight' and if you don't fight within the hour you get off it.
Interviewer:	Do you think that works?
Martin:	Sometimes.

(Martin, aged 14)

Often sanctions were viewed by young people as a given, but often highly unpopular, aspect of residential life. Sanctions represented a highly explosive area within many homes. Young people often challenged staff's grounds for imposing sanctions and most knew what sanctions were applicable. In addition, young people spoke at length about perceived injustices against both themselves and others regarding sanctions that had been inconsistently imposed. A constant area of interest and discussion within the peer groups we observed concerned which young people had what sanctions against them. Policing of such sanctions by young people was extensive, generally against their less well-liked peers. Overall younger children focused more attention on scrutinising others; whilst older adolescents seemed more concerned with collectively gaining an advantage over staff, for example, where a previously assigned sanction was overlooked by subsequent workers.

Many (41) young people stated that sanctions were used inconsistently within their homes, although about half of the above evaluations came from young people who, according to them, had been unjustly sanctioned for what they deemed to be a legitimate use of violence. Other reasons that young people provided in their explanations for these inconsistencies included staff having favourites, individual staff employing different thresholds, time of day, mood of the staff member, type of work shift and presence of senior staff in the home. Young people complained that it was unfair if sanctions imposed on individuals affected the whole group. Thus, if a number of young people were banned from extra activities, this sometimes meant that external outings had to be abandoned due to staff having to stay in the home, or a video could not be watched.

Some staff (18) also felt that sanctions were often used inconsistently within their establishment, with some of their colleagues being more lenient than others. This caused problems within the homes when more serious behaviour sometimes received a reduced sanction than less worrying incidents. These staff felt that young people were well aware which staff were more lenient in their allocation of sanctions than others. Three homes had developed *sanction books* in which all incidents had to be documented, including the sanction imposed, who was involved, which worker imposed the sanction, the young people's reaction and other relevant factors. These books could then be used to determine if any inconsistencies were present in working practices.

In three homes there seemed little recognition between staff shifts concerning which young people had sanctions imposed against them. We observed cases where sanctions imposed on an earlier shift were disregarded. Indeed, in one home, although all the young people had been placed on a 'no activity' sanction due to their behaviour, it was decided by a senior worker that, as the home had no formal policy concerning sanctions, this had to be lifted. Although the young people were obviously delighted by this decision, and taking into account the fact that no formal policy was in place, the actions of this senior worker still severely undermined colleagues' earlier attempts to control these young people's very disruptive and violent behaviour. This was evident the next day, when the young people spent a full morning telling these more junior staff that they could do what they liked as their superior had told them they had no authority to control their behaviour; not one of the most productive team-building experiences we witnessed.

Two homes used a system of 'time-out' where a young person was removed from their current home to a temporary placement in another children's home to provide the young person 'time to think' and the wider group a break from their behaviour. It did seem, however, that often the young person did not return from this break, and that if they did they were generally removed at a later date due to their continued violent or abusive behaviour. Some more successful outcomes were also reported, although these seemed to involve incidents of lower impact violence.

Physical restraint

Young people generally felt that staff only used physical restraint when it was appropriate to do so, with most accounts stating that it was necessary for the protection of the young people concerned. Only six young people in three homes complained to us that physical restraint had been used inappropriately by staff. In all these cases, young people felt the physical restraint was either used prematurely by certain staff or that they had received physical injuries. In one home, where staff had only recently been trained in the use of physical restraint, children commented on how safe they now felt compared to before when staff were unable physically to control violent residents.

Grant: He did it less at the end (physical violence) 'cause staff stopped him. Before they didn't 'cause they weren't allowed to get hold of him.
Interviewer: Why was that?
Grant: 'Cause they hadn't been shown how to do it so that's why they weren't allowed to help us...but now they can, so that's better 'cause they can stop us if we hit each other... before fights used to get bad, but not now.

(Grant, aged 11)

Most staff stated that the physical restraint of young people was the last resort, only employed if other methods had failed, and physical injury was imminent. However, although national minimum standards (Department of Health 2002a) emphasise that staff should be trained in the use of restraint (in the wider context of behavioural management strategies), a number of staff we interviewed stated that either they or other staff members had not received such training. In four homes it was reported that over the last year problems had occurred due to the insufficient numbers of staff trained in the use of physical restraint techniques. For example, in one private home where physical violence was common, only two full-time staff had received training in the use of restraint techniques. In another (voluntary) home for younger children, prior to the arrival of the current manager the home had according to one worker few staff trained in restraint techniques and an informal ban on using such control mechanisms. At this time one of the boys in the home was physically bullying and intimidating other children and, according to the worker's account, staff were unable to secure their safety. It was not, however, clear if the informal policy was in place to stop untrained staff from endeavouring to physically restrain a child or if it reflected some wider principle concerning the use of physical restraint.

Some staff (11) felt that their colleagues were sometimes too eager to use restraint rather than reach a positive outcome through the use of alternative methods.

> Some here use restraining more quickly than I would. I prefer to try and calm the situation down verbally before jumping in physically. Give the kids a chance to take control over themselves, that seems more productive, although I'd jump in if I thought someone was going to really get hurt, but I do feel that staff are too eager to use restraint. (Residential Social Worker, male)

Some participants felt that male staff were more likely to use physical restraint at an earlier stage than female workers. Both female and male staff stated the difficulties of having to restrain older adolescent boys due to their physical strength, although this was physically more problematic for females. Additionally, many participants highlighted the problems surrounding male workers physically restraining girls, and particularly young women, due to the possibility of inappropriate touch inadvertently occurring during a restraint and the associated worry of having an allegation of sexual abuse brought against them. To reduce the need for male staff members to physically restrain female residents, nearly all homes tried to ensure that a female member of staff was always working.

A minority of female staff stated that they did not generally physically intervene unless their male colleagues were unable to respond or the violence involved a girl. This was not necessarily related to their lack of physical strength. Instead, it seemed that these female workers perceived their role within the homes as being fundamentally different to that of their male counterparts, reflecting traditional gender roles.

> I would possibly use restraint, but I wanna be the person who picks up the pieces. Let the men do the physical bit and I'll do the loving bit. (Residential Social Worker, female)

The female approach is totally different from the male staff. I think we're approaching it from a mothering sort of situation, whilst with male staff it's more an ego sort of thing. Males do the restraining and then females do the caring afterwards, it's more normal isn't it that way? (Residential Social Worker, female)

In practice these very definite gender roles within homes may come to reinforce young people's ideas concerning gender appropriate roles and may possibly obstruct their ability to relate emotionally to males. However, we found such extreme gender distinctions in only a minority of homes, although more subtle gender distinctions were evident in others.

Staff used a range of conciliatory strategies to deal with physical and non-contact violence and verbal attacks. In many instances staff reported that in cases of minor verbal insults and low-level spontaneous retaliatory violence, a swift separation of young people followed by a 'stiff' word by staff was sufficient. Often staff reported that within a short period the young people involved would be on amicable terms once again, although young people's previous assessments seem to contradict this optimistic view.

But in other cases staff needed to undertake more in-depth discussions with young people in their attempts to resolve situations both in the short- and long-term. In their descriptions of these processes staff routinely distinguished between *informal discussions* surrounding isolated low-level acts of violence and verbal insults, and more *formalised meetings* in response to high-level or recurrent violence or verbal attacks or actions rooted in wider power dynamics.

Informal meetings

Informal meetings between staff and young people in response to isolated incidents of low-level violence were generally concerned with:

- Achieving some form of consensus between each party in the dispute, often through highlighting how all parties concerned had to a greater or lesser extent exacerbated the situation, if only by failing to inform staff earlier.
- Ensuring that all parties recognised that violence is not tolerated in any context.
- Determining the level of culpability on each side, if any, and ensuring the young people concerned acknowledge their role within this (without this degenerating into a 'slanging match').
- Attempting to stop young people from using physical violence to resolve disputes by trying to make them aware of the inappropriateness of a physical response even in situations of extreme provocation.

- Highlighting the potential consequences of using violence, including the possibility of criminal charges and transfer from the home.
- Ensuring that thoughts of retaliation are discouraged.
- Identifying that this is not an indicator of wider power issues between the young people involved.
- Determining what sanctions or loss of privileges, if any, would result.

Staff members who intervened or observed the incident generally held these discussions in private, directly after the incident and usually with both parties together. In most homes, staff stated that these discussions would be noted in the young person's file and would be mentioned at staff 'handover' meetings to ensure that staff on the next shift were aware of any possible ramifications. The young person's key worker was generally viewed as having responsibility for undertaking any further work required. We observed some instances involving what seemed to us significant disputes where this information-sharing procedure was not adhered to. However, in general, staff's vigilance in sharing information was impressive. Although the above process seemed to operate more or less similarly in most of the children's homes in the sample, the more formalised response was more varied.

Formal meetings

Most often these meetings followed the use of serious physical violence or concerns around bullying or intimidation. Generally these occurred individually with the young people involved. The key worker was usually present, often with a senior staff member, and less often the head of home. The young person's social worker also attended, although this varied between homes. The more serious or persistent the behaviour, the greater the representation of senior staff at these meetings. There was considerable variation between homes regarding whether the keyworker or the senior staff member presided over the meeting. The most serious outcome, transfer from the home, tended to occur most frequently in cases of persistent, long-term, severe, physical violence or sexual violence and to a lesser extent non-physical, persistent bullying.

Perpetrator meetings generally focused on
- Homes' policies on the unacceptability of physical violence and/or bullying behaviour;
- Acknowledgement of their actions and their unacceptable use of power/domination;
- Recognition of harm caused obtained through empathy with victim;
- Further implications if behaviour persists, including transfer and the possibility of criminal charges;

- The sanctions or preventive measures to be taken by staff, including increased staff surveillance of their actions and 'exclusion zone' around the victim;
- Possible reasons for their use of violence or power and resolutions to this;
- Devising a contract between the young person and staff detailing what changes needed to occur;
- Removal from placement.

Victim meetings concerned

- Determining what occurred if the young person is willing to disclose.
- Exploring any previous incidents.
- Discuss mechanisms to keep the young person safe in the future and the role of staff and the individual in this process.
- What, if any, formal action they wished to take, including making a complaint or involving the police.

A record of these meetings would normally be placed in the young person's file for future reference. Some homes operated a hierarchical system of meetings where young people progressed from one level to another if their behaviour did not improve.

We found that differential thresholds were employed between homes in relation to triggering a formal rather than informal meeting. Unsurprisingly perhaps the homes situated towards the upper end of the violence continuum generally exhibited higher thresholds than those positioned nearer the bottom. This may be due to their heightened exposure and subsequent desensitisation to violence. Linked to this, it appeared from close scrutiny of the data that homes with increased levels of violence and higher thresholds also generally shared lower expectations of behaviour, an issue raised in previous research (Brown *et al.* 1998).

One manager in a local authority home felt that she and her colleagues should not have to determine when an incident warranted external involvement. This was because their close relationships with young people may subconsciously impede judgements regarding what level of behaviour needed a broader response. Instead she felt that all incidents should be externally reported so that independent assessment could be undertaken.

Child protection procedures

Official guidelines contained in *Working Together Under the Children Act* guidance (Department of Health, Home Office Department for Education and Employment 1999) makes it clear that an allegation of sexual abuse by a child should result in child protection procedures being invoked. The main aims of a child protection conference involving relevant professionals are to establish if the abuse occurred and if so how, including any organisational factors; the support requirements of the victim; and an assessment of the perpetrator's needs and how these will be best met, including the provision of specialist therapeutic assistance. Importantly, the investigation can also examine if the abuse could have been avoided, if any other children or young people may be at risk, and identifying any preventative mechanism that needs to be implemented to ensure the future safety of young people in the establishment under investigation. In addition, if the young people are from the same local authority which is also providing the care it may be necessary to have an independent body undertake the investigation to ensure its impartiality (Barter 1998).

In our study the only 'serious risks' that initiated a child protection conference were sexual in nature, and in all cases these incidents were deemed to be 'serious' by both managers and ourselves. Overall, we identified that of the 20 cases of serious sexual violence recognised, only 8 resulted in a formal child protection conference taking place. All these except 2 concerned recurring sexual violence, and most (6) involved some form of penetration. Thus, even 'serious' sexual incidents, as defined by staff and/or ourselves, did not receive a child protection investigation. The implications of this are significant both for the victim and the assailant.

Research findings, as well as experts working with children and young people who display sexually harmful behaviour, conclude that all incidents should be investigated and that decisions about the use of the criminal justice system should be made in the light of the best way to secure assessment and treatment for the young person (National Children's Home 1992, Brown 1993, Morrison 1994).

However, many staff stated that, even when a child protection investigation was enacted, this did not necessarily always resolve the problem. Most often this concerned sexual abuse when the victim was reluctant to participate. Many felt that these investigations lost impetus once the perpetrator had been removed. In three cases managers were unsure of the investigation's outcomes as the child was no longer in their care. Thus, although the victim was still in placement, they could not be informed of the investigation's conclusions. Police involvement was usually minimal and quickly declined due to lack of evidence.

In most cases when a child protection conference had been initiated, the alleged perpetrator had already been removed from the home. However, in a small number of instances (3) we were told that both the alleged perpetrator and victim had remained within the same placement and in two of these cases this was still the situation at the time of our fieldwork.

In the final section of this chapter we now move on to look at ways in which homes sought not simply to intervene in violence but to work proactively towards reducing or stopping it occurring at all. Some of the challenges and barriers to doing this are raised as well as examples of good working practices.

Proactive working practices

Overall, there was reliance on reactive rather than proactive strategies within homes. The main strategies employed in all homes to prevent violence occurring were through the supervision of young people's contact, restriction of their movements and through staff interactions with young people.

Supervision

We found that the direct supervision of young people's interactions was undertaken with great determination in many of the 14 homes. Staff seemed to spend a significant amount of their time supervising or observing young people's behaviour and interactions. In all homes with younger children, staff were generally present wherever the children were in the house. In many of the homes for older adolescents, staff remarked that it was essential to at least know where all young people were at any time, even if they were not directly with them. Many senior staff and managers stated they would periodically check on the level of supervision being undertaken.

> I keep my eye on what's going on. If staff are not with the kids, I want to know exactly why and who is supervising them. (Manager, male)

In a minority of homes, however, some staff seemed to use the office as a refuge; and certain individual staff appeared to spend more time talking with each other than observing, let alone interacting with, the young people. Many staff, in mitigation emphasised that to maintain this degree of oversight, especially when this also involved frequent intervention, could be very stressful, especially if due to low staffing levels they were unable to have a proper break. In some establishments, low staff numbers, the physical structure of the building, disinclination of some staff to be with young people and internal inconsistency reduced effectiveness (see Chapter 6). Similarly, young people were aware of the limitations of supervision as a method of keeping them safe, especially in relation to hidden forms of violence.

Restriction of young people's freedom was a key mechanism to increase surveillance. Rules governing movements included restriction to communal areas, controlling access to bedrooms, and requiring consent to use certain internal and external areas of the building. Often young people disliked these restrictions imposed on their movements, especially to bedrooms. One main complaint, especially from girls, was that they were not allowed to socialise with others in their bedrooms, or only with permission and if they left their bedroom door open. This was generally perceived as a violation of their right to privacy. Although all stated that they knew the restriction was in place to protect them, they nevertheless felt their privacy was more important. Often young people simply sneaked into others' rooms without staff knowledge. In only two homes we visited could same-sex peers sleep over in each others' rooms at weekends with staff's permission. This was a popular activity amongst girls, reflected in wider society, and was seen by staff as a way of trying to deinstitutionalise peer interactions.

Two private homes and one local authority home had more sophisticated surveillance methods. One private home had alarms on bedroom doors to warn staff of children's movements and another had CCTV surveillance in communal areas. Young people did not seem to mind this electronic monitoring of their movements and none complained to us about it. In the later home the CCTV monitors were positioned along the dining room wall, providing a popular alternative to TV at mealtimes. Indeed, young people frequently used the monitors to their own advantage, for example, as a convenient mechanism for signalling to staff downstairs (generally by jumping in the air) that they had 'misplaced' their bedroom key and needed to be let in. The local authority home had CCTV cameras on the front door only, although a number of staff in this home felt that it would be useful to extend this to communal areas of the building. A few staff in homes with very restrictive practices questioned the long-term consequences this might have on young people's social development.

> Sometimes you need to let it ride, I call it living in a fishbowl, 'cause they're observed a lot more than kids out in the community would be, and if we observe them too much and stop them too much, they won't ever learn to protect themselves. If we do it for them all the time, when they go out in society they're going to fail because they won't have learnt them skills. (Residential Social Worker, male)

Keywork system

All homes operated a keyworker system, used to address individual problems concerning violence. However, support in relation to violence seemed to address the physical rather than emotional aspects, reflected in both young people's as well as staff's accounts. This is not surprising given how reluctant many young people were to discuss personal aspects of their lives with staff. Keywork counselling of young people seemed to be based on 'common sense' rather than any formal training or methods. The degree and skills of individual staff varied considerably, as did insights into the impact of violence and the subsequent needs of young people in this area. Individual staff talked about the need to provide support but in a covert manner as any attempts at 'counselling' would be met with great resistance; the phase most often used in relation to formal counselling was 'they'd run mile'. This was especially true concerning issues of power in sexual relationships or encounters. Many staff justifiably felt they did not hold the necessary skills to undertake intensive work with young people, and this was made especially clear in relation to sexual abuse, and especially young people with a history of sexually harmful behaviour (Farmer and Pollock 1998). Given the general lack of external professional support in homes, many young people did not receive the level of assistance staff felt they required for any substantial changes to occur (Department of Health 1998a). Indeed, many staff questioned whether they were in a position to effect long-term change at all, especially with adolescents.

> There's a huge difference between being able to see something and being able to change it. They maybe can see the harm they've done, but they're not able to change it 'cause they're too used to acting that way and they do get benefits from it. It's a huge risk for them to question their behaviour, and it's an enormously slow process, and we don't really have enough time or expertise here, so we just end up as a holding station. (Residential Social Worker, female)

As the participant below added, you may be able to realise eventually that something is wrong, but being able to change that behaviour is far more difficult.

> You have some hope with the youngsters, but for the older lot it's too late really, you just can't get through to them anymore. They've got into an aggressive pattern that works for them and they don't want to change, especially if it means that they're not being picked on. (Senior Residential Social Worker, male)

Indeed, this pessimism has some support in the research literature. Sinclair and Gibbs (1998) found that homes that appeared more effective did not necessarily lead to better outcomes and improvements were often temporary. Berridge and Brodie (1998) concluded that young people living in children's homes often needed specialist, external, professional help but were unlikely to get it.

Some staff in homes showed little insight into the possible damage that violence could have beyond general assumptions concerning making young people feel unhappy, and effects on their self-esteem and confidence. As we have already seen many staff, and especially more junior staff, often disassociated young people's use of violence from both their background experiences and wider influencing factors. This meant that, in practice, keywork sessions were often focused on situational motivations, such as determining the individual reasons behind a particular act of violence, rather than also looking at wider issues involving the young person's past experiences and social worlds.

External professional help

Overall, we found very little evidence of external professional help. When it was provided it most commonly addressed young people's recognised mental health problems or educational needs (generally not directly related to violence). To a lesser extent, some external counselling was offered to victims of familial sexual abuse and perpetrators of severe physical (and in two cases sexual) violence. It appeared that the provision of external professional help was most likely to occur in homes where this was an agreed prerequisite to the referral being accepted. However, as we have already seen in Chapter 6, only 6 out of the 14 homes were routinely able to control referrals on these grounds; of these four accepted referrals of young people with challenging behaviour. Once a young person was in placement staff felt that the provision of external support was more difficult to secure. This finding is especially disconcerting when we consider that senior staff in ten homes stated that they often lacked adequate information at the time of referral, including previous involvement in violence. The general impression from staff was that many young people who required professional external help did not receive it. Only two units, the role of which was to undertake detailed assessments of young people's long-term needs, provided intensive residential psychiatric support, both individually and in groups. Young people's evaluations of the benefit of this mandatory provision varied. Six young people we talked with had, at some point in their residential experience, received external professional assistance to deal with their behaviour. Generally this provision was viewed positively by the young people.

> Interviewer: Do you find your temper runs away with you?
> Robert: Yeah
> Interviewer: Is it quite hard to control?
> Robert: Yeah
> Interviewer: Do the staff help you with that?
> Robert: My psychiatrist does
> Interviewer: Is that working?
> Robert: Yeah, it's going all right
>
> (Robert, aged 14)

> Interviewer: Some children's home have independent visitors don't they, people who...
> Fergus: Independent visitor? I got one. Well we don't really take each other as an independent visitor really.
> Interviewer: And what's your relationship with them like?
> Fergus: Good
> Interviewer: Yes?
> Fergus: Yeah because not many of my colour down (name of town) so they thought get him an independent visitor what's black.

Interviewer: And how long have you been seeing him?
Fergus: About two years.
Interviewer: Can you talk to him about your problems?
Fergus: Not really, but we do talk sometimes, not about problems, just about bullying or something like that.
Interviewer: So you talk about the bullying with him?
Fergus: Yeah.

(Fergus, aged 15)

In all these young people's assessments the importance of the help being external to the residential setting was central to their positive evaluations. As the above young man explained to us, young people may not wish to divulge very sensitive personal information to someone they have to see daily. In addition, as this role would generally be undertaken by a keyworker who has considerable influence over a young person's residential experience, many young people felt uncomfortable with this situation, even when a positive relationship had been established. This may be why young people who received residentially based psychiatric help were often less than positive, especially as they were aware that the assessment could have far-reaching implications for their subsequent placement.

In both of the above positive examples, external professionals worked closely with residential staff (whilst respecting boundaries of confidentiality) to ensure that their individual work was complementary, and that residential staff benefited from the specialist guidance. This was viewed by staff as an essential element of good practice in this area. Unfortunately, we also encountered some cases where external professional help had been counterproductive to residential attempts to control young people's behaviour. Often a breakdown in information-sharing between external professionals and residential staff, alongside a lack of commitment by external professions to working together with residential workers, left staff feeling unrecognised and undermined.

> We have had a couple of quite negative experiences of working with external professionals... In one case we tried to set sanctions and boundaries for this lad who was becoming completely out of control, unfortunately the psychiatrist just ignored these, never consulted with us and really, I feel, made the whole situation reach crisis point due to her inconsistency in practice. (Manager, female)

Group work

We found few examples of formal group work activities aimed at decreasing young people's involvement in violence. Staff often lacked the training or confidence to undertake group work on sensitive issues, relying instead on reactive intervention rather than working towards primary prevention alongside young people. Of those who had experienced group work, most stated that there seemed little impetus in homes to engage in such activities. One exception to this in our study was a voluntary home where staff were about to make a number of videos concerning issues such as bullying, intimidation and sexualised behaviour, which were then to be used in group work with young people. It was unfortunate that this imaginative initiative was still being developed at the time of our fieldwork and, thus, we were unable to explore young people's responses. In another home for younger children staff had undertaken some group work with the children concerning different aspects of good/bad touch strategies about how to keep safe and issues of telling. In addition, and as we have already described, a third home ran formalised group work as part of their assessment of young people's longer term needs.

One benefit claimed by young people in residential care is the emotional support they receive from their peers who share similar experiences (Kahan 1979a). It seems unfortunate that this resource is not considered more often, although as we have seen the peer group is not always benign. Although formal group work was rare, this did not mean that individual staff did not engage young people in group discussions on topics, including violence. Many examples were produced of informal gatherings where a worker 'spontaneously' raised, or encouraged discussion, about a specific topic subject. Often the most non-threatening place to do this was when young people were gathered for a specific reason. The smoking room, minibus and TV room were all favourite venues for staff to initiate discussions and generate debate around specific issues. Yet, when we suggested to staff who routinely engaged with young people in this manner that they could perhaps use these skills to undertake more formalised group work, this was generally met with resistance due to their perceived lack of ability in this area.

> I think taking groups formally can seem very daunting for many staff here...I know I'd feel quite unsure about undertaking it, although as you say I do talk with the young people about issues all of the time. (Residential Social Worker, female)

Positive reward systems

Although nearly all homes had formal rules in place covering the use of negative sanctions, few had systems in place based on rewards for positive behaviour. Two homes operated a complex 'token economy system', where good behaviour earned points and continuing good behaviour was rewarded by progression to a higher level (marked by different coloured cards) with more privileges attached. At the end of each day points could be 'cashed-in' for privileges, for example, an external activity or the use of a TV in the young person's bedroom. Evaluations of the usefulness of this system seemed to be dependent on the age and background of the young person.

In a home for younger children a major change had occurred since a new manager had arrived. Prior to his appointment physical violence, intimidation and 'bullying' had been pervasive, and staff's intervention had been inconsistent and ineffective. The new manager implemented procedures, working practices, behaviour management including physical restraint training, and undertook team-building work. Alongside this, a reward system was introduced whereby stars were awarded for positive behaviour. When a child reached the prescribed number a small ceremony was held and a prize given. This system allowed staff to identify problem areas for each individual child and target the reward at this specific behaviour. No stars were removed for negative behaviours. These combined measures resulted in significantly lower levels of physical violence and verbal attacks being present in the home over a five-month period. The children themselves stated they now felt much safer and praised the new reward system, proudly showing the researcher their star books and the rewards they had received.

> I didn't like it when we all have to suffer 'cause somebody's kicked off and 'cause of that we didn't have our outing. But I'm really well behaved, staff are always saying to me how good I am, I've got three stars this week so if I do good for the next two days I'll get a prize. (Dwight, aged 8)

The manager confirmed that the move away from focusing on children's negative behaviour patterns and instead concentrating attention (both staff and peers) on positives had completely transformed the atmosphere in the home. In our observations, children were very concerned with demonstrating to staff, researchers and each other their good behaviour. Whilst negative behaviour received a swift intervention from staff, their focus concentrated on encouraging constructive interactions rather than providing young people with attention for violent behaviour. So, although violent behaviour was discussed with children after the event, the overall emphasis was on reinforcing positive behavioural patterns through staff attention and rewards. Nevertheless, despite the apparent success of this scheme, the manager raised doubts about the applicability of this system for adolescents.

Wider perspectives on reducing violence

Wider perspectives on reducing violence and abuse within placement concerned two main areas; the importance of developing positive relationships with young people and meeting the needs of residents.

Positive relationships

We have already seen the extent to which young people valued wider relationships with staff in relation to their interventions. In all cases, young people emphasised that they preferred interventions undertaken by staff whom they trusted and respected. Staff who were inconsistent (except in relation to provocative-victims), who were seen as biased or uninterested in young people's wider lives were much more likely to be viewed negatively. Although residents still complained about sanctions, if the worker was perceived more favourably, they were more likely to accept their decision. An important area of concern for young people was negative relationships with their keyworker. Many stated that they felt they should be able to choose their keyworker rather than have one imposed on them. In addition, young people who said that they had confided in staff always picked an individual they felt close to, especially in relation to sexual violence.

Staff emphasised the importance of developing positive relationships, where young people feel they are listened to and where their views are taken into account. Research had confirmed that young people value these qualities in professionals (Triseliotis *et al.* 1995). This enables a trusting relationship to develop where young people feel able to talk openly about their problems and concerns, including issues relating to violence and abuse. Staff acknowledged that this can take some considerable time as many barriers may have to be overcome before young people feel safe enough to trust an adult again.

> It all starts with how staff relate to young people. It's essential to develop a trusting and positive relationship with young people, where staff are interested in a young person's life and they sit and talk with them properly. It takes a long time to gain that trust, but without that you've got nothing to work with... We've developed very good relationships here, without that groundwork you'll never stop bullying or violence. (Manager, male)

Only in two homes did young people consistently say they would regularly disclose personal issues and problems to staff, as discussed in-depth at the beginning of this chapter. Although individual young people in other homes used staff in this way, they represented the minority view in these settings.

Meeting the needs of young people

In addition many staff (56), including all managers, argued that unless the young person's needs are being met within the placement, it is very difficult to work proactively with them to reduce violence. Furthermore, if the placement is unable to meet their needs, this will often lead to acting-out behaviour, including the use of violence, against both staff and their peers.

> If you get a referral who is very disruptive or has needs that this team can't meet, due to the present client group or due to lack of expertise in the team, whatever reason, then, instead of working with young people,

what you end up doing is managing violent crisis after crisis after crisis and you end up not even meeting the existing needs of the group and it all escalates very quickly. (Senior Residential Social Worker, male)

You have to balance the needs of the new person with the needs of the wider group. If these are not compatible with each other, then commonly nobody gets what they require and more often than not this leads to young people acting out their frustrations through violence. (Manager, female)

I want to be part of the solution not the problem, so I'll act in the best interest of the children. I'd rather walk than accept a child whose needs I felt could not be accommodated here, for their own sake and the sake of the kids here. (Manager, female)

As we have already seen in Chapter 6, a number of factors may mitigate against effectively meeting young people's needs. Often, their needs were not recognised at the time of referral. The lack of control over referrals experienced by many homes meant that young people with contrasting requirements were often placed together: a situation exacerbated by emergency admissions and an absence of clarity for homes regarding their wider function. Alongside this the lack of external help, coupled with residential workers' understandable apprehension at being able to provide the intensive support they felt many residents required, meant that young people's needs may not be adequately addressed. In these situations staff felt that their role became one of containment rather than help. This led to frustration on both sides and often resulted in an increase in negative, often violent, behaviour from the young people concerned. The subsequent escalation in violent behaviour can also impact on the wider residential group, and consequently, other residents' needs may be overlooked due to the concentration on containing the violent behaviours. The effect can be much more far-reaching beyond those individuals directly involved in the violent incidents. In contrast, where young people's needs were more adequately met, staff felt that violent behaviour was more likely to diminish, and that young people were more able to concentrate on the implications of their behaviour, both for themselves and others.

The majority of these staff stressed that this was a precarious process. We saw in Chapter 6 that such work can be quickly undone if the residential dynamic changes, generally through the admission of an 'unsuitable' referral. However, some young people were very aware of the demands that residential staff were under, and praised their efforts to meet the diverse needs of the young people in their care.

> Interviewer: Is there anything you think staff could do more to support you while you're living here?
> Gail: I think they're doing everything they can 'cause they have to look after everyone that's in here and it is a hard job.

> I understand that they're doing their best. If they didn't care about us they wouldn't be here. It's because they care about us that they look after us properly. All the staff are great. I think they're all top.
>
> (Gail, aged 14)

Summary points

- Homes mostly relied on reactive rather than proactive strategies to deal with violence.
- A main strategy to respond to violence was the use of sanctions, such as early bedtimes and restricting leisure activities. Many young people and some workers felt that staff applied these inconsistently.
- Young people believed that physical restraints were used appropriately. More training was required in their proper use.
- Only a minority of cases of serious sexual violence received a formal child protection response, as the law requires.
- Efforts were made to supervise closely young people within the homes. Young people did not object to the electronic monitoring (CCTV) in three of the homes.
- There was little use of specialist, external, professional help to deal with young people's violent behaviour. Residents were positive about this when delivered by outside specialists but did not like it as part of residential regimes.
- It was generally acknowledged that wider strategies such as developing positive relationships and meeting young people's needs were important precursors to preventing violence.

9
Conclusion

The evidence that young people are often the targets of physical, sexual and psychological attack from age peers, in most settings where the young congregate, has focused research attention on the nature and meaning of the violence. There is evidence that violence between young people is universal, at least in modern western society: for example, an internet search for information on 'bullying' produced over 500 000 hits, on websites from many countries. The overview of research on violence in institutional and community settings given in Chapter 1 identified some parameters defining aggressors and victims which have been explored in this study, but it raised as many questions as answers. A number of recent quantitative surveys identify the high levels of victimisation of adolescents by other young people (Graham and Bowling 1995, Flood-Page *et al.* 2000, Beinart *et al.* 2002) and the link between youth violence and bullying in schools (Youth Justice Board 2002, 2003). The evidence is consistent that young people are both the most common victims and offenders, though violent offences are still very much a minority of youth offences.

There have been attempts to examine in greater depth the nature and causes of school bullying (Smith and Sharp 1994, Eslea and Smith 1998) and racist attacks between young people (Barter 1999, Virdee *et al.* 1999, Pitts *et al.* 2000, Cline *et al.* 2002). Outside school, however, more effort appears to have been put into deploring youth violence than in attempting to understand it, to disentangle the influences and thinking that lie behind the statistics. There has been some research attention to sexual violence between young people within the child protection discourse, focusing on the background and treatment of 'young abusers' (Vizard *et al.* 1995, Fergusson *et al.* 1997, Grubin 1998, Epps 1999) but much less exploration of the circumstances in which sexual assault occurs. Little attention has been given to young people's perspectives on violence either as a perpetrators or as victims, to the specific context of violence within children's culture or to the influence which adults can or do have in the process either for the worse or the better. There is evidence that children and young people's experience of violence is largely hidden from adults (Butler and Williamson 1994, Smith and Sharp 1994, Aye Maung 1995). Young people, far from being conveniently divisible into aggressors and victims, are likely to be both on different occasions (Smith and Sharp 1994, Browne and Falshaw 1996, Menesini *et al.* 1997, Eslea *et al.* 2004, also included on the website: Bullyweb.co.uk).

The limited attention paid to children's perspectives on violence reflects a wider tendency to ignore the importance of children as social actors, found more generally in social science until recently (James *et al.* 1998). Age as a determining issue for social organisation has been acknowledged almost since the birth of sociology, but only in the past quarter century have the views and cultures of children and young people received significant attention from sociologists.

Summary of the research

Residential care has several different purposes in the care system, offering long-term care to some young people, emergency accommodation in a crisis to others, and preparation for independence to young people leaving care. It takes many forms, from large campus-based establishments to small domestic scale houses accommodating at most half a dozen residents. Children and young people may be admitted in a wide range of circumstances, from those immediately removed from home following abuse to those held on remand awaiting trial on serious criminal charges. Many have experienced a series of previous unsuccessful placements.

The research described in this book aimed to develop understanding of children's violence towards peers in residential settings by exploring children's perspectives on the meaning and effects of violence whether as perpetrators, recipients or observers. We were interested in protective strategies adopted by children and the extent to which children and the staff caring for them had shared reference systems for dealing with violence. There were two objectives:

- To contribute to the sociology of childhood and to treat the children's perspectives as important in their own right;
- To contribute to the development of policy and practice which would safeguard children in residential settings from peer violence.

Fieldwork was conducted in 14 residential units from the local authority, voluntary and private sectors. We held interviews with 71 children (ages ranging from 6 to 17 years), in which they discussed experiences of violence between children in residential care, as victims, witnesses and perpetrators, and with 71 staff, including managers, team leaders and residential social workers. Semi-structured interviews and vignettes of violent scenarios were used to explore interviewees' experience. Interviews were introduced as being about young people's behaviour towards each other in residential care. No definition of violence was given and the interview was structured around respondents' accounts and definitions. The standard of confidentiality adopted and explained to all participants was that the interview was in confidence unless there was reason to believe that a young person was in danger, when the researchers would have to act to protect the individual concerned, by informing a senior manager in the agency responsible for the home. Appropriate contacts were identified in each agency taking part in the study for this eventuality.

Young people were asked about, and described, positive and negative aspects of their contact with fellow residents, but in almost all interviews hostility from other residents was quickly identified as one of the biggest problems of their contact with peers in residential care. Follow-up discussion explored the circumstances in which this arose, and how it was dealt with, by young people themselves and by staff, and sources of support which were available from peers, staff or elsewhere.

A conceptual framework was used from Kelly's (1987) definition of violence as a continuum of physical, emotional, verbal and sexual abuses of power. It was clear that the study could not be restricted to physical violence, since violent cultures are often underpinned and maintained by fear and threat. Discussions included all forms of attack involving direct physical assault, intimidation by looks or gestures, forceful invasions of personal space and attacks on personal property, unwelcome behaviour experienced as both abusive and sexual and spoken words hurting or intending to hurt. The discussion was not intended to obtain a measure of the frequency of violent incidents, but to clarify the context within which particular types of violence occurred and their meaning to those involved.

Young people's experience of peer violence in residential care

Nearly all young people described verbal attack as being a common feature of life in residential care, but most also described incidents of physical attack (more than half as victims) and almost half described attacks on personal property or invasions of personal space. Reports of unwanted sexual behaviour were the least common, but girls were far more likely to report this than boys, with more than one-quarter of the girls having had some experience, either directed towards themselves or observed towards others. Although the form of the interview enabled young people to choose and describe events in either present or previous homes, most were able to describe something that had taken place in their present placement. Young people described different levels of impact of violence, according to the severity of the force used, and whether the behaviour was an isolated, transitory event or part of a pattern of sustained and targeted attack.

In the homes studied, the incidents taking place during the fieldwork period were not at a level which would lead to risk of serious or life-threatening injury, and there were no occasions when researchers had to use the reporting line to senior managers in order to protect residents. While there were some descriptions of extremely serious incidents, these had become known to staff and had been dealt with, usually by removal of the aggressor. Physical violence described by residents and staff was most often punches and kicks during fights. Verbal attack predominantly took the form of name-calling concerning gender, sexuality, ethnicity, family and appearance, but could include other threat or insult. Other kinds of psychological intimidation included damaging property, or trashing personal space such as bedrooms. Sexual assault or other unwelcome sexual behaviour was usually inappropriate touching or offensive, insulting words. However some examples described by both young people and staff were serious by any standard: for example, one girl described an incident of rape in a previous placement, following which a boy had been arrested and charged; in another home residents described how a former resident had forced younger boys to swim in a nearby lake at night, while in a third, a boy had tied other children to hot radiators. These extremes were not the normal patterns of behaviour in the homes, but give an indication of the risks which some young people encounter, and for which staff need appropriate responses.

Violence as a structured element of the group culture

The present research suggests that there are indeed identifiable and coherent perspectives on peer violence among young people, which reflect values and beliefs shared within a group, and holding consequences for the group's behaviour, rather than simply being individual viewpoints. However these are not uniform among all young people, even within a single home, and certainly not for residents in the study as a whole. Very often more than one perspective could be identified, sometimes gender-linked, sometimes with a prevailing view ascribed to by most young people and a small group with a different outlook.

The difficulties faced by young people who held views different from those of the majority or who did not 'fit in', found by Frosh et al. (2002) in a community sample, were described graphically by some young people in the present study. The residential setting offered them few escapes. We found examples of young people who experienced continuous misery of regular attacks from others that they did not know how to deal with, and for which staff, even if they knew about it, sometimes also had no solutions.

In each home some young people confidently spoke out to the researchers against bullying, violence and hostility between residents, rejecting the patterns and stereotypes adopted by many of their peers. In the confines of the present study it was not possible to tell the origins of their different views, how far it reflected greater maturity, a more positive experience before and since admission to care, or the availability of support from adults or peers with a different outlook.

As well as there being separate, parallel cultures among young people, there were parallel but distinctive staff cultures. In many ways young people and staff agreed on the nature of violence. But while there are many points of similarity between the perspectives of young people and staff there are also differences, some obvious, some subtler and easily over-looked or misread.

The young people's and staff's perceptions of violence were shown to be strongly influenced by two features of life in the children's homes: the gendered nature of interaction, and the hierarchical structure of relationships within the group.

The gendered nature of violence

Both young people's and staff's perceptions were influenced by stereotypes of 'normal' behaviours within a group of young people and by gender. Physical and sexual aggression were understood and described in a context where specific expectations of 'normal' male and female behaviour set the rules within which words and actions were judged as understandable, if not always acceptable. Behaviour which was expected and tolerated as an expression of youthful masculinity was not accepted when coming from girls and young women. On the other hand, strong views of 'normal' masculinity and femininity also restricted options available to boys and young men, due to the strongly homophobic culture of the residents and their disapproval of male behaviour judged as effeminate. This stereotyping affected behaviour ranging from sexual and physical assault through verbal insult to choice of dress and language, and ways of dealing with offence given by others.

The stereotypes were often supported by accounts of actual events and by the interpretation of events given both by young people and by staff. In the specific incidents described by young people, boys were more often involved in physical fights and assaults, and girls in verbal attacks and forms of intimidation such as ignoring and excluding other young people, or damaging their property. The stereotypes that boys were more likely to use physical violence and girls more likely to resort to verbal and other forms of psychological attack were, therefore, supported by the young people's account of their own experience, in which incidents often fitted the expected pattern. For both young people and staff, boys and girls behaving true to type was expected.

Seeing what really happens or what is expected?

Obviously this data is influenced by selective choice of incidents to describe, with a possible greater tendency to focus on the familiar and expected traditionally 'masculine' or 'feminine' incidents. There were, however, also many accounts where events contradicted stereotype. Yet the element of truth in the stereotypes enabled any experience or information which contradicted them to be discounted or minimised by both young people and staff. One result was that staff underestimated female involvement in physical attack and the male use of psychological attack.

The perception of psychological attack as 'feminine' and therefore less dangerous, seemed to contribute to a general underestimation of its importance as compared to physical or sexual attack. In fact some of the worst examples of sustained attack on property and trashing residents' bedrooms were found in single-sex male units. Many young people in this study reported that the long-term effects of being threatened, or insulted, or intimidated by attacks on property and personal space was greater than that of physical assault. There is evidence from previous studies of violence in other contexts, including peer violence, that psychological assault is both more hurtful at the time and more damaging in the long-term, at least where physical assaults are at a level unlikely to cause serious injury or threaten life (Tomison and Tucci 1997, Cawson 2002). Adult failure to take verbal aggression seriously has been noted in research on bullying at school, where it also made children reluctant to seek help from staff (Oliver and Candappa 2003).

Similarly, the perception of girls as mainly choosing psychological means of intimidation led to a tendency for staff to underestimate girls' involvement in physical aggression, and to regard it as unnatural when it did occur. The problematic nature of response to physical violence by females has been identified in research on offending by girls and women. Social responses range from trivialising it and treating minor offences less seriously in some contexts, to demonising women and girls once behaviour reaches a level which cannot be ignored. Penalties for female offenders are harsher than those applied to males exhibiting the same behaviour, especially violent behaviour (Heidensohn 1995, Howard League 1997, 2000, YWCA 2001, Home Office 2002). While all research on offending shows much higher levels of violent offending by males than by females, the difference is much smaller in self-report studies than in official records. In the present study, use of violence by girls was not at a level likely to cause serious injury. However, while there might have been greater potential for some kinds of physical violence in boys' relationships, there was also a task for adult carers in confronting some aspects of girls' relationships and use of physical violence.

The gender stereotypes also led to some young people and staff minimising sexually offensive behaviour, especially verbal insult, predominantly from males to females. This was often seen as normal behaviour for male adolescents, or as being provoked and therefore instigated by the young women who were, therefore, defined as offenders rather than victims. This reflects a view of young males' inability to control their sexual behaviour, and of young women as being responsible for male behaviour, which remains in the popular belief system, even though it has long been disputed by research on sexual behaviour and sex offenders (Epps 1999, Thomas 2001, Calder *et al.* 2001).

Equally, homophobia was such a sensitive issue that most young people were not even willing to talk about it, and response to a vignette describing sexually ambiguous behaviour between boys was almost uniformly hostile. Several staff also showed considerable reluctance to discuss the issue of sexual violence between young people, raising questions about their ability to confront it if they observed it or if young people consulted them about difficulties they experienced.

Frosh *et al.* (2002) point out that the traditional 'macho' male stereotypes are harmful to the development of boys, as well as setting the scene for inappropriate treatment of girls and women. The stereotypes make it harder for boys to seek help if in difficulties and to confide in friends or seek emotional support with the uncertainties and dilemmas of maturation. Other studies have found that boys are less likely to have anyone they can talk to about a personal problem, because boys are meant to be 'tough' and able to cope (McLeod *et al.* 1996). Boys have been shown to be less likely to discuss problems with friends (Ghate and Daniels 1997, Fuller *et al.* 2000, Balding 2002).

The greater ease with which girls assume supportive and mature friendships has been used as an argument in favour of mixed- rather than single-sex environments in many contexts, including schools and children's homes. Similar arguments used to advocate co-educational day schools and mixed children's homes stress the importance of girls in ameliorating aggressive macho cultures. A generation ago, the Dartington studies of boarding schools noted that in co-educational schools, girls performed a pastoral function for boys which was quite separate from and in some respects more important than their roles as potential sexual or romantic partners (Lambert *et al.* 1975).

While the arguments that girls' presence reduces aggression in boys also reflect adult gender stereotypes, they additionally place on girls the responsibility for civilising and controlling boys (O'Neill 2001). Frosh *et al.* (2002) note the importance of adults responsible for the upbringing and education of boys being able to work on boys' relationships with each other, rather than expecting girls to solve the boys' problems. These issues also assumed importance in the present study. Mixed groups in children's homes may have many benefits for both boys and girls, but it is important to be clear about what those benefits are, and aware of the associated responsibilities for adults; most especially in a context where many young people will have had personal experience of gender-linked abusive relationships in their home environments before entering care.

Hierarchies and the pecking order

There were consistent accounts of the importance of hierarchies within the resident group. Young people and staff both described this feature of relationships between residents, identifying 'top dogs' and describing the pecking order in some detail. Whether the current hierarchy was described as oppressive and destructive or as a force for maintaining order varied, but there was strong agreement from both young people and staff that it existed.

The concept that group relationships among the young are a matter of hierarchies and pecking orders was supported by the amount of detail that the young people could give on the hierarchies in their homes, naming positions at present and identifying power figures 'in waiting'. The phenomenon was expected by young people as part of their group relationships, but it was not seen as beneficial, especially by those low in the hierarchy, for whom the hierarchy was linked with their understanding of bullying and abuse of power.

The findings from this study seriously challenge adult assumptions about the inevitability, normality and acceptability of the 'pecking order' as a feature of social relationships in groups of children and young people. For the young people hierarchies were a fact of life, but one which was more likely to cause them problems than to help them. Among those who saw the process as most intimidatory were the younger children, a common finding also in studies of bullying in schools (Balding 2002, Youth Justice Board 2003), indicating one of the particular vulnerabilities in the power structure. It is unusual for young children to be placed in residential care, and most agencies have a general policy of placing them, especially under 12s, in family placements. A young child placed in a residential home would usually be there either as an emergency placement while more suitable alternatives are sought, because their behaviour or their history of abuse in families was thought to make them 'unfosterable' (Sinclair and Gibbs 1998) or due to fostering disruptions (Berridge 1997). Either way, younger children placed in residential homes could be expected to be among the most vulnerable in the care system, and the frequency with which young people and staff described younger children as deliberately 'winding up' the older residents testified to this. When the older residents may themselves have personal experience leading to them lacking some of the inhibitors that contain violence, this is potentially a risky situation. Although younger children were among the most vulnerable, they were not the only ones: those with low status in the hierarchy due to other personal characteristics, for example, appearance or lack of 'street cred', could also have a miserable time.

For the staff the hierarchy reflected a natural social process of young people finding their place, and learning to cope with group conflict was part of 'growing up'. As long as 'top dogs' did not resort to violence and bullying, the pecking order was seen as presenting no problems, and could indeed be an asset. In the present study we did not see staff exploiting or relying on physical control by 'top dogs', as has been described over many years in studies of very large institutions, in particular of all-male institutions ranging from prisons to public schools (Lambert *et al.* 1970, Bramham 1980). There were, however, instances when staff appeared to value the influence and pressure that 'top dogs' could put on the group as a support in maintaining calm and order, or in persuading young people to accept staff guidance. It was the practice in some homes for staff to ask existing residents to take on the introduction of new residents, showing them around and introducing them to the group. In other contexts this might be a positive strategy, but in the children's homes it was common for young people to describe meeting the other residents as a primary source of anxiety when entering a new placement, and staff support at that time was important to them.

This raises a number of issues about the nature of peer authority in a group. There is a difference between the use of 'authority' and 'leadership' by young people in a hierarchy with unequal power, and the availability of support from peers in an equal relationship, in which 'authority' comes from individual respect and value for each other. Positive peer support was mentioned and valued by young people as one of the benefits of being in a children's home. This was not in itself a contradiction, since the young people distinguished quite clearly between supportive and controlling behaviour from peers. It could be a difficulty when their own need for support overrode caution and judgement over confiding in peers whom they barely knew, or who had complex emotional needs of their own.

Peers as both oppressors and supports

Peers were most likely to be the first port of call for support when young people were experiencing any kind of violence. Given the short-term nature of placements and the constantly shifting populations of many homes this is perhaps a surprising finding. In a family, older and more powerful siblings might also be sometimes experienced as oppressive while at other times supportive. Several years spent together at school is often the basis for lifetime friendship and support networks, but can also expose children to long-term pressure from bullies (Smith and Sharp 1994, Cline *et al.* 2002). Yet there is a fundamental difference in this situation, where a relationship has grown through years of childhood into adolescence, and the situation in most of the residential homes where relationships were essentially transitory. It is not a coincidence that some of the homes where peer relationships were most positive were also those where placements were longer term, or the group was smaller, and placements seemed less likely to be made at short notice without involvement of staff. But something about the residential home context enabled young people to seek some level of peer support from fellow residents known only for a short time. When asked at the beginning of the interview about the good points of living in a children's home, the young people often commented that it was helpful meeting others with similar experience and problems to their own. Possibly this common bond and the closeness of the residential setting enables a short cut to a relationship of mutual support that would take far longer to forge in other circumstances.

Nevertheless this readiness to trust peers who share the adversities of family breakdown and loss of their own homes also made residents especially vulnerable to hostility and rejection by peers. Staff commented on the way that young people would set themselves up for future distress by being too ready to confide very personal information on themselves and their families, and said that they would often warn newly admitted residents to avoid confiding in others until they had got to know them better. This emphasises the importance of an approach from adults that facilitates the positive aspects of peer support, encourages and enables young people to help each other, while reducing the opportunities and incentives for physical and psychological exploitation by peers.

The finding that peer support may be used in preference to adult support is not unique to the present study. Other research on young people in the community and away from home shows that they often are circumspect in what they will tell adults, especially professionals (Butler and Williamson 1994, Smith and Sharp 1994, Aye Maung 1995, Wattam 1999, Cawson et al. 2000). There are many reasons for this and it does not necessarily reflect lack of trust in adults. Young people may fear that they will not be believed, or that their freedom will be curtailed by adults seeking to protect them through supervision. They may have experienced well-intentioned adults taking action which has worsened their situation rather than ameliorated it (Butler and Williamson 1994, Oliver and Candappa 2003). They may lack confidence in the adult's ability to protect them. All of these effects may be enhanced in a group of young people in children's homes. Although Fuller et al. (2000) found that young people in residential care were more likely to go to their keyworkers with problems than to friends, parents or other adults, it was still only a small proportion prepared to approach professionals about anything that worried them. Just as young people in the community may conceal abuse because they are afraid of removal to care, so may many conceal it in a residential placement because they fear their own rather than the abuser's removal.

As well as these pragmatic reasons for concealing what happens, there is a powerful culture among young people which governs 'telling tales' or 'grassing' and which is linked to an understanding of the effects of such behaviour on the social organisation of the home and the peer group. Wattam (1999) analyses the complexities of 'telling' secrets in the context of children reporting sexual abuse, especially in the family or close social network. She describes the complex mesh of unwritten rules that affect what is said, and to whom, as well as the problems which surround expectations of confidentiality, for both children and professionals. Sexual assaults, by their nature, take place in a context of secrecy and guilt which may affect children's self-perception and self-esteem, or the way they think others will see them. Part of the reluctance to 'tell' is their desire to appear 'normal' and reluctance to identify themselves as 'victims'. In the context of peer violence, the young people in the present study were similarly affected by a mesh of expectations and assumptions about 'telling', when there were clearly defined and well understood shared codes about 'bullying'. They were equally reluctant to identify themselves as 'bullies' – abusers of power – or as weak, low status members of the hierarchy who were vulnerable to others.

Justification narratives

This research found, as also have studies of bullying in schools, that young people cannot be neatly divided into bullies and the bullied. There is considerable overlap between those who suffer attacks and those who inflict them, with some young people simultaneously describing both experiences. But the meaning attached to the two experiences reflects an ability to partition events in the young people's lives in a way which justifies the use of violence by themselves and condemns it for others while having no sense of the illogicality of this position. This provides a perfect context for the cyclical development and continuation of peer violence.

One thing became very clear, that violence among the young is not 'mindless' or 'senseless', but on the contrary highly socialised, operating within strict rules and moral codes. Unfortunately the moral code regulating the use of violence for many of the young people was one which supported violence in some circumstances, and victimised those already disadvantaged.

In addressing the features of children's culture which maintain and support violence, the central issue is clearly that of the belief that violence is justified in retaliation for insults or provocation, aligned with a very wide definition of what comprised provocation. The young people's accounts often reflected the double standard in the construction of an irregular verb: 'I stand up for myself and defend my honour; you hassle and provoke people; he/she bullies and abuses power'. The rejection of the label of 'bully' as a description of their own behaviour, even when describing attacks on younger and smaller children who were 'winding them up', or rejection and exclusion of peers who just didn't 'fit in', sat alongside a very articulate understanding of what bullying was when carried out by others. A consistent moral and practical response to confronting this offers the only possibility that staff can intervene in the self-perpetuating cycle. The consequences of this particular discourse of justified retaliation are potentially far greater than the immediate resolution of conflicts within the children's home. The assumption that some people deserve physical, sexual or psychological attack is the foundation of many other forms of interpersonal violence, including street violence, domestic violence and child abuse. A recent survey of young people's attitudes to offending found that almost three-quarters thought it was not wrong to hit someone who insults you (Youth Justice Board 2003). Many of the young people in children's homes will have come from backgrounds where this cycle has formed the context to their family life and their neighbourhood relationships. Their placements in care may offer them their last chance of avoiding being trapped in it into adult life.

The permeable institution and the community culture

Although the young people in the study were living in institutional settings, they were most definitely not in a glass bubble. Their views about violence were formed against a backdrop of broader social experience and norms of the families and communities from which they came. Children's homes are not total institutions in Goffman's (1961) sense. In ten of the homes young people attended local schools; though attendance was sometimes poor and some had been excluded from school. Many came from the neighbourhood close to the home, with some visiting home regularly, and keeping in contact with local friends. Some young people joined local community activities in their free time. It was sometimes difficult for the young people to find time to grant us an interview amid their hectic after school social lives, or their visits to their families. Placements were often short, interspersed with periods at home or in foster families.

This situation places great demands on staff, who also operate as members of families and communities, and bring into the home cultures and expectations from the wider world. It was common for both young people and staff in interview to draw on experience outside the home, including their own families, for explanations and analogies when describing events in the home: 'It's the same everywhere', 'It happens at school as well, not just here'.

Furthermore, in most of the homes the young people had a culture of verbal insult and swearing, developed outside the home but brought into it. It was not taken particularly seriously by most young people and was regarded by them as normal life and normal language. Yet it created a constant atmosphere of aggression, which was initially difficult for some young people when they first entered the homes, although they said that they had 'got used to it'. Staff hesitated to challenge this as they might have done in other contexts, because they were aware it was part of many residents' home background cultures, and because it was so constant that challenging it strongly could have involved permanent confrontation, and perhaps nonstop nagging (Colton 1988). This was not seen as a helpful or realistic way to work with the young people. Children's home staff are not alone in facing this dilemma. O'Neill (2001) reports similar findings of routine aggressive language in children's secure units causing distress to young people. Frosh *et al.* (2002), in a study of a community sample of boys, discuss the difficulty that constant moralising with adolescents serves only to alienate and is unlikely to change their thinking or their behaviour. They suggest that adults need to find a way to challenge harmful attitudes and behaviour without moralising, but that it is important for them not to avoid that responsibility if anything is ever to change.

Combatting racism among young people

One aspect of the findings which surprised the research team was the low level of expressed racism and the rarity with which young people in the homes seemed to deploy racist insults and attacks. Although there was a general culture of name-calling between residents which sometimes used racist language as well as other insults, young people were clear that this could be distinguished from serious, real, hurtful psychological attack. This seemed similar to the pattern described by Troyna and Hatcher (1992), exploring the complex nature of racism in young children's school experience and social relationships with each other. They describe the 'contradictory dynamics' in which children can simultaneously express both racist and egalitarian views. In their study, children used racist language in short-term quarrels with children who were otherwise good friends, as they might use other personal insults, without this necessarily representing fully formed racist views or being intended to cause serious hurt. The different experience of racism which black and white children brought to the situation meant that insults involving race had different meanings for the two groups of children. White children in Troyna and Hatcher's research had little conception of the emotional impact of their taunts on black children who had experienced or seen serious racist attacks and insults from adults towards themselves and their parents. We found the young people in children's homes (for the most part older than those in Troyna and Hatchers' study) very conscious that racism was not acceptable and was a serious and hurtful form of attack which would be taken seriously by staff. Although some groups, particularly South Asians, seemed more vulnerable, other minorities were not, and were as likely to be seen as leaders and role models.

This was unexpected because studies of adolescents in day schools, youth clubs and custodial institutions have consistently found racism between young people at high levels and a cause of distress (Barter 1999, Virdee *et al.* 1999, Pitts *et al.* 2000, Cline *et al.* 2002). In a random sample of young people in the community (Cawson *et al.* 2000), while young people from minority ethnic groups reported no more bullying at school than white respondents, more than 70 per cent of those who were bullied identified their race or ethnicity as one of the main reasons for the bullying. O'Neill (2001) reports the use of racist language in children's secure units as causing problems for young people. The young people in our sample of children's homes came predominately from socially disadvantaged and excluded groups among whom expression of racism is often found to be high.

So why was it apparently different in these children's homes? One possibility is the closeness of daily living in a multi-cultural group. In a large secondary school, custodial institution or a neighbourhood it is possible for young people to avoid close association with other ethnic groups, and Barter's (1999) review of research identified the extent to which young people segregated themselves in separate youth clubs, leisure activities and gangs. In a small children's home, however, avoidance of other residents is difficult, and the attempt would be likely to result in isolation. Another possibility is that racism was under-reported by the minority group young people to the researchers, all of whom were white. Nevertheless this does not explain why the white young people in the study should have felt unable to express racist views to the researchers if they had such views, nor why the staff accounts should have concurred so markedly with those of the young people in stating that racist attack was rare.

It was notable that racism was one area where staff were well prepared in these homes. Most homes had multi-cultural staff groups, and there were clear anti-racism policies which were written down, and with which both young people and staff were familiar. There were clearly stated sanctions against racism of which young people were aware, and staff had often received in-service training on how to deal with racism. Consequently it was an area in which they felt confident in setting a lead for young people and in responding to unacceptable behaviour. In such a complex area, staff were successful in challenging unacceptable behaviour by clear policies and expectations, leadership and consistency. Presumably such strategies could be more generally applied to other areas of residential life.

What is different about the residential setting?

The triggers for violence which were identified in the homes showed similarity to those described in other youth group contexts (e.g. Kendrick 1997, Frosh *et al.* 2002). Although the settings in schools, children's homes, youth clubs and custodial institutions are very different; the feature that they have in common is that they bring together children and young people in groups which are decided primarily by their age, and in which their interactions are subject to adult rules, mediated for group, rather than individual control. Issues concerning gender, race, sexuality and homophobia, and insults to family, especially mothers, are noted in several settings as primary sources of conflict. In many respects the young people in the homes described their peer culture and involvement in peer violence in similar terms to that found in other contexts, whether community-based, school-based, or in more enclosed custodial institutions (Virdee *et al.* 1999, Cawson *et al.* 2000, Pitts *et al.* 2000, Cline *et al.* 2002). When these issues for conflict are brought into children's homes, however, they acquire a dimension which is not present in the day school or youth club: the enforced closeness of daily living with strangers, creating round-the-clock vulnerability to the peer group. The residential children's home has a unique combination of characteristics which is different from other settings in which bullying and other peer violence has been studied. These are: the quasi-domestic setting for daily life, combined with the troubled experience of personal and small group relationships which 'looked after' children often bring with them into the care placement; the short-term, transitional nature of many placements and the resulting fluctuation in group membership. Any of these characteristics can be found singly in other settings. Only in the children's home do they come together.

Some young people in day schools and other community settings will have strained and difficult family situations, and may have experiences of abusive, violent relationships in domestic contexts. In the personal histories of residents in children's homes these are common experiences, and homes admit young people who are likely to be particularly sensitive to triggers for violence due to previous experiences of abuse and sexual exploitation. Children's homes, with their small, mixed-gender groups and daily access to the community, also differ from the large all-male boarding schools and custodial institutions in which much previous research has taken place. The children's home settings create specific vulnerabilities, and these were evident in young people's accounts of their distress at the invasion of their personal space which sometimes happened, and at peers' exploitation of their strained family situations, to wound and torment. The children's home imitates the day-to-day currency of family living but without a base of shared family knowledge, relationships and affection to mediate the frictions, conflicts and lack of privacy intrinsic to shared living space. Furthermore, the family experience of many 'looked after' children may not have given them much positive experience of harmonious family life or close relationships on which they can draw when coping with the pressures of small groups and domestic life. Many also come into residential care from a background of unsuccessful foster care placements to compound their negative experience of family and quasi-family relationships.

Another feature of the scene is the mixture of change and constancy. During the period of the fieldwork, national statistics showed that almost one-fifth of 'looked after' children in England had three or more placements in a year, with some local authorities recording much higher figures (Department of Health 2003). With an average length of placement being 8–9 months, and an average number of placements being just over two for each period of care, this represents considerable movement around the care system, including movements in and out of residential care. Nearly all the homes in our sample recorded considerable fluctuations in the frequency of violent incidents over time. Much of this appeared to be linked to the transitional status of residential placement in the young people's care careers, and the inevitable results of population change. This has implications for the group processes in homes and for the tactics needed to work with relationships between a relatively fluctuating group membership. Recent statistics indicate that the 'Quality Protects' targets to reduce numbers of placements may have begun both to reduce the numbers of placement moves and increase the length of stay (Department of Health 2002c) but the pattern is still of considerable instability of placements for many children.

Children's homes by their nature are likely to be admitting many young people in crisis, following the breakdown of their family situation or a previous placement disruption. It is the homes' task to help them to settle in, stabilise and mature. When greater stability is achieved, young people often move on, either to return home or to family placements or independent living. Consequently the home may be continuously discharging the most stable residents and replacing them with troubled newcomers, while at the same time coping with other residents who do not settle, and whose placements end abruptly and unhappily. This feature of establishments with caring and therapeutic functions has been noted previously in research on therapeutic communities (Rapoport *et al.* 1960). Studies of children's homes which include a perspective over time rather than a 'snapshot' describe some of the problems of homes with residents constantly in flux (Brown *et al.* 1998). Recent research, however, has largely ignored the effect of changing populations as a system variable, which both has effects on residents, and requires specific, targeted approaches to address its consequences.

The present research showed that, in spite of these changing groups, there was a clearly identifiable children's culture which was passed on within a home, which at times supported or led to considerable violence and at others appeared to reject violence. Although conclusions are tentative, there did appear to be a pattern in which the more violent cultures persisted over time in some homes, in spite of the inevitable short-term fluctuations due to change in populations. While we are a long way from being able to explain fully the conditions for this, in the context of previous research and of similarities in accounts from staff in the present study, it seems likely to reflect the management context for the homes. Staff in the present study gave similar explanations to those identified in Sinclair and Gibbs' (1998) study of children's homes as distinguishing good from poor homes. The extent to which staff felt empowered in managing the intake and discharge of residents, and in having a say in whether placements were appropriate, were identified by staff as affecting their ability to control and influence the young people, and to protect those in their charge. This is linked to their ability to maintain commitment to the stated purpose of a home, rather than allowing it to be used to solve all urgent placement problems. Bullock *et al.* (1993) identify a number of studies over a 30-year period with similar findings on the importance of staff involvement in decisions, raising questions about our inability to learn the lessons from research and incorporate them into practice and management of services.

Understanding the roots of violence

The extent to which both young people and staff interpreted peer violence solely in the context of the immediate situation and the triggers for violent incidents, is a cause for concern. Only the managers and most experienced workers commonly drew links between young people's previous histories and their current behaviour. Inevitably this would make it harder for staff to address behaviour in a way that would have meaning for young people. These difficulties are likely to be compounded by the gendered assumptions discussed earlier, which rated behaviour as typical or untypical of boys and girls, and which therefore under-estimated the amount of physical violence among girls and psychological attack among boys. It is also notable that staff were more likely to think of previous history as relevant for girls than for boys, perhaps linked to their perception of boys' physical violence as being immediate and short-term whereas girls' psychological violence was seen as long-term and persistent. A number of staff said that they did not like working with girls, which appeared to reflect a perception of girls as more devious and complicated than boys. This could also perhaps reflect a greater expectation of pathology among girls who are physically violent, since such behaviour is not expected of girls.

There were some aspects of peer violence where the consensus among the young people appeared greater than that among staff. It is not immediately clear why this should be so. Although there was high turnover among staff in some of the homes, the staff group probably was more stable then the resident group in most homes. Differences between staff sometimes appeared to reflect differences between staff and management thinking. Practice is also informed and regulated by a whole host of external influences ranging from professional training, previous experience and different residential settings, and the policies and guidance issued by the agency responsible for the home.

The more sophisticated understanding of the roots of violence by the managers and more experienced staff may be linked to training. One of the questions arising from this research is whether it makes a difference to combatting or controlling violence as distinct from understanding violence. It may also make a difference to the long-term development of coherent staff strategy. Sinclair and Gibbs (1998) questioned whether training was significant in distinguishing between good and bad homes, but this was in a context similar to that of the present study, where very few staff had full professional training. It is impossible to do more than speculate about the likely effects of training for residential staff in the homes in the present study, as in none was there a majority of staff qualified in social work or other work with young people. Although in eleven homes the Heads/Managers were qualified social workers, only one deputy and one residential social worker had this level of training. Most of the other staff interviewed were undertaking National Vocational Qualification (NVQ), the recently introduced in-service training for residential work, usually at Level 3.

There are issues about the nature of training needed. In the recent past training in residential work meant the Diploma in Social Work, which, like its predecessors, was largely a training for working with individuals and families, not with groups of children or adolescents. Training for teachers and youth workers, another common background for residential workers with children, is training for educational and developmental objectives but does not prepare students to deal with bullying in schools, let alone the kinds of trauma experienced – or generated by – young people in the care system (e.g. Baginsky 2000a). Sharp and Thompson (1994) show the difference that six short specialist sessions of in-service training for teachers could make to reducing bullying in day schools, but also comment on the problems of organising training and the importance of management commitment to the process. The change recently introduced into residential social work training through NVQ can only ensure that staff in group care situations with children and young people are given the right preparation to deal with peer violence if group care issues, and conflict between young people, are addressed in sufficient depth. Recent critiques of the introduction of NVQ for residential social work suggest reasons to be concerned over whether this model will be adequate (Hopkins 2003, Sharpe 2003).

Tackling different levels of violence

Children's homes admit young people with challenging behaviour and conflicting needs. Those with histories of abuse and of abusing others may be placed together (Farmer and Pollock 1998, O'Neill 2001). As fewer young people are admitted to residential care and family placement increasingly becomes the primary choice for young people living away from home, the likelihood that those with the most troubled histories will be placed together, in enforced close contact in small residential homes, is probably increasing rather than decreasing. Farmer and Pollock (1998) show that neither children's home staff nor foster carers were trained to work with young sexual abusers in the care system. The response they described was usually to make sure the abuser was not placed with younger children, or to place them in foster care. Neither solution protected potential victims.

The violence described in this study operated on a number of different levels. Most was casual low impact violence, of a kind that operates in many group settings for children, and was usually triggered by the immediate situation. Strategies to deal with violence of this nature could be very similar to those found useful in tackling bullying in schools and custodial institutions, although there is a need to develop the tools and techniques for use in a small group residential setting.

Some of the more serious incidents described, however, had a very different feel. There were examples which seemed to reflect the kind of physical, sexual and psychological domination found in domestic violence and other family violence. In other instances there were physical and sexual assaults which were serious criminal offences, and in some cases of threat where no physical violence had taken place, there were concerns about the mental health of the young people making the threats. There rarely seemed to have been specialist help available either to young people or staff in these more pathological situations. Usually they were resolved either by the perpetrator being arrested and transferred to custody, or simply being moved on to another placement.

The problem of placing children and young people who pose a serious risk to others is one that all services face constantly, but around which there has been little open discussion or development of best practice. These young people are themselves vulnerable and they have to live somewhere. They cannot be placed appropriately in services for adults, out of contact with age peers, nor kept in solitary confinement. It is imperative that we address the issue of what is a safe and effective placement, and what are the skills needed to confront their behaviour.

Confronting peer violence – strategies and standards

Social work has lagged behind other services in confronting the implications of peer violence. Only in 2002 did inspection standards for children's services incorporate for the first time specific requirements for children's homes and secure units to prevent and counter bullying among residents (Department of Health 2002a). Although previous standards did cover child protection practice, the boundaries between this and the management of behaviour to ensure children's welfare and good order in the home, were not spelled out.

The absence of strategic approaches to peer violence is in marked contrast to the approach taken in education and young offender services, which both began a decade ago to address issues of violence and bullying between young people. In recent years this has led to very specific and national anti-bullying initiatives, guidance and training for schools and young offender institutions. There is a specific duty placed on head teachers, enshrined in legislation, of 'encouraging good behaviour and respect for others on the part of pupils and in particular preventing all forms of bullying among pupils' (S61(a) Schools Standards and Framework Act 1998). There is a specific duty on Local Education Authorities (LEAs) to combat bullying, and detailed guidance is offered to staff, pupils and parents by the Department for Education and Skills (2002). A recent inspection and survey, focused specifically on bullying, reported that all LEAs that were visited employed staff with specific responsibilities for supporting anti-bullying work in schools and that most provided in-service training on the topic for teachers and for pupils involved in peer mentoring (Office for Standards in Education 2003).

Similarly, the Prison Service has had an anti-bullying strategy since 1993, and revised it comprehensively in 1999 (HM Prison Service 1999). While there is no equivalent reference in legislation to bullying or peer violence, Rule 55 of the Young Offender Institution Rules specifically prohibits assaults and fights, action endangering the health or personal safety of others and the use of threatening, abusive, insulting and racist words or behaviour. Attention to peer violence and other bullying is a major part of the Prison Service inspection regime, and is monitored regularly, including the use of surveys of young prisoners to identify whether and where they feel safe or unsafe in their establishment.

For children's homes strategic development is at a much earlier stage. Children's homes are now required to have a policy which is known to children and staff (Department of Health 2002a). There is no more general strategic guidance available so far other than a single paragraph (Para. 18, 1–5, pp. 26/7) in the standards document. Since inspection reports, formerly published on the Social Services Inspectorate website, are no longer freely available on the National Care Standards Commission website, it is not easy to check how rigorously this is enforced. Having a national strategy document is not in itself enough to protect young people; inspections in young offender institutions and surveys of pupils at school still continue to suggest high levels of bullying in both (HM Chief Inspector of Prisons for England and Wales 2002, Children's Rights Alliance for England 2002, Balding 2002, Youth Justice Board 2003). Nevertheless it is the first step to establishing a climate within which staff recognise the problem and know what they should do to counter it. Evaluations of different approaches have shown that effective management, intervention and support to victims can reduce levels of peer violence. Managers need to ensure that staff hold high expectations of young people's behaviour (Hicks et al. 2003). In school settings, the most effective responses to bullying were found when the head teacher gave the lead in dealing with any incidents (Cline et al. 2002). In the present study the role of the Head of Home was also crucial in setting standards. Examples of good practice included homes where there was emphasis on building positive and trusting relationships between staff and young people, and on positive reward systems rather than focusing only on negative behaviour.

Services which have, and evaluate, strategies to combat peer violence stress the importance of a 'whole' institution approach which involves all players: management, staff, students and parents, residents or inmates.

Without consistency in delivering the messages, supporting the victims and providing the necessary resources, human and material, strategies and policies are just paper exercises.

Clear definitions and descriptions of the unacceptable behaviour and its consequences are a prerequisite. The present research has shown that in the children's home context the term 'bullying' is not sufficient to encompass the full range of physical, sexual and psychological assault which can harm and distress residents. Young people use it to refer only to one aspect of peer violence, and rarely to describe either their own use of aggressive tactics or their experience as victims. The review of evidence in Chapter 1 identified the lack of clarity and consistency with which the terms 'bullying' and 'peer abuse' were used in government and professional literature. Identifying the appropriate boundaries between the use of child protection procedures and the use of other measures to prevent harm, control unacceptable behaviour, or mediate conflict between young people, is crucial. In the present study, staff in some homes had undertaken in-service training in child protection, and had little difficulty in identifying situations where peer assaults had crossed the boundaries of child protection concerns, at least in relation to physical and sexual assault. In other homes staff were much less confident. Children's homes are not the only settings in which this dilemma is found. As the Children's Rights Alliance for England (2002) points out in the context of young offender institutions, it would clearly not be practical to refer every fight between young people for a S47 enquiry and child protection conference, but the availability of clear guidance is crucial to the protection of young people. There is a need for social work to develop clearer guidelines for the use of child protection procedures in relation to peer assaults in group care.

Experience in working with groups of young people in residential and non-residential contexts has now explored many possible approaches to reducing bullying and other peer violence, including mentoring, peer counselling and 'listener' schemes, mediation, group education and discussion, 'no blame' approaches, adult counselling, helplines and confidential reporting systems (Smith and Sharp 1994, Eslea and Smith 1998, HM Prison Service 1999, Department for Education and Skills 2002). Techniques that work in one setting are not necessarily amenable to direct transfer to other settings, but there is a good enough evidence base to make a start on identifying the most hopeful approaches for the children's home setting. Monitoring and evaluating the effectiveness of any strategy may need different methods and be more complex and difficult in these small group settings than in a large school or young offender institution, where confidential questionnaires have been used to good effect. Meetings with inspectors, as required by the inspection standards for children's homes, may be of relatively limited use to obtain information on bullying in a very small group, when young people know that inspection findings will be reported back to management and form part of a public report. Inspections have in the past failed to identify abusive regimes by such means (Cawson 1997). But the care system is now developing more experience in the use of independent, confidential advice, advocacy and representation schemes, and in working with young people to address and resolve problems and complaints on sensitive topics. The building blocks of a more comprehensive, coherent and inclusive approach to addressing violence are there.

Using the strengths of young people's culture

In developing strategies and guidance and working to reduce peer violence it is essential to use the experience and insights of young people as well as of staff. The young people in the children's homes we visited showed themselves well able to differentiate between attacks by peers in terms of their seriousness, impact and potential for harm, though their assessment was not necessarily identical to that which would have been made by adults. This too is a dilemma that faces many child protection services. If young people lack confidence in the protective systems set up by adults, or fear that major decisions affecting them will be made over their heads, and regardless of their wishes, they are likely to deal with the situation by concealing what is happening to them or to other residents. Evaluation of interventions with both young people's and adults' behaviour in relation to offending, bullying, child maltreatment and other problems also stresses the importance of recognising people's strengths and building on their skills, rather than focusing on their failures. Turnell and Edwards (1999) point out that professionals often make the mistake of focusing on the small proportion of someone's behaviour that is problematic, and ignoring the much larger proportion that is socially acceptable and competent. They cite Thomas's (1995) description of his work with delinquent children: 'Directing 100% of my attention to roughly 5% of these boys' behaviour was the worst investment I ever made.'

The young people in the care system have often been excluded in many ways from responsible participation in their own futures. Many are not in school, have low educational achievements, and poor employment prospects, damaged self-esteem and difficulties in social relationships on many fronts. They may have little choice over present and future placement, or the direction their lives will take when they leave care. Yet the young people in this study demonstrate that when given the opportunity, they are able to give an articulate, detailed and insightful analysis of situations that cause them grief. They show understanding of complex rules and social pressures, the capacity to see through false attempts to engage, consult or control them, and extraordinary resilience in the face of adversity and unhappiness. They surely deserve to have their experience, skills and understanding taken seriously by the managers and policy makers who set the agenda for the care system.

Supporting residential care

Many young people will have had histories that have given them little reason in the past to trust adults, whether parents or professionals. Frequent moves of placement, combined with frequent staff changes in residential care, mean that there is often little chance to establish continuity of relationships with staff, enabling trust to be built up over time. Residential staff in some respects have everything stacked against them in the struggle to win trust from the young people for whom they care. In many respects the present study shows how well they did. Most young people named at least one member of staff as someone they could talk to and almost all expressed confidence in staff's intervention to protect them from physical violence.

Two recent accounts of research on residential staff presented polar opposite views of residential social work, and illustrate the different conclusions that can be reached from similar data. Mainey (2003a,b) reports staff experiences and morale very similar to those reported in the Department of Health (1998) research programme, and found in the present study. She noted that while many residential staff expressed frustration at the lack of support they often experienced from colleagues outside the home and other services such as education, they were for the most part 'motivated, committed and generally satisfied in their work' (2003b, p. 37), gaining much satisfaction from contact with the young people and from teamwork with supportive colleagues and managers. This, she considered, presented a cheering message, indicating a service which should be more highly valued. However a similar study published almost simultaneously with Mainey's reported a depressing picture of life in residential children's homes in which staff felt they achieved little, were apathetic and had no role in tackling children's problem behaviour (Heron and Chakrabarti 2002). While the specific problems described by staff in Heron and Chakrabarti's study seem quite similar to those reported by Mainey and other studies of children's homes, and in our study, the authors say that they raise fundamental questions about the value of children's homes.

Yet to suggest this is to imply that there are other services that are available and able to do better. The reality is that most young people who spend substantial periods in children's homes have already had breakdowns of foster care, sometimes several. For many of them neither family placement nor immediate return home is an option, and many whose experience of family life has been negative express a preference for residential care in spite of the pressures they experience (Berridge and Brodie 1998). Sinclair and Gibbs (1998, p. 5) note that the 'combination of cost and scandal mean that residential care may not survive. That it has survived so far reflects the difficulty of doing without it'. In the past, studies of care careers showed that a high proportion of the young people entering public care would spend some time in a residential establishment, even if they subsequently settled in a family placement (Rowe, et al. 1989). Although no recent comparable figures are available on the total use of residential care, the 'looked after children' statistics still show almost twice as many young people leaving residential placements in the course of a year as are in residence on 31 March, the date used for recording placements. In 2000–01, over 12 000 young people left a children's home placement, and this figure does not include the unknown number who were in residence for the whole year (Department of Health 2002b). We have therefore to address the issues which residential care presents now; they cannot be permanently avoided in pursuit of a probably illusory future in which there will be ideal family placements for all. There is certainly no evidence, in this or other recent research which includes the views of young people, to support the stereotype that residential care is always a negative experience, or that family placement would always be the better option or the one that the young people would have chosen. There is considerable evidence that longstanding failure to address some of the substantive issues about training, management, poor placement planning, and integration of homes with other services for children often makes life in children's homes far more difficult than it need be, both for residents and staff (Utting 1997).

The concerted effort made in recent years through government programmes such as 'Quality Protects', and now 'Choice Protects', the development of more rigorous and consistent criteria for inspection, and the introduction of NVQ standards should all contribute to making children's homes safer and happier places. These changes can only do so, however, if there also is a change in the management culture in some agencies towards a greater recognition of the level of need and the potential contribution of the young people, combined with greater valuing of the work of residential homes and investment in their staff.

Children's homes have had a chequered history in the recent past, with much bad publicity due to poor and often abusive standards of care. The major scandals of 'historic abuse' in Staffordshire, Leicestershire and North Wales, in which children were abused by staff, have contributed to a perception of homes as dangerous and uncaring environments, able to offer young people only negative experiences (Levy and Kahan 1991, Kirkwood 1993, Waterhouse 2000). This perception can be found both in the media and in professional social work contexts. Yet the picture presented in research is often very different, of homes where there are great variations in standards, in the competence of management and staff and in the quality of experience given to young people. As we have seen, a preoccupation with abuse by adults has underplayed the damage caused by violence between children and young people. The present research adds to the body of evidence that the way a children's home is run does make a difference to the quality of experience for the children and young people who live there.

Peer violence: an aspect of social relations

The organisation of human social life is largely under the control of adults, and adults create the contexts where children and young people's primary interactions and relationships are in age-layered groups. Yet that process by its nature sets up a dynamic which adults are not necessarily in a position to oversee, and in which children become independent actors. The links between the culture of children and young people and those of the adults charged with their day to day care form a context to the present study, due to the way in which 'children are relentlessly subjected to the law, and especially the politics of adult life, which works to position them firmly in their particularity' (James et al. 1998, p. 43). At times in the past research has suggested that children's beliefs and opinions reflect those of the adults around them, at others that they are independently operating in their own world, and that all that adults can do amounts to minor influence. Opinions have differed on whether there is a collective and identifiable culture shared by all or most young people, as some previous research suggests, or a fragmented culture in which adults can divide and rule; where young people's own distressed and troubled histories militate against them developing coherent and co-operative strategies (Millham et al. 1975). Yet, neither of these extremes can be the whole picture. Children's development is a process of learning from the world around them, both from adults and other children. The present study shows the way in which cultures brought into the children's home are developed and modified in interaction with other players, both young people and staff.

The evidence cited earlier that violence between young people is common in a variety of contexts is not matched by convincing evidence that it is an inevitable feature of peer relationships. Rather, the recent evidence, including that from the present study, suggests that it is an aspect of social relations, amenable to influence and socialisation. Sinclair and Gibbs (1998, p. 235) note that bullying and sexual harassment in children's homes was linked, not only to the young people's happiness or unhappiness while in the homes, but to their long-term happiness and progress. A similar conclusion was reached in a study which included measures of peer violence and bullying in the community (Cawson 2002). It is evident that neither children's homes nor the care system can resolve the most fundamental problems of peer violence, which have their origins in much deeper rooted aspects of social relations involving children and young people. These are bound up with wider social norms concerning gender relationships, power and culture passed between generations, carried into the homes by both residents and staff but given new dimensions within the context of a residential home.

It is important to keep the evidence on children's violence in perspective. The conclusion from the Gulbenkian Commission on children and violence, that children 'are far more often victims of violence than perpetrators of violence' (Gulbenkian Foundation 1995, p. 10) was noted at the beginning of this book. It has been reinforced by substantial research evidence since the Gulbenkian report was written (Flood-Page *et al.* 2000, Beinart *et al.* 2002, Simmons 2002). The Commission also noted that violence to children and violence by children are inextricably linked. In the situation of peer violence in children's homes we see the connection at its most obvious, and the young people who live in the homes should be able to expect that the adults responsible for their care will work with them to find a solution.

Appendix A – Researching Violence

Feminist researchers have placed considerable emphasis on the integral role that reflexivity plays within the research process (Holland and Ramazanoglu 1994, Maynard 1994). Amongst other things, this entails a consideration of the emotional impact of doing research. Within our study, the emotional impact of researching violence manifested itself in a number of significant ways. These not only impacted on us personally, in ways that were sometimes difficult to acknowledge, but also had implications for the research process itself and, ultimately, on how we conceptualised violence within the study.

For example, a central concern in the design of our methodology was to minimise the potential distress for children that talking about violence may bring, and ultimately our role as researchers was to 'discover' and explore these violent incidents. Inevitably, some of these experiences were very painful for children to talk about and for us to listen to. Throughout the process, we tried to ensure that the young person remained in control over what was discussed and in how much detail, however in practice this was not always so clear-cut. While as a team we are experienced researchers, the need to continue to probe into what is obviously a distressing experience, no matter how sensitively this is undertaken, is difficult and generates contradictory feelings. In these instances, we had to make rapid judgements about whether or not to stop the interview, take a break, change the direction of the interview and return to the 'distressing' part later. We were also acutely aware of the possibility of giving an inappropriate comment or remark, or that our body language may have contradicted our (verbal) efforts to be 'non-judgmental' or 'comfortable' with what participants were saying, especially when they were discussing their own use of violence.

Linked to this was the need to maintain some sort of emotional distance and avoid being perceived by the children as counsellors. This was an especially problematic stance to maintain when children were using the interview to unburden themselves. Although we practised 'active listening' where we acknowledged the children's experiences and pain, our role was not to provide counselling. We did, however, offer participants information regarding services that would be able to provide this specialist support if they wished. We also asked the young person if they would like a worker or a friend to stay with them after the interview, or if there was anyone we could contact on their behalf. However, despite all our efforts, and even though many children stated they valued the opportunity to talk and to have their views taken seriously, we were both acutely aware that ultimately some of these children would have to deal with the impact of revisiting these painful experiences.

We also had to contend with issues of personal safety due to physical violence. For example, in one home a physical fight broke out between two young men in a narrow corridor, which trapped one of us in the middle. Feelings for personal physical safety were heightened in this case after we found out that one of the boys had a knife with him. There were also times when children confronted us directly with their own use of violence, through verbal and non-contact forms of intimidation, such as spitting at us, making jokes at our expense and through the use of verbal insults. Generally, such 'attacks' were initiated against us only when the children concerned had an audience to perform for, often individually they acted very differently with us.

We found this a difficult position to be in, not only due to the effect such behaviour had on us personally, but also due to the fact that our presence was being manipulated to reinforce directly and perpetuate violent reputations.

Fundamental to the aims of our research was the positioning of ourselves as less 'adult-centric' (Mandell 1988, Mayall 2000). This involved us being non-judgemental and stopping ourselves from intervening, even when comments were deliberately aimed to harm others. We found not intervening immensely difficult at times, particularly when children were being physically violent, or verbally attacking or humiliating another young person in our presence. Often in these instances we felt distinctly uneasy in our passivity, as a swift intervention from us could have halted the abusive interactions. Thus, when our least adult-centric position became too uncomfortable, we sought to project ourselves into the abusive encounter and thereby remove or at least divert attention away from the 'victim'. And in some instances, direct intervention was necessary for the protection of children from physical injury. For a fuller description, we have written a 'confessional' and reflexive account of the methodological and ethical implications of undertaking fieldwork in situations of on-going violence and the impact upon the researcher and ultimately the research process and design (Barter and Renold 2002).

Appendix B – Analysing the Data

All of the interviews were tape-recorded and fully transcribed for detailed analysis. Given the thousands (over 3000) of pages of interview data, we chose to employ NUD*IST4 as one of the most suitable computer packages to assist in the organisation, management and analysis of large qualitative data sets (Richards 1995). Furthermore, it allows for speedy code, search and retrieval techniques from which data, codes and categories can be rigorously theorised. The vast quantity of interview data means that it is impossible to analyse and explore in-depth all of the themes, categories and relationships between and within them throughout the duration of the research. However, what we do provide is a comprehensive and thorough overview of the key themes that have arisen from our 'interactive reading' (Dey 1993) and thematic analysis of the interviews. From our initial reading of the data and early impressions, a temporary coding frame was constructed. We then took a sub-sample of interviews and reconstructed the coding frame to enable us to explore the following.

Definitions and conceptualisations of violence (what, how and why)

This allowed us to map not only researcher definitions of different types of violence (such as verbal violence, physical violence, property attacks) but also participants' own definitions (such as 'bullying', 'cussing', 'acting out'). We also coded for the impact of violence, rationales for engaging in violent behaviour, young people's coping strategies and management of violence and violent behaviours.

Contextualisation of violence (where and when)

Young people's accounts would then be coded at a number of structural levels to examine and differentiate between the location and timing of violence.

Experience of violence (who)

Staff and young people drew not only upon their own experiences of violence, but also others' experiences, including witnessing or hearing about peer violence within the home. The 'who' category enabled us to distinguish personal or indirect experiences of violence, alongside the number (e.g. one to one or group violence), gender (male to female, female to male), age and ethnicity of the young people involved.

Coding at these different thematic and structural levels enabled us, through NUD*IST4's powerful search tools, to ask quite complex questions of the data and explore many different relationships between codes and categories, such as:

- To what extent does 'bullying' include verbal, physical, emotional and sexual behaviours?
- Do young people and staff define 'bullying' in different ways?
- How are these definitions shaped by age, gender, ethnicity and context?

- To what extent are 'bullying' accounts personal experiences only?
- How many young people report experiences from current children's homes?

To overcome the fragmentation and de-contextualisation often inherent in the coding process (Tesch 1990), *summary profiles* were written and accounts of *single events* were maintained. We produced one-page summaries of each interview, which allowed us to maintain the continuity and linearity of young people's narratives. This was especially important, not only to gain an overview of a young person's experience and background, but enabled us to pull together different and often multiple interpretations of a single incident within the same children's home – thus maintaining the complexity and contradiction of experience. With many accounts being divided in terms of incident, experience, impact, coping strategy and management and others, and with some young people and staff finding it difficult to remember when or where an incident may have occurred, we felt it was necessary to keep hold of experiences of violence that incorporated both contextual and conceptual codes within a single incident.

While NUD*IST4 enabled, and some of the data analysis involved, a quantitative element insofar as it was possible to state how many young people had reported experience of or engaged in particular types of violent behaviours, or how many reported disclosing incidents to staff and so on, the main thrust of the analysis is qualitative. That is, we have been guided by and have produced and grounded our understandings and theorisations from the accounts and interpretations of young people's (and staff's) own experiences.

Appendix C – Sample Breakdown

Young people

Table C1 Age and gender of young people

Age (years)	Male	Female	Total
6	1	0	1
7	1	0	1
8	1	0	1
9	1	2	3
10	1	2	3
11	1	2	3
12	2	0	2
13	7	6	13
14	9	7	16
15	14	4	18
16	4	4	8
17	2	0	2
Total	44	27	71

Table C2 Gender and ethnic origin of young people

Ethic origin	Male	Female	Total
White	32	23	55
Mixed parentage	4	2	6
North African	3	2	5
African Caribbean	4	0	4
East European	1	0	1
Total	44	27	71

Staff

Table C3 Grade and gender of staff

Grades	Male	Female	Total
Manager	4	9	13
Deputy	3	4	7
Senior	6	4	10
Residential social worker	19	22	41
Total	32	39	71

Table C4 Type of home by grade of staff

Home	Manager	Deputy	Senior	Residential social worker	Total
Local Authority	9	4	8	26	47
Private	2	3	1	8	14
Voluntary	2	0	1	7	10
Total	13	7	10	41	71

Table C5 Grade and ethnic origin of staff

Grade	White English	African Caribbean	Irish	South Asian	African	Total
Manager	12	0	0	1	0	13
Deputy	5	0	0	1	1	7
Senior	7	3	0	0	0	10
Residential social worker	29	4	4	2	2	41
Total	53	7	4	4	3	71

Bibliography

Ackland, J. (1982) *Girls in Care*, Aldershot, Gower.
Aiers, A. and Kettle, J. (1998) *When Things Go Wrong: Young People's Experience of Getting Access to the Complaints Procedure in Residential Care*, London, National Institute for Social Work.
Alexiadou, N. (2001) 'Data analysis in institutional contexts', *International Journal of Social Research Methodology*, 4 (1), 51–69.
Alldred, P. (1998) 'Ethnography and discourse analysis: Dilemmas in representing the voices of children', in J. Ribbens and R. Edwards (eds), *Public Knowledge and Private Lives*, London, Sage.
Archer, J. (1992) 'Childhood gender roles: Social context and organisation', in H. McGurk (ed.), *Childhood Social Development: Contemporary Perspectives*, Hillsdale, USA, Lawrence Erlbaum Associates: 31–61.
Arora, C.M.J. and Thompson, D.A. (1987) 'Defining bullying for secondary school', *Education and Child Psychology*, 4 (3), 110–20.
Askew, S. (1989) 'Aggressive behaviour in boys: To what extent is it institutionalised?' in D.P. Tattum and D.A Lane (eds), *Bullying in Schools*, Stoke-on-Trent, Trentham Books.
Astor, R. (1994) 'Children's moral reasoning about family and peer violence: The role of provocation and retribution', *Child Development*, 65, 1054–67.
Aye Maung, N. (1995) *Young People, Victimisation and the Police: British Crime Survey Findings on Experiences and Attitudes of 12- to 15-Year-Olds*. London, HMSO.
Back, L. (1994) 'The "White Negro" revisited', in A. Cornwall and N. Lindisfarne (eds), *Dislocating Masculinity*, London, Routledge.
Baginsky, M. (2000a) *Child Protection and Education*, London, NSPCC.
Baginsky, M. (2000b) 'Training teachers in child protection', *Child Abuse Review*, 9 (1), 74–81.
Balding, J. (2002) *Young People in 2001: The Health Related Behaviour Questionnaire Results for 15 881 Young People Between the Ages of 10 and 15*. Exeter, University of Exeter, Schools Health Education Unit.
Baldwin, N. (1990) *The Power to Care in Children's Homes: Experiences of Residential Workers*, Aldershot, Avebury.
Barter, C. (1996) *Nowhere to Hide: Giving Young Runaways a Voice*, London, Centrepoint.
Barter, C. (1997) 'Who's to blame: Conceptualising institutional abuse by children', *Early Child Development and Care*, 133, 101–4.
Barter, C. (1998) *Investigating Institutional Abuse of Children: An Exploration of the NSPCC Experience*, London, NSPCC.
Barter, C. (1999) *Protecting Children from Racism and Racial Abuse: A Research Review*, London, NSPCC.
Barter, C. and Renold, E. (1999) 'The use of vignettes in qualitative research', *Social Research Update*, 25, University of Surrey.
Barter, C. and Renold, E. (2000) 'I wanna tell you a story: The application of vignettes in qualitative research with young people', *Social Research Methodology, Theory and Practice*, 3 (4), 307–23.

Barter, C. and Renold, E. (2002) 'Dilemmas of control: Methodological implications and reflections of foregrounding children's perspectives on violence', in E. Stanko and R. Lee (eds), *Researching Violence*, London, Routledge, 88–106.

Batchelor, S., Burman, M. and Brown, J. (2001) 'Discussing violence: Let's hear it from the girls', *Probation Journal*, 48 (2), 125–34.

Beinart, S., Anderson, B., Lee, S. and Utting, D. (2002) *Youth at Risk?: A National Survey of Risk Factors, Protective Factors and Problem Behaviour Among Young People in England, Scotland and Wales*. London, Communities that Care.

Bell, V. (1993) *Interrogating Incest, Feminism, Foucault and the Law*, London, Routledge.

Belle, D. (1989) *Children's Social Networks and Social Supports*, Chichester, Wiley.

Berger, P.L. and Luckman, T. (1966) *The Social Construction of Reality: A Treatise in the Sociology of Knowledge*, Harmondsworth, Penguin.

Berndt, T.J. (1986) 'Children's comments about their friendships', in M. Perlmutter (ed.), *Cognitive Perspectives on Children's Social and Behavioural Development: The Minnesota Symposia on Child Psychology*, Volume 18, Hillsdale, USA, Lawrence Erlbaum Associates, 189–212.

Berridge, D. (1985) *Children's Homes*, Oxford, Blackwells.

Berridge, D. (1994) 'Foster and residential care reassessed: A research perspective', *Children & Society*, 8 (2), 132–50.

Berridge, D. (1997) *Foster Care: A Research Review*, London, Stationery Office.

Berridge, D. and Brodie, I. (1998) *Children's Homes Revisited*, London, Jessica Kingsley.

Borland, M., Laybourn, A., Hill, M. and Brown, J. (1998) *Middle Childhood: The Perspectives of Children and Parents*, London, Jessica Kingsley.

Braithwaite, J. and Daly, K. (1994) 'Masculinities, violence and communitarian control', in T. Newburn and E. Stanko (eds), *Just Boys Doing Business? Men, Masculinities and Crime*, London, Routledge.

Bramham, P. (1980) *How Staff Rule*, Aldershot, Saxon House.

Brannan, C., Jones, J. and Murch, J. (1993) 'Lessons from a residential special school enquiry: Reflections on the Castle Hill Report', *Child Abuse Review*, 2 (4), 5.

Brannen, J. and O'Brien, M. (1996) *Children in Families: Research and Policy*, London, Falmer Press.

Brinkworth, L. and Burrell, I. (1994) 'Sugar 'n Spice.... Not at all Nice', *Sunday Times*, 27 November.

Brown, A. (1993) 'Caution assessments for adolescent sexual offenders: Shropshire Adolescent Sexual Offenders Programme', *Nota News* (March), 24–36.

Brown, E., Bullock, R., Hobson, C. and Little M. (1998) *Making Residential Care Work: Structure and Culture in Children's Homes*, Aldershot, Ashgate.

Browne, K. and Falshaw, L. (1996) 'Factors related to bullying in secure accommodation', *Child Abuse Review*, 5, 123–7.

Bullock, R., Little, M. and Millham, S. (1993) *Residential Care for Children: A Review of the Research*, London, HMSO.

Burman, M., Batchelor, S. and Brown, J. (2001) 'Researching girls and violence: Facing the dilemmas of fieldwork. Centre for Crime and Justice Studies', *British Journal of Criminology*, 41 (3), 443–59.

Butler, I. and Williamson, H. (1994) *Children Speak: Children, Trauma and Social Work*, London, Longmans.

Butler, J. (1990) *Gender Trouble*, Cambridge, Polity Press.

Butler, J. (1997) *Gender as Performance: An Interview with Judith Butler for Identity and Difference*, Milton Keynes, Open University Press.

Calder, M. (2001) *Juveniles and Children who Sexually Abuse: Frameworks for Assessment*, Lyme Regis, Dorset, Russell House Publishing.

Calder, M., Hampson, A. and Skinner, J. (1999) *Assessing Risk in Adult Males who Sexually Abuse Children: A Practitioner's Guide*, Lyme Regis, Dorset, Russell House Publishing.
Cameron, D. and Fraser, E. (1987) *The Lust to Kill: A Feminist Investigation of Sexual Murder*, Cambridge, Polity.
Carabine, J. (2000) 'Constituting welfare subjects through poverty and sexuality' in G. Lewis, S. Gerwirtz and J. Clark (eds), *Rethinking Social Policy?*, London, Sage Publications.
Carlen, P. (1987) 'Out of care into custody' in P. Carlen and A. Worrell (eds), *Gender, Crime and Justice*, Milton Keynes, Open University Press.
Cawson, P., Wattam, C., Brooker, S. and Kelly, G. (2000) *Child Maltreatment in the United Kingdom: A Study of the Prevalence of Child Abuse and Neglect*, London, NSPCC.
Cawson, P. (2002) *Child Maltreatment in the Family: The Experience of a National Sample of Young People*, London, NSPCC.
Cawson, P. (1997) 'Who will guard the guards? Some questions about the models of inspection for residential settings with relevance to the protection of children from abuse by staff', *Early Child Development and Care*, 133, 57–71.
ChildLine (1997) *Children Living Away from Home*, London, ChildLine.
The Children Act 1989, London, HMSO.
Children and Young People's Unit (2001a) *Building a Strategy for Children: A Review of the Research*, London, HMSO.
Children and Young People's Unit (2001b) *Learning to Listen: Core Principles for the Involvement of Children and Young People*, London, Department for Education and Skills, Children and Young People's Unit.
Children's Fund (2001) *The Work of the Children's Fund*, www.cypu.gov.uk
Childern's Rights Alliance for England (2002) *Rethinking Child Imprisonment: A Report on Young Offender Institutions*, London, Children's Rights Alliance for England.
Cline T. de Abreu, G., Fihosy, C., Gray, H., Lambert, H. and Neale, J. (2002) *Minority Ethnic Pupils in Mainly White Schools*, London, Department of Education and Skills.
Cohen, J. (1994) ' "The Great Moll Reversal": Violent Crime by Women', *Sunday Times*, 20 February.
Colton, M. (1988) Dimensions of foster care and residential care practice, *Journal of Child Psychology and Psychiatry*, 1 (5), 589–600.
Colton, M. (2002) 'Factors associated with abuse in residential child care institutions', *Children & Society*, 16, 33–44.
Connell, R. (1987) *Gender and Power: Society, the Person and Sexual Politics*. Cambridge, Polity Press.
Connell, R. (1995) *Masculinities*, Cambridge, Polity Press.
Cooper, D. (1993) 'An engaged state: Sexuality, governance and the potential for change', *Journal of Law and Society*, 20, 257–75.
Cowie, J., Cowie, V. and Slater, E. (1968) *Delinquency in Girls*, Heinemann, London.
Daly, M. and Wilson, M. (1988) *Homicide*, New York, Aldine de Gruyter.
Dawkins, J. (1996) 'Bullying, physical disability and the paediatric patient', *Developmental Medicine and Child Neurology*, 38, 603–12.
Department for Education and Skills (2002) *Bullying: Don't Suffer in Silence*, London, Department for Education and Skills. http://www.dfes.gov.uk/bullying/
Department of Health and Social Security (1972) *Care and Treatment in a Planned Environment: A Report on the Community Homes Project*, London, HMSO.
Department of Health (1991) *The Children Act 1989 Guidance and Regulations*, Volume 4, London, HMSO.

Department of Health (1992) *Choosing with Care: The Report of the Committee of Inquiry into the Selection, Development and Management of Staff in Children's Homes*, London, Department of Health.
Department of Health (1995a) *Child Protection: Messages from Research*, London, HMSO.
Department of Health (1995b) Support Force for Children's Residential Care. *Residential Care for Children and Young People – A Positive Choice?* Final report to Secretary of State for Health, London, Department of Health.
Department of Health (1997) *The Control of Children in the Public Care*, London, Department of Health.
Department of Health (1998a) *Caring for Children Away from Home: Messages from Research*, Chichester, Wiley.
Department of Health (1998b) *Quality Protects: Framework for Action*, London, Department of Health.
Department of Health (2001) *Children Looked After by Local Authorities. Year Ending 31 March, England*, London, Department of Health.
Department of Health (2002a) *Children's Homes: National Minimum Standards*, London, Department of Health.
Department of Health (2002b) *The Children Act Report 2001*, London, Department of Health.
Department of Health (2002c) *The Personal Social Services Performance Assessment Framework*, London, Department of Health.
Department of Health (2003) *Children Looked After by Local Authorities, Year Ending 31 March 2002*, London, Department of Health.
Department of Health, Home Office Department for Education and Employment (1999) *Working Together to Safeguard Children: A Guide to Inter-agency Working to Safeguard and Promote the Welfare of Children*, London, Stationery Office.
Dey, I. (1993) *Qualitative Data Analysis: A User Friendly Guide for Social Scientists*, London, Routledge.
Dobash, R.E. and Dobash, R.P. (1992) *Women, Violence and Social Change*, London, Routledge.
Douglas, J. (1971) *American Social Order*, New York, Free Press.
Duncan, N. (1999) *Sexual Bullying: Gender Conflict and Pupil Culture in Secondary Schools*, London, Routledge.
Edgar, K. and O'Donnell, I. (1997) 'Responding to victimisation', *Prison Service Journal*, 109, 15–19.
Eisenberger, N., Lieberman, M. and Williams, K. (2003) 'Does rejection hurt? An FMRI study of social exclusion', *Science*, 10 October, 290–2.
Emond, R. (2002) 'Understanding the resident group', *Scottish Journal of Residential Child Care*, 1, 30–40.
Epps, K. (1999) 'Causal explanations: Filling the theoretical reservoir' in M. Calder (ed.), *Working with Young People who Sexually Abuse: New Pieces of the Jigsaw Puzzle*, Lyme Regis, Russell House Publishing.
Epstein, D. and Johnson, R. (1998) *Schooling Sexualities*, Buckingham, Open University Press.
Eslea, M. and Smith, P. (1998) 'The long-term effectiveness of anti-bullying work in primary schools', *Education Research*, 40 (2), 203–18.
Eslea, M., Menesini, E., Morita, Y., O'Moore, M., Mora-Merchan, J., Pereira, B., Smith, P. and Wenxin, Z. (2004) 'Friendship and loneliness among bullies and victims: data from seven countries', *Aggressive Behaviour*, (30), 71–73. Also see Bullyweb at www.uclan.ac.uk/facs/science/psychol/bully/bully.htm.

Farmer, E. and Pollock, S. (1998) *Sexually Abused and Abusing Children in Substitute Care*, Chichester, Wiley.

Farrington, D. (1993) 'Understanding and preventing bullying' in M. Tonry and N. Norris (eds), *Crime and Justice: An Annual Review of Research*, Volume 17, University of Chicago Press, 381–458.

Featherstone, B. and Trinder, L. (1997) 'Familiar subjects? Domestic violence and child welfare', *Child and Family Social Work*, 2, 147–59.

Fever, F. (1994) *Who Cares? Memories of a Childhood in Barnardo's*, London, Warner.

Fergusson, D., Horwood, L., and Lynskey, M. (1997) 'Childhood sexual abuse, adolescent sexual behaviours and sexual revictimization', *Child Abuse and Neglect*, 21 (8), 789–803.

Finch, J. (1989) *Family Obligations and Social Change*, Cambridge, Polity.

Flood-Page, C., Campbell, S., Harrington, V. and Miller, J. (2000) *Youth Crime: Findings from the 1998/99 Youth Lifestyle Survey*. Research Study 209. Home Office, Research, Development and Statistics Directorate.

Frosh, S., Phoenix, A. and Pattman, R. (2002) *Young Masculinities: Understanding Boys in Contemporary Society*, Basingstoke, Palgrave.

Frydenberg, E. (1997) *Adolescent Coping: Theoretical and Research Perspectives*, London, Routledge.

Fuller, R., Hallett, C., Murray, C. and Punch, S. (2000) *Young People and Welfare: Negotiating Pathways*. End of Award Report to the Economic and Social Research Council (ESRC), University of Stirling.

Gabe, J., Denney, D. and Elston, M. (2001a) *Violence Against Professionals Working in the Community*. End of Award Report no. L133251036, ESRC.

Gabe, J., Denney, D., Lee, R., Elston, M. and O'Beirne, M. (2001b) 'Researching professional discourses on violence', *British Journal of Criminology*, 41 (3), 460–71.

Gallagher, B., Bradford, M. and Pease, K. (1998) *The Nature, Prevalence and Distribution of Physical and Sexual Abuse by Strangers: Results of a School Based Study*. Final Report submitted to the ESRC.

Gardner, C. Brooks (1995) *Passing By: Gender and Public Harassment*, Berkeley, CA, University of California Press.

Geertz, C. (1973) *The Interpretation of Cultures*, New York, Basic Books.

Ghate, D. and Daniels, A. (1997) *Talking About My Generation*, London, NSPCC.

Gilmore, D. (1990) *Manhood in the Making, Cultural Concepts of Masculinity*, Yale University Press.

Glass, D. (1995) *All My Fault*, London, Virago.

Godenzi, A. (1994) 'What's the big deal? We are men and they are women' in T. Newburn and E. Stanko (eds), *Just Boys Doing Business? Men, Masculinities and Crime*, London, Routledge, 135–52.

Goffman, E. (1961) *Asylums*, New York, Doubleday.

Goffman, E. (1990) *Stigma*, Harmondsworth, Penguin.

Graham, J. and Bowling, B. Home Office Research Statistics Department (1995) *Young People and Crime*, Home Office Research Study 145, London, Home Office Research and Planning Unit.

Grubin, D. (1998) *Sex Offending Against Children: Understanding the Risk*, Police Research Series Paper 99, London, Home Office.

Gulbenkian Foundation (1995) *Children and Violence: Report of the Commission on Children and Violence Convened by the Gulbenkian Foundation*, London, Calouste Gulbenkian Foundation.

Hanmer, J. and Saunders, S. (1984) *Well-Founded Fear*, London, Hutchinson.

Hanna, C. (1999) 'Ganging up on girls: Young women and their emerging violence', *Arizona Law Review*, 41 (1), 37–42.

Hanney, L. (1996) 'Homeboys, babies, men in suits: The state and the reproduction of male dominance', *American Sociological Review*, 61 (5), 759–78.

Harden, J., Beckett-Milburn, K., Scott, S. and Jackson, S. (2000) 'Scary faces, scary places: Children's perspectives on risk and safety', *Health Education Journal*, 59, 12–22.

Hawker, D. and Boulton, M. (2000) 'Twenty years research on peer victimization and psychosocial maladjustment: A meta-analytic review of cross-sectional studies', *Journal of Child Psychology and Psychiatry*, 41 (4), 441–55.

Hearn, J. (1998) *The Violences of Men*, London, Sage.

Heidensohn, F. (1985) *Gender and Crime*, London, Macmillan.

Heidensohn, F. (1995) *Women and Crime*, London, Macmillan.

Heron, G. and Chakrabarti, M. (2002) 'Examining the perceptions and attitudes of staff working in community based children's homes: Are their needs being met?', *Qualitative Social Work*, 1 (3).

Hicks, L., Gibbs, I., Byford, S. and Weatherly, H. (2003) *Leadership and Resources in Children's Homes*, Report to the Department of Health, University of York.

Hill, M. (1997) 'Ethical issues in qualitative methodology with children' in D. Hogan and R. Gilligan (eds), *Researching Children's Experiences: Qualitative Approaches*, Trinity College Dublin, The Children's Research Centre.

HM Chief Inspector of Prisons for England and Wales (1997) *Young Prisoners: A Thematic Review*, London, Home Office.

HM Inspectorate of Prisons for England and Wales (2002) *Inspections of Young Offenders Institutions 2000–2002*, London, Home Office.

HM Prison Service (1999) *Anti Bullying Strategy*. Prison Service Order 1702, London, H.M. Prison Service.

Hodges, E., Malone, M. and Perry, D., (1997) 'Individual risk and social risk as interacting determinants of victimisation in the peer group', *British Journal of Developmental Psychology*, 33, 1032–9.

Hodgkin, R. and Children's Rights Alliance for England (2002) *Rethinking Child Imprisonment: A Report on Young Offender Institutions*. London, Children's Rights Alliance for England.

Holland, J. and Ramazanoglu, C. (1994) 'Coming to conclusions: Power and interpretation in researching young women's sexuality' in M. Maynard and J. Purvis (eds), *Researching Women's Lives from a Feminist Perspective*, London, Taylor and Francis.

Holland, J., Ramazanoglu, C., Sharpe, S. and Thompson, R. (1998) *The Male in the Head*, Tufnell Press.

Home, L., Glasgow, D., Cox, A. and Calam, R. (1991) 'Sexual abuse of children by children', *The Journal of Child Law*, 3 (4), 147–51.

Home Office (2001) *Criminal Statistics: England and Wales. Supplementary Tables 1998 Vol. 3: Recorded Offences, Fire Arms Offences and Court Proceedings by Police Force Area, Cautions*, London, Government Statistical Service.

Home Office (2002) *Statistics on Women and the Criminal Justice System*, London, Home Office.

Hood, S., Kelly, P., Mayall, B. and Oakley, A. (1996) *Children, Parents and Risk*, London, Social Science Research Unit, Institute of Education.

Hopkins, G. (2003) 'The training now arriving', *Community Care*, (1466), 34–35.

House of Commons: Home Affairs Committee (2002) *The Conduct of Investigations into Past Cases of Child Abuse in Children's Homes: 4th Report of Session 2001–2002*. Volume 2: Memoranda, London, HMSO.

Howard League for Penal Reform (2000) *The Use of Imprisonment for Girls*. Factsheet 18. London, Howard League for Penal Reform.

Howard League for Penal Reform (1995) *Banged Up, Beaten Up, Cutting Up: Report of the Howard League Commission of Enquiry into Violence in Penal Institutions for Teenagers Under 18*, London, Howard League for Penal Reform.

Howard League for Penal Reform (1997) *Lost Inside: The Imprisonment of Teenage Girls: Report of the Howard League Inquiry into the Use of Prison Custody for Girls Aged Under 18*, London, Howard League for Penal Reform.

Hoyle, C. (1998) *Negotiating Domestic Violence: Police, Criminal Justice and Victims*, Oxford, Clarendon.

Hudson, B. (1984) 'Adolescence and femininity', in A. McRobbie and M. Nava (eds), *Gender and Generation*, London, Macmillan.

Hughes, R. (1998) 'Considering the vignette technique and its application to a study of drug injecting and HIV risk and safer behaviour', *Sociology of Health and Illness*, 20 (3), 381–400.

Jackson, D. (1995) *Destroying the Baby in Themselves: Why Did the Two Boys Kill Jamie Bulger?*, Nottingham, Mushroom Publications.

James, A. (1993) *Childhood Identities: Self and Social Relations in the Experience of the Child*, Edinburgh, Edinburgh University Press.

James, A. and Prout, A. (eds) (1990) *Constructing and Reconstructing Childhood*, Basingstoke, Falmer.

James, A., Jenks, C. and Prout, A. (1998) *Theorizing Childhood*. Cambridge, Polity.

Jefferson, T. (1994) 'Theorising masculine subjectivity' in T. Newburn and E. Stanko (eds), *Just Boys Doing Business? Men, Masculinities and Crime*, London, Routledge.

Jenks, C. (1996) *Childhood*, London, Routledge.

Kahan, B. (1979a) *Growing Up in Care: Ten People Talking*, Oxford, Blackwell.

Kahan, B. (1979b) *Growing Up in Groups*, London, HMSO.

Kelly, L. (1987) 'The continuum of sexual violence' in J. Hammer and M. Maynard (eds), *Women, Violence and Social Control*, London, Macmillan.

Kelly, L. (1988) *Surviving Sexual Violence*, Cambridge, Polity Press.

Kemshall, H. and Pritchard, J. (1996) *Good Practice in Risk Assessment and Risk Management: Volume 1*, London, Kingsley.

Kendrick, A. (1997) 'Safeguarding children living away from home: A literature review', in R. Kent (1997) *Children's Safeguards Review for the Scottish Office*, Edinburgh, The Stationery Office.

Kendrick, A. and Mair, R. (2002) 'Developing focused care: A residential unit for sexually aggressive young men' in M. Calder (ed.), *Young People who Sexually Abuse: Building the Evidence Base for your Practice*, Lyme Regis, Russell House Publishing.

Kent, R. (1997) *Children's Safeguards Review for the Scottish Office*, Edinburgh, The Stationery Office.

Kirkwood, A. (1993) *The Leicestershire Inquiry 1992*, Leicester, Leicester County Council.

Kochenderfer, B. and Ladd, G. (1997) 'Victimized children's responses to peers' aggression: Behaviours associated with reduced versus continued vicitimization', *Development and Psychopathology*, 9, 59–73.

La Fontaine, J. and Morris, S. (1992) *The Boarding School Line*, London, ChildLine.

Lambert, R. (1968) *The Hothouse Society*, London, Weidenfeld and Nicolson.

Lambert, R., Millham, S. and Bullock, R. (1970) *Manual to the Sociology of the School*, London, Weidenfeld and Nicolson.

Lambert, R., Bullock, R. and Millham, S. (1975) *The Chance of a Lifetime? A Study of Boarding Education*, London, Weidenfeld and Nicolson.
Laming, H. (2003) *The Victoria Climbié Report*, London, Stationery Office.
Lees, S. (1986) *Losing Out: Sexuality and Adolescent Girls*, London, Hutchinson Education.
Lees, S. (1993) *Sugar and Spice: Sexuality and Adolescent Girls*, London, Penguin.
Levy, A. and Kahan, B. (1991) *The Pindown Experience and the Protection of Children*, Stafford, Staffordshire County Council.
Lindsay, M. (1991) 'Complaints procedures and their limitations in the light of the "Pindown" inquiry', in *Journal of Social Welfare and Family Law*, Issue 6, 432–41.
Little, M. with Kelly, S. (1995) *A Life Without Problems: The Achievements of a Therapeutic Community*, Aldershot, Arena.
Lofland, J. and Lofland, L. (1995) *Analysing Social Settings: A Guide to Qualitative Observation and Analysis* 3rd edition, Belmont, CA, Wadsworth Publishing Company.
Lunn, T. (1990a) 'Pioneers of abuse control', *Social Work Today*, 22 (3), 9.
Lunn, T. (1990b) 'Solution or stigma', *Social Work Today*, 22 (9), 20–1.
MacLeod, M., Barter, C. and ChildLine (1996) *We Know It's Tough to Talk: Boys in Need of Help: A ChildLine Study*, London, ChildLine.
McNeil, S. (1987) 'Flashing: It's effects on women' in J. Hanmer and M. Maynard (eds), *Women, Violence and Social Control*, London, Macmillan.
McRobbie, A. (1990) *Feminism and Youth Culture from 'Jackie' to 'Just Seventeen'*, London, Macmillan.
Mac an Ghaill, M. (1994) *The Making of Men: Masculinities, Sexualities and School*, Buckingham and Philadelphia, Open University Press.
Madriz, E. (1998) *Nothing Bad Happens to Good Girls*, Berkeley, CA, University of California Press.
Mainey, A. (2003a) *Better Than You Think: Staff Morale, Qualifications and Retention in Residential Child Care*, London, National Children's Bureau.
Mainey, A. (2003b) 'Winning against the odds', *Community Care*, (1466), 36–37.
Majors, R. (1989) 'Cool pose: The proud signature of black survival' in M. Kimmel and M. Messner (eds), *Men's Lives*, New York, Macmillan.
Majors, R. and Billson, J.M. (1992) *Cool Pose*, New York, Lexington Books.
Mandell, N. (1988) 'The least-adult role in studying children', *Journal of Contemporary Ethnography*, 16 (4), 433–67.
Marr, N. and Field, T. (2001) *Bullycide: Death at Playtime*, Didcot, Oxfordshire, Success Unlimited.
Mayall, B. (2000) 'Conversations with children: Working with generational issues' in P. Christensen and A. James (eds), *Research with Children: Perspectives and Practices*, London, Falmer.
Mayall, B. (2002) *Towards A Sociology for Childhood: Thinking from Children's Lives*, Buckingham, Open University Press.
Mayer, M. and Blum, A. (1971) (eds), *Healing Through Living: A Symposium on Residential Treatment*, Springfield, Illinois, U.S.A, Thomas.
Maynard, M. (1993) 'Violence towards women', in D. Richardson and V. Robinson (eds), *Introducing Women's Studies: Feminist Theory and Practice*, London, Macmillan.
Maynard, M. (1994) 'Methods, practice and epistemology: The debate about feminism and research' in M. Maynard and J. Purvis (eds), *Researching Women's Lives from a Feminist Perspective*, London, Taylor and Francis.
Maynard, M. and Winn, J. (1997) 'Women violence and male power', in V. Robinson and D. Richardson (eds), *Introducing Women's Studies: Feminist Theory and Practice* 2nd edition, London, Macmillan.

Menesini, E., Eslea, M., Genta, M., Gianetti, E., Fonzi, A., Costabile, A. and Smith, P.K. (1997) 'A cross-national comparison of children's attitudes towards bully/victim problems in school', *Aggressive Behaviour*, 23, 245–57.

Messner, M. and Sabo, D. (eds) (1990) *Sport, Men, and the Gender Order: Critical Feminist Perspectives*, Champaign, Illinois, USA.

Miedzian, M. (1992) *Boys Will be Boys: Breaking the Link between Masculinity and Violence*, London, Virago.

Millham, S., Bullock, R. and Cherrett, P. (1975) *After Grace – Teeth: A Comparative Study of the Residential Experience of Boys in Approved Schools*, Brighton, Chaucer.

Millham, S., Bullock, R. and Hosie, K. (1976) 'On violence in community homes', in Tutt (ed.), *Violence*, London, HMSO.

Millham, S., Bullock, R. and Hosie, K. (1978) *Locking Up Children: Secure Provision within the Child-Care System*, Farnborough, Saxon House.

Millham, S., Bullock, R., Hosie, K. and Haak, M. (1981) *Issues of Control in Residential Child-Care*, London, HMSO.

Mills, M. (2001) *Challenging Violence in Schools: An Issue of Masculinities*, Open University Press, Buckingham UK.

Morris, S. and Wheatley, H. (1994) *Time to Listen: The Experience of Young People in Foster and Residential Care*, London, ChildLine.

Morrison, T. (1994) 'Context, constraints and considerations for practice' in Morrison, T., Erooga, M. and Beckett, R. (eds), *Sexual Offendings against Children: Assessment and Treatment of Male Abusers*, London, Routledge.

Morrow, V. and Richards, M. (1996) 'The ethics of social research with children: An overview', *Children & Society*, 10, 39–49.

Moss, M., Sharpe, S. and Faye, C. (1990) *Abuse in the Care System. A Pilot Study by the National Association of Young People in Care*, London, National Association of Young People in Care.

Naylor, P. and Cowie, H. (1999) 'The effectiveness of peer support systems in challenging school bullying: The perspectives and experiences of teachers and pupils', *Journal of Adolescence*, 22 (4), 467–79.

National Children's Home (1992) *The Report of the Committee of Enquiry into Children and Young People who Sexually Abuse Other Children*, London, National Children's Home.

Newburn, T. and Stanko, E. (eds) (1994a) *Just Boys Doing Business? Men, Masculinities and Crime*, London, Routledge, 1–9.

Newburn, T. and Stanko, E. (1994b) 'Introduction: men, masculinities and crime' in T. Newburn and E. Stanko (eds), *Just Boys Doing Business? Men, Masculinities and Crime*, London, Routledge, 153–65.

Newburn, T. and Stanko, E. (1994c) 'When men are victims: The failure of victimology' in T. Newburn and E. Stanko (eds), *Just Boys Doing Business? Men, Masculinities and Crime*, London, Routledge.

O'Neill, T. (2001) *Children in Secure Accommodation: A Gendered Exploration of Locked Institutional Care for Children in Trouble*, London, Jessica Kingsley.

Office for Standards in Education (2003) *Bullying: Effective Action in Secondary Schools*. London, OFSTED.

Oliver, C. and Candappa, M. (2003) *Tackling Bullying: Listening to the Views of Children and Young People*, Summary Report for Childline. London, Department for Education and Skills.

Olweus, D. (1993) *Bullying at School: What We Know and What We Can Do*, Blackwell, Oxford.

Olweus, D., Block, J. and Radke-Yarrow, M. (eds) (1986) *Development of Antisocial and Prosocial Behaviour*, Orlando, Academic Press.

Olweus, D. and Endresen, I. (1998) 'The importance of sex-of-stimulus object: Age trends and sex differences in empathic responsiveness', *Social Development*, 3, 370–88.

Padley, D. (2000) *Keeping Our Children Safe. Child Victimisation: Key Issues and Implications for Community Safety Policy*. University of Portsmouth thesis for MSc in Criminal Studies.

Parker, R. (1998) 'Residential childcare', in I. Sinclair (ed.), *Residential Care: The Research Reviewed*, London, HMSO.

Parker, R., Ward, H., Jackson, S., Aldgate, J. and Wedge, P. (1991) *Assessing Outcomes in Child Care*, London, HMSO.

Parkin, W. (1989) 'Private experiences in the public domain: Sexuality and residential care organisations' in J. Hearn, D. Sheppard, P. Tancred-Sheriff, and G. Burrell, (eds), *The Sexuality of Organisation*, London and Newbury Park, CA, Sage.

Parkin, W. and Green, L. (1997) 'Cultures of abuse within residential child care', *Early Child Development and Care*, 133, 73–86.

Pitts, J. (1995) 'Public issues and private troubles: A tale of two cities', *Social Work in Europe*, 2 (1), 3–11.

Pitts, J. and Smith, P. (1995) *Preventing School Bullying*, London, Home Office Police Department.

Pitts, J., Marlow, A., Porteous, D. and Toon, I. (2000) *Inter-group and Inter-racial Violence and the Victimisation of School Students in a London Neighbourhood*, funded by the Economic and Social Research Council and Violence Research Programme, University of Luton. Reports can be accessed at http://www.regard.ac.uk.

Plummer, K. (1995) *Telling Sexual Stories: Power, Change and Social Worlds*, London, Routledge.

Randall, P. (1996) *A Community Approach To Bullying*, Stoke-on-Trent, Trentham Books.

Rapoport, R., Rapoport, R. and Rosow, I. (1960) *Community as Doctor: New Perspectives on a Therapeutic Community*, London, Tavistock Publications.

Renold, E. (2001) 'Coming out: Gender, (Hetero) sexuality and the primary school', *Gender and Education*, 12, 309–26.

Renold, E. and Barter, C. (2003) ' "Hi, I'm Ramon and I run this place": Challenging the normalisation of violence in children's homes from young people's own perspectives' in E. Stanko (ed.), *The Meaning of Violence*, London, Routledge.

Richards, L. (1995) 'Transition Work!: Reflections on a three-year NUD*IST project', *Studies in Qualitative Methodology*, 5, 105–40.

Richardson, D. (1996) 'Heterosexuality and social theory', in D. Richardson (ed.), *Theorising Heterosexuality*, Buckingham, Open University Press.

Richardson, D. and May, H. (1999) 'Deserving victims?: Sexual status and the social construction of violence', *Sociological Review*, 47 (2), 308–331.

Rigby, K. (1996) *Bullying in Schools And What to Do About It*, London, Jessica Kingsley.

Rivers, I. (1995) 'Mental health issues among young lesbians and gay men bullied in school', *Health and Social Care in the Community*, 3, 380–3.

Rowe, J., Hundleby, M. and Garnett, L. (1989) *Child Care Now: A Survey of Placement Patterns*, London, British Agencies for Adoption and Fostering.

Rutter, M., Giller, H. and Hagell, A. (1998) *Antisocial Behaviour by Young People*, Cambridge, Cambridge University Press.

Salmivalli, C., Lagerspetz, K., Björkqvist, K., Österman, K. and Kaukiainen, A. (1996) 'Bullying as a group process: Participant roles and their relations to social status within the group', *Aggressive Behaviour*, 22, 1–15.

Salmon, G., James, A. and Smith, D.M. (1998) 'Bullying in schools: Self reported anxiety, depression, and self esteem in secondary school children', *British Medical Journal*, 317, 924–5.
Schaffner, L. (1998) 'Female juvenile delinquency: Sexual solutions, gender bias, and juvenile justice', *Hastings Women's Law Journal*, 9 (1), 1–25.
Schaffner, L. (1999) Violence and female delinquency: Gender transgressions and gender invisibility, *Berkeley Women's Law Journal*, 14, 40–65.
Schoenberg, N. and Ravdal, H. (2000) 'Using vignettes in awareness and attitudinal research', *International Journal of Social Research Methodology, Theory and Practice*, 3 (1), 63–75.
School Standards and Framework Act (1998), London, HMSO.
Sereny, G. (1998) *Cries Unheard: The Story of Mary Bell*, London, Macmillan.
Sewell, T. (1997) *Black Masculinities and Schooling: How do Black Boys Survive Modern School?*, Stoke-on-Trent, Trent Books.
Sharpe, C. (2003) 'NVQ fails test of child care skills', *Community Care*, 1466, 21.
Sharpe, S. (1994) *Just Like a Girl: How Girls Learn to be Women, from the Seventies to the Nineties*, 2nd edition, London, Penguin.
Sharp, S. and Thompson, D. (1994) 'The role of whole school policies in tackling bullying in schools', in P.K. Smith and S. Sharp (eds), *School Bullying: Insights and Perspectives*, London, Routledge.
Sibbitt, R. (1997) *The Perpetrators of Racial Harassment and Racial Violence*, Home Office Research Study 176, London, Home Office.
Simmons, J. (ed.) (2002) *Crime in England and Wales 2001/2002*. Home Office Statistical Bulletin 07/02. London, Home Office Research and Statistics Directorate.
Sinclair, I. and Gibbs, I. (1998) *Children's Homes: A Study in Diversity*, Chichester, Wiley.
Smart, C. (1976) *Women, Crime and Criminology: A Feminist Critique*, London, Routledge and Kegan Paul.
Smith, P.K. (2000) 'Bullying and harassment in schools and the rights of children', *Children & Society*, 14 (4), 294–303.
Smith, P.K. and Myron-Wilson, R. (1998) 'Parenting and school bullying', *Clinical Child Psychology and Psychiatry*, 3, 405–17.
Smith, P.K., Morita, Y., Junger-Tas, J., Olweus, D., Catalano, R. and Slee, P. (eds) (1999) *The Nature of School Bullying: A Cross-National Perspective*, London, Routledge.
Smith, P.K. and Sharp, S. (eds) (1994) *School Bullying: Insights and Perspectives*, London, Routledge.
Smith, P.K. and Shu, S. (2000) 'What good schools can do about bullying: Findings from a survey in English schools after a decade of research and action', *Childhood*, 7, 193–212.
Soothill, K. and Walby, S. (1991) *Sex Crime in the News*, London, Routledge.
Spradley, J. (1979) *The Ethnographic Interview*, Boston, MA, Holt, Rinehart and Winston.
Stacy, M. and Davis, C. (1983) *Division of Labour in Child Health Care*. Final report to the SSRC, Coventry, University of Warwick.
Stanko, E. (1985) *Intimate Intrusions: Women's Experiences of Male Violence*, London, Routledge and Kegan Paul.
Stanko, E. (1990) *Everyday Violence*, London, Routledge.
Stanko, E. (1995) 'Women, crime and fear', *The Annals of the American Academy of Politics and Social Science*, 539, 46–59.
Stanko, E. (2000) 'Rethinking violence, rethinking social policy' in G. Lewis, S. Gerwirtz, and J. Clark, (eds), *Rethinking Social Policy*, London, Sage, 245–58.

Stanko, E. (2002) *Taking Stock: What do We Know about Interpersonal Violence?* Egham, Surrey: Economic and Social Research Council Violence Research Programme.

Strauss, M. and Hotaling, G. (1980) *The Social Causes of Husband-Wife Violence*, Minneapolis, University of Minnesota Press.

Support Force for Children's Residential Care (1995) *Residential Care for Children and Young People – A Positive Choice?* Final Report to Secretary of State for Health, London, Department of Health.

Sutton, J., Smith, P.K and Swettenham, J. (1999) 'Social cognition and bullying: Social inadequacy or skilled manipulation?', *British Journal of Developmental Psychology*, 17, 435–50.

Tattum, D. (1995) 'Bullying in prisons', *Young Minds Newsletter*, 22, 18–19.

Tesch, R. (1990) *Qualitative Research: Analysis Types and Software Tools*, London, Falmer.

Thomas, G. (1995) *Travels in the Trench between Child Welfare Theory and Practice*, New York: Sage. Cited in: A. Turnell and S. Edwards (1999) *Signs of Safety: A Solution and Safety Oriented Approach to Child Protection Casework*, New York, W.W. Norton.

Thomas, T. (2001) *Sex Crime: Sex Offending and Society*, Cullompton, Devon, Willan Publishing.

Thorne, B. (1980) 'You still takin' notes?: Fieldwork and problems of informed consent', *Social Problems*, 27 (3), 284–97.

Tizard, B. and Phoenix, A. (2002) *Black, White or Mixed Race? Race and Racism in the Lives of Young People with Mixed Parentage*, London, Routledge.

Tomison, A. and Tucci, J. (1997) 'Emotional abuse: The hidden form of maltreatment', *Issues in Child Abuse Prevention,* (8) Spring, 16.

Triseliotis, J., Borland, M., Hill, M., and Lambert, L. (1995) *Teenagers and the Social Work Services*, London, HMSO.

Troyna, B. and Hatcher, R. (1992) *Racism in Children's Lives*, London, Routledge.

Turnell, A. and Edwards, S. (1999) *Signs of Safety: A Solution and Safety Oriented Approach to Child Protection Casework*. New York, W.W. Norton.

Tutt, N. (ed.) (1976) *Violence*, London, HMSO.

Utting, W. (1991) *Children in the Public Care*, London, HMSO.

Utting, W. (1997) *People like Us: The Report of the Review of the Safeguards for Children Living Away from Home*, London, HMSO.

Virdee, S., Modood, T., Newburn, T. and Shaw, C. (1999) *Understanding Racial Harassment in Schools*. Funded by the ESRC. University of Strathclyde and Bristol. Reports can be accessed at http://www.regard.ac.uk

Vizard, E., Monck, E. and Misch, P. (1995) 'Child and adolescent sex abuse perpetrators: A review of the research literature', *The Journal of Child Psychology and Psychiatry*, 36 (5), 731–56.

Wade, J. and Biehal, N. with Stein, M. and Clayden, J. (1998) *Going Missing*, Chichester, Wiley.

Walby, S. (1990) *Theorizing Patriarchy*, Oxford, Basil Blackwell.

Wallis, L. and Frost, N. (1998) *Cause for Complaint: The Complaints Procedure for Young People in Care*, London, Children's Society.

Warner, N. (1992) *Choosing with Care: The Report of the Committee of Inquiry into the Selection, Development and Management of Staff in Children's Homes*, Department of Health, London, HMSO.

Waterhouse, R. (2000) *Lost in Care: Report of the Tribunal of Inquiry into the Abuse of Children in Care in the Former County Council Areas of Gwynedd and Clwyd Since 1994*, HC 201, London, Stationery Office.

Wattam, C. (1999) 'Confidentiality and the social organisation of telling' in N. Parton and C. Wattam, *Child Sexual Abuse: Responding to the Experiences of Children*, Chichester, Wiley.

Westcott, H. and Clement, M. (1992) *NSPCC Experience of Child Abuse in Residential Care and Educational Placements: Results of a Survey*, London, NSPCC.
Whitaker, D. (1998) *Working in Children's Homes: Challenges and Complexities*, Chichester, West Sussex, Wiley.
Whitaker, D., Archer, L. and Hicks, L. (1998) 'The prevailing culture and staff dynamics in children's homes: Implications for training', *Social Work Education*, 17 (3), 361–73.
Whitney, I. and Smith, P.K. (1993) 'A survey of the nature and extent of bullying problems in junior/middle and secondary schools', *Educational Research*, 35 (1), 3–25.
Whitney, I., Smith, P.K. and Thompson, D. (1994) 'Bullying and children with special educational needs', in P.K. Smith and S. Sharp (eds), *School Bullying: Insights and Perspectives*, Routledge, London, 213–40.
Whyte, W. (1984) *Learning from the Field: A Guide from Experience*, London, Sage.
Wise, S. and Stanley, L. (1987) *Georgie Porgie: Sexual Harassment in Everyday Life*, London, Pandora.
Wolmar, C. (2000) *Forgotten Children: The Scandals in Britain's Children's Homes*, London, Vision.
Young, A. (1996) *Imagining Crime*, London, Sage.
Youth Justice Board (2002) *Youth Survey 2002: Research Study Conducted for the Youth Justice Board by MORI*, London, Youth Justice Board for England and Wales. http:/www.youth-justice-board.gov.uk
Youth Justice Board (2003) *Youth Survey 2003: Research Study Conducted for the Youth Justice Board by MORI*. London, Youth Justice Board. http:/www.youth-justice-board.gov.uk
YWCA (2001) 'Bad girls or bad laws?: Young women in the criminal justice system', *Briefings*, (2) Summer 2001, London, YWCA.

Index

African-Caribbean males 94–5
age and violence 76–7, 95–9

boarding schools 13–14
boys *see* gender, masculinity
bullying 5–8, 42–4, 50–1, 62–3, 15–16, 203–4
   associated factors 7–8, 120
   inevitability of 65–7, 227–8

child protection procedures 191–2
children and young people
   as victims of violence 4
   backgrounds 99–102
   using strengths of children's culture 224
children's backgrounds and violence 99–102, 135–6, 227–8
children's perspectives 18, 59–78, 104–38, 140–5
   on staff interventions 167–72
children's rights 145–6
childhood
   perspectives on 2–3
   sociology of 2–3, 60–1, 204
conceptualisation of violence 22, 24, 29–57, 104–38
continuum of violence 56–7, 157–60
custody, violence in 20–21

disclosure of violence 161–7

ethics 27
external professional help 196–7

gender
   and physical violence 32, 34–6, 67–9
   and sexual violence 122, 134
   and verbal attacks 42
   and violence 23–4, 34–7, 42, 67–9, 72–6, 87–93, 122–34, 161–3, 208–9

girls *see* gender
group work 197–8

'hard masculinities' *see* masculinity
hierarchy *see* peer group hierarchies
high-level violence 34–6, 46

individualised explanations of violence 134–5
inquiries into child abuse 13–14, 19–20
homophobia 132–3, 209
institutional factors 139–60

justification narratives 69–74, 107–9, 137, 213–14

keywork system 194–6

levels of violence in residential homes 44–56
listening to children 2–3
low-level violence 33, 45–6

masculinity 35–6, 67, 74–6, 87–8
meetings
   formal 190–1
   informal 189–90
   young people's meetings 146–9
methodology *see* research methodology

normalisation 60–3

organisational factors *see* institutional factors

'pecking order' *see* peer group hierarchies
peer group hierarchies 63–7, 80–7, 210–11
peer violence
   as child protection 11
   in boarding schools 13–14
   rates of 21
   research on in residential care 11–19

physical contact violence 31–6, 67, 106–13, 167–74
physical non-contact violence 31, 36–7, 47–9, 103–22, 174–9, 206
physical restraint 187–9
'play-fighting' 172–4
policy, on peer violence in children's homes 19–20, 140–5
'positioning' *see* peer group hierarchies
property attacks 36–7, 49

qualitative research 25

racial violence 16, 41, 56, 93–5, 120–2, 136, 215–16
racist abuse *see* racial violence
research methodology 24–7, 131
  data analysis 231–2
  ethics 27
  researching violence 229–30
  sample 26–7, 233–4
  vignettes 25–6
residential care for children 8–21, 216–21, 225–7
  admission procedures 152–4
  buildings 154
  bullying in residential care 10–11
  changing population and realignment in peer group hierarchies 84–7
  functions 155–6
  institutional factors 139–60
  inquiries into abuse at residential homes 13–14, 19–20
  referrals 149–52
  residents of 9–10
  sexual abuse in 17

staffing levels 156–7
statistics on 9
responding to violence 221–4
  child protection procedures 191–2
  external professional help 196–7
  group work 197–8
  keywork system 194–6
  meetings 189–91
  physical restraint 187–9
  positive rewards 198–9
  relationships 199–200
  sanctions 184–7
  supervision 193–4
retaliation 69–74, 107–9, 137

sanctions 184–7
sexual violence 31, 37–9, 51–4, 122–34
  female responsibility for male sexual violence 123–6
  male on male sexual violence 130–4
sociology of childhood 2–3, 60–1, 204
staff perspectives on peer violence 79–103, 104–38
  girls' violence 88–93
  girls' use of sexuality 93
  normalisation of male violence 87–8

thresholds 137
'top dog' *see* peer group hierarchies

verbal attacks 31, 39–42, 49–50, 54–6, 179–81, 205
  and race 56
  against family 41–2, 55
victim status 134
vignettes 25–6, 104–38
violence as social justice 69–74